Textual Practice

Contents

Volume 9 Issue 1

Articles

Reviews

Stephen Orgel

Insolent women and manlike apparel

My title invokes one of the most commonplace Renaissance juxta-positions, identifying socially offensive behaviour in women with masculinity – what Leontes in *The Winter's Tale* implies by calling the argumentative Paulina 'a mankind witch', not merely a witch, the essence of feminine wickedness, but something even worse, one who behaves like a man. In social contexts, the complaint focused particularly on fashions in clothing. The locus classicus here is King James's well-known admonition to the London clergy, requiring them

> to inveigh vehemently and bitterly in their sermons against the insolency of our women, and their wearing of broad-brimmed hats, pointed doublets, their hair cut short or shorn, and some of them stillettos or poniards . . . adding withall that if pulpit admonitions will not reform them he would proceed by another course.[1]

This admonition was directed against what was seen as a masculine style of dress; but the ministers did not invariably understand the point of the royal injunction. 'The Dean of Westminster', John Chamberlain reported, 'hath been very strict in his church against Ladies and gentlewomen about yellow ruffs, and would not suffer them to be admitted into any pew.' Yellow ruffs being particularly stylish at the moment, the fashionable parishioners appealed at once to the king, who was obliged to explain that 'his meaning was not for yellow ruffs, but for other man-like and unseemly apparel.'[2]

What constitutes masculinity, however, in apparel as in everything else, is a matter of opinion. Figure 1 shows Paul van Somer's 1617 portrait of the queen, with broad-brimmed hat, short hair and pointed doublet. The picture, roughly contemporary with the king's expostulation, was painted for her, and shows her own palace of Oatlands in the background; it presents her as she wanted to see herself. Is the real object of King James's outburst, then, his wife's

Textual Practice 9:1, 1995, 5–25

taste in fashion? The possibility is not inconceivable; husband and wife had few tastes in common, and by 1617 were maintaining both different households and different religions – indeed, Queen Anne's conversion to Catholicism had been a problem for the king for two decades, even threatening to compromise his accession to the English throne. Manlike and unseemly clothes in this case would be an index to a much more dangerous kind of independence. And if every Englishman was a king in his own household, was every English woman by the same token a version of the unmanageable queen?

Figure 1 Paul van Somer, *Anne of Denmark*, 1617. HM the Queen.

Here is the same issue in reverse. Barnabe Riche in his *Farewell to the Military Profession* indicates as one of the major changes driving him from his calling the effeminization of the military:

> It was my fortune to walk through the Strand towards Westminster, where I met one came riding towards me ... appareled in a French ruff, a French cloak, French hose, and in his hand a great fan of feathers, bearing them up very womanly against the side of his face. And for that I had never seen any man wear them before that day, I began to think it impossible that there might a man be found so foolish as to make himself a scorn to the world, to wear so womanish a toy, but rather thought it had been some shameless woman that had disguised herself like a man in our hose and our cloaks; for our doublets, gowns, caps, and hats they had got long ago.

For comparison with Riche's description of unsuitable masculine fashion, Figure 2 is a miniature of Lord Mountjoy, elaborately curled and ear-ringed – this is the military hero who succeeded in the pacification of Ireland after Essex failed. Riche focuses his disapproval on the fan; to the best of my knowledge, no gentleman in the period had himself depicted with such an accessory, but the association of military and aristocratic masculinity with feathers is easy enough to document. Figure 3 shows a Polish rider liberally furnished, and in Figure 4 the feathered hat is clearly an important element in the lavish costume of Edward Sackville, Earl of Dorset. Riche's larger point, about what he sees as the feminization of the military, is amply attested by any number of other portraits, ranging from George Clifford, Earl of Cumberland, the Queen's champion, shown in Figure 5 in jousting costume, to Essex himself, in Figure 6, as he was portrayed after his victory at Cadiz. Any of these images might do for the 'certain lord' who so outrages Hotspur on the battlefield, 'neat and trimly dressed, / Fresh as a bridegroom. . . / perfumèd like a milliner.'[3] Riche's diagnosis of the new social disease places its etiology securely in heterosexuality, observing that the fashion is adopted 'to please gentlewomen'.

But of course Clifford, Essex and Mountjoy are not simply gentleman-soldiers; they are the equivalent of four-star generals, and all these portraits are documents in the creation of a set of idealized public selves. The essential question here is not so much what constitutes masculinity or femininity, but what constitutes glamour in the representation of the stars of the 1590s. Figure 7 shows the most widely circulated portrait of King James's elder son Prince Henry, who saw himself as a military hero. He is presented as manly and

Figure 2 Nicholas Hilliard, *Charles Blount, Lord Mountjoy, later Earl of Devonshire*. Sir John Carew Pole, Bt. Reproduced in Erna Auerbach, *Nicholas Hilliard* (Routledge, 1961), plate 73.

Ein Polonischer Hofiuncker . Nobilis Polonus . ꝟ. 41

Figure 3 Abraham De Bruyn, *Polish Rider*, from Frances Yates, *The Valois Tapestries* (Routledge, 1975), plate 7b.

Figure 4 William Larkin, *Edward Sackville, 4th Earl of Dorset*, 1613. The Executors of the Estate of the late Countess of Suffolk and Berkshire. Reproduced in Roy Strong, *The Elizabethan Image* (Tate Gallery, 1969), no. 128.

Figure 5   Nicholas Hilliard, *George Clifford, 3rd Earl of Cumberland*, c. 1590.
National Maritime Museum, Greenwich. Auerbach, *Nicholas Hilliard*, plate 89.

Figure 6 Marcus Gheeraerts the Younger, *Robert Devereux, 2nd Earl of Essex*, *c.* 1596. The Duke of Bedford. Reproduced in Strong, *The Elizabethan Image*, no. 157.

athletic, practising at the lance. Figure 8, on the other hand, is his investiture portrait as Prince of Wales, painted only a year earlier – the lace collar, the pompoms on the shoes, the richly embroidered doublet and pants, the dainty gloves, the accentuation of the hips with even a suggestion of a farthingale, all indicate how undifferentiated with regard to gender the idealizations of fashion were in the period. It is clear that these two representations of the heir to the throne do not contradict each other. Just to make it even clearer, here is some mythographic evidence: two plates from the popular mid-sixteenth-century iconology of Georg Pictor. Figure 9 is Pallas Athena, the martial goddess – that the woodcut was originally intended to depict her is clear from the presence of the owl at her feet. But Pictor also used the same image for Hercules (Figure 10). Doubtless this conjunction has more to do with the exigencies of early printing than with any theory of the interchangeability of genders in the Renaissance; but it is also clear that in the representation of heroism and divinity, as of royalty, gender was not an exclusive category. Figure 11 is an even more striking illustration: Cornelis van Haarlem's sumptuous *Venus and Adonis* (1619), in which, save for the slight accentuation of Venus's breasts, the two figures are mirror images of each other, down even to the pearl ear-ring, and it appears that the same model was used for both hero and heroine.

Gender, moreover, is not the only relevant issue here. Barnabe Riche's scorn is directed at the sartorial pretensions of an ordinary gentleman. Would he take the same line about Essex, or Mountjoy, or the Prince of Wales? Let us return to Queen Anne in her hunting dress: is the king's indictment of 'man-like and unseemly apparel' really directed at her? Perhaps; but perhaps too the politics of gender are more complex than this. For all the pulpit rhetoric about the evils of cross-dressing, sumptuary legislation said nothing about the wearing of sexually inappropriate garments. It was concerned with violations of the sartorial badges of class, not those of gender. Tradesmen and their wives were enjoined from wearing the satins and velvets of aristocrats, people below the rank of gentry were limited to clothing made of certain kinds of wool and other plain cloth (the legislation, not surprisingly, works only in one direction; it does not prohibit the gentry from wearing frieze jerkins). The statutes were finally acknowledged to be unenforceable in the civil law, and were repealed in 1604, but this only complicated matters further: it did not mean that there were no longer any sumptuary regulations, it only transferred the jurisdiction over questions of appropriate dress, as an issue of public morality, from the criminal courts to the ecclesiastical ones, where the guidelines were much less clear.

Figure 7 William Hole, *Henry Frederick Prince of Wales*, dedicatory engraving from Michael Drayton, *Poly-Olbion* (London, 1613).

Figure 8 Robert Peake, *Henry Frederick Prince of Wales*. National Portrait Gallery.

In so far as sumptuary legislation in the period generalizes about women, it insists on just the distinctions the king refuses to make: it declares that all women are not the same; what is proper dress for ladies is not proper for women of the middle class – indeed, it says the same of men, and thereby declines to distinguish the sexes. King James didn't have much use for women, but perhaps the point of his reproach is really the same as the point of van Somer's painting: that the queen sets her own style; and that what is appropriate for the queen is not appropriate for other women. The royal outrage would be, in this reading, against presuming to imitate the style of royalty, and thereby encroaching on the prerogatives of the crown – a danger the king throughout his reign saw as ubiquitous.

This may well be giving the king too much credit. But the idea that masculine dress could serve as a potent mode of female

Figure 9   Minerva, from Georg Pictor, *Apotheoseos* (Basel, 1558), p.44.

Figure 10 Hercules, from Georg Pictor, *Apotheoseos* (Basel, 1558), p. 96.

idealization is clear from Figure 12, a piece of Caroline anti-pacifist propaganda, showing Elizabeth rallying her troops before the antici-pated invasion of the Armada in 1588. The engraving was done in the 1630s, and as Susan Frye has shown, it is pure fantasy: there is no evidence that Elizabeth wore armour on this or any other occasion; but the image of the late queen as an Amazon – or, depend-ing on your point of view, a virago – served as an effective rebuke to the effeminate Charles I, who was felt by his critics to be con-trolled by his French Catholic queen.[4]

What, then, are the limits of social imitation? Figure 13 shows a particularly ambiguous Elizabethan example, coming this time from below. The title-page of *Pleasant Quips for Upstart Newfangled Gentle-women*, attributed on not very good evidence to Stephen Gosson,

Figure 11 Cornelis van Haarlem, *Venus and Adonis* (Baltimore Art Museum).

Figure 12 Thomas Cecil, *Elizabeth I in Armour*, c. 1625–30. The Mansell Collection.

displays a woodcut of a woman elaborately dressed and accessorized. The obvious assumption that this image represents the upstart newfangled gentlewoman of the title is, however, seriously complicated by the fact that two of her accessories are the orb, in her left hand, and the sceptre in her right: this is a woodcut of Elizabeth, or at least it must have started out as one – the only change has been the replacement of her crown with a tiara and feathered headdress. The model for it, from a popular broadside, is shown in Figure 14. Is the point that upstart gentlewomen are approaching dangerously close to the royal style? Or is the real object of attack the queen herself, illegitimate child of a mother executed for adultery and incest, granddaughter of a mere London merchant, the model for all upstart newfangled gentlewomen?

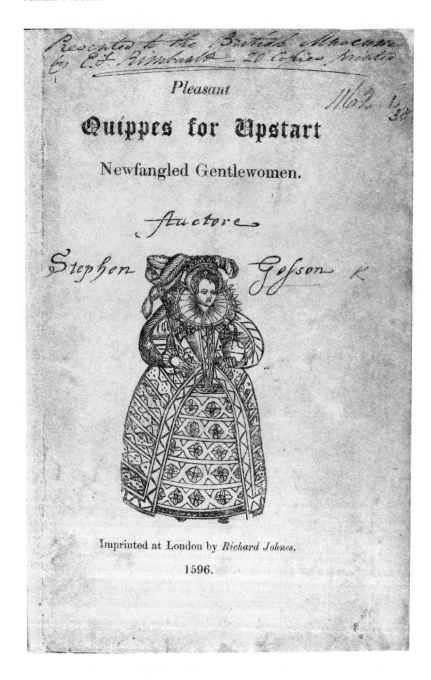

Figure 13 *Pleasant Quips for Upstart Newfangled Gentlewomen* (London, 1596), title-page. The British Library.

Figure 14 *Queen Elizabeth I, c.* 1588, woodcut. The British Library.

It is in the nature of social hierarchies that the rules descend from above, and this is as true of the laws of fashion as of those of commerce and domestic arrangements. Theatre was under aristocratic and ultimately royal patronage, but it constituted both an obvious violation of the sumptuary laws – it presented middle-class actors and working-class apprentices dressed as aristocrats – and a powerful stimulus to society as a whole to violate them. Polemicists from John Stubbes to William Prynne record in compulsive and fascinated detail the ungodly finery characteristic of London theatre audiences, and Sir Henry Wotton's reaction to Shakespeare's *Henry VIII* at the Globe, that it was 'sufficient in truth within a while to make greatness very familiar if not ridiculous',[5] puts the case against the imitation of royalty, whether by players or audiences, succinctly. Marion Trousdale, in a brilliant discussion of the interrelations of sumptuary legislation, fashion and the stage, quotes the correspondence of Philip Gawdy, resident in London from the 1580s until his death in 1617, who moves in the world of the court and the City, frequents the playhouses, observes the fashions of the great and sends stylish apparel home to his family in Norfolk. With a shipment of clothing he writes to his sister that 'I can assure you that both the queen and all the gentlewomen at the court wear the very fashion of your tough [i.e. stiffened] taffeta gown with an open wired sleeve and such a cut, and it is now the newest fashion.'[6] Fashion, even in Elizabethan Norfolk, descends directly from the queen.

To imitate the queen and the court aristocracy, however, was, as Trousdale shows, in the most literal way also to imitate the theatre. In 1572 Thomas Giles (or Gylles), a haberdasher (not, apparently, the same Thomas Giles who was the Master of Paul's at the time) lodged a complaint against the office of the queen's revels. He charges that the Yeoman of the Revels leases out masquing costumes that are the property of the crown to 'all sorts of persons'; that these courtly clothes are then worn not only 'in the court', but 'into the city or country', where they are subjected to

> the great press of people and foulness both of the way and weather and soil of the wearers, who for the most part be of the meanest sort of men, to the great discredit of the same apparel, which afterward is to be showed before her highness and to be worn by them of great calling.

The point of this complaint is not a demand for enforcement of the sumptuary laws; Giles claims his concern is for the welfare of the costumes, not for the social hierarchy. But his real purpose, as he readily admits, is to protect his own business from royal competition – he too has fancy dress for hire, and he is, he says, 'greatly hindered of his living hereby ... having apparel to let and cannot so cheaply let the same as her highness's masques be let.'[7] The fact that the queen's revels could do a thriving business in renting out aristocratic clothes at cut rates to 'the meanest sort of men' indicates both what kind of investment the culture had in the semiotics of clothing and how little regulations about who could wear what represented social practice.

For us, the prime instance of the misrepresentations of costume in the period are the innumerable disguises that constitute so large an element in the plots of Elizabethan drama. If costume was essential to theatre, the wrong costume was even more essential. This is a case, moreover, where clothes really do make the man: there are scarcely a handful of instances in which anyone sees through a disguise in English Renaissance drama. In the England of Elizabeth, the most highly charged misrepresentations were those of class, hence the legislation against wearing clothes that admitted one to an undeserved place in the hierarchy, and hence also the endemic flouting of the legislation. On the stage, however, the egregious misrepresentations are those of gender, the playing of women by boys, and within the drama the playing of boys by women. But this practice was clearly just as thoroughly naturalized in Renaissance England as the violation of the semiotics of class: the only people who found it reprehensible were those for whom theatre itself was reprehensible.

I have said in another context that there was an analogy between boys and women in the culture.[8] This has been taken to mean that I am arguing that boys were substitutes for women, but in fact I am arguing just the opposite: both are treated as a medium of exchange within the patriarchal structure; and both are (perhaps in consequence) constructed as objects of erotic attraction for adult men. Boys and women are not in competition in this system; they are antithetical not to each other, but to men. This is clear, for example, in Lady Mary Wroth's well-known passage in *Urania* describing a lover seeing his mistress in another man's arms, and observing that he was 'unmoveable, no further wrought than if he had seen a delicate play-boy act a loving woman part, and knowing him a boy, liked only his action.'[9] The accuracy of the generalization is not the issue here; there is ample evidence that homosexual peder-asty was a strong element in the erotic life of Renaissance England, and Mary Wroth to the contrary notwithstanding, it is demonstrable that many men in the period did find boys sexually exciting. But the point is that Wroth doesn't see the boy as threatening – and it should probably be added that the lover in *Urania* is being duped: he *ought* to be jealous; he is a fool not to be, the equivalent of a cuckold. (It is at least arguable that this reflects on Wroth's own sexual complacency.) When Lear issues his warning about the untrust-worthiness of a boy's love, he is asserting a commonplace (that is, falling in love with boys is commonplace in this society); and like the proverbial wisdom declaring the unreliability of women, it is asserted in the ultimate interest of defining and stabilizing the nature not of boys and women, but of men.

But what allows boys to be substituted for women in the theatre is not anything about the real nature of boys and women, but precisely the costume, and more particularly, cultural assumptions about costume. Orsino's love for the youth he knows as Cesario is paralleled by Antonio's love for Sebastian, the youth he knows as Roderigo, and despite the fact that there were no twins in Shakespeare's company, the two are represented on stage as being indistinguishable – an effect achieved, doubtless then as now, by dressing them, quite illogically from the point of view of the plot, in identical costumes. Twins are people who *dress* alike. The flummery at the play's conclusion about the impossibility of proceeding with the marriage of Orsino and Viola – the impossibility of concluding the plot – until Viola's clothes have been found, declares in the clearest possible way that, whatever Viola says about the erotic realities of her inner life, she is not a woman unless she's dressed as one; and even here, it is a *particular* costume that matters, her *own* dress that was left with the sea-captain: this is the dress that *is* Viola. The costume is the real thing; borrowing a dress from Olivia or buying a new one to get married in are not offered by the play as options. Clothes make the woman, clothes make the man: the costume is of the essence.

When Prospero tempts Stefano and Trinculo to their destruction with a closetful of 'glistering apparel', he invokes a central cultural topos. Caliban declares the garments to be 'trash'; but they are trash only because the conspirators are not yet entitled to wear them – robes of office, aristocratic finery, confirm and legitimate authority, they do not confer it. There is obviously, however, a widespread conviction in the culture that they do. Caliban may well be revealing here just how much of an outsider he is – the costumes, after all, are Prospero's. Prospero himself invests his cape with the enabling power of his magic: 'Lie there, my art' (I.ii.25). Analogously, the wardrobe of Henslowe's company included 'a robe for to go invisible',[10] asserting in a culturally specific way how powerfully garments determined the way one was to be seen, and not seen. These fictions, moreover, reflect an economic reality: the theatre company has its largest investment, its major property, in its costumes; and since the costumes themselves are for the most part the real cast-off clothes of real aristocrats, the legitimating emblems of authority, they possess a kind of social reality within this culture that the actors, and indeed much of their audience, can never hope to have.

Notes

1 *Letters of John Chamberlain*, ed. Norman E. McClure (Philadelphia: American Philosophical Society, 1939), vol. 2, pp. 286–7.
2 ibid., p. 294.
3 *King Henry IV, Part 1*, I.iii,33–6.
4 See Susan Frye, 'The myth of Elizabeth I at Tilbury', *Sixteenth Century Journal*, 23 (1992): pp. 95–114.
5 The letter is reprinted in E. K. Chambers, *William Shakespeare* (Oxford: Oxford University Press, 1930), vol. 2, pp. 343–4.
6 *Letters of Philip Gawdy*, ed. I. H. Jeayes (London: Nichols, 1906), p. 28. See Marion Trousdale, '*Coriolanus* and the playgoer in 1609', in Murray Biggs (ed.), *The Arts of Performance* (Edinburgh: Edinburgh University Press, 1991), pp. 124–34.
7 Albert Feuillerat, *Documents Relating to the Office of the Revels in the Time of Queen Elizabeth* (London: David Nutt, 1908), vol. 3, p. 409. William Ingram discusses the complaint, which, however, he takes to mean that the Queen's Revels is renting out the costumes to playing companies. This is not what Gylles says. 'The "evolution" of the Elizabethan playing company', in John H. Astington (ed.), *The Development of Shakespeare's Theater* (New York: AMS Press, 1992), pp. 16–17.
8 See 'Nobody's perfect, or Why did the English stage take boys for women?', *South Atlantic Quarterly*, 88,1 (Winter 1989), pp. 7–29.
9 *The Countesse of Mountgomeries Urania* (London, 1621), p. 60. Michael Shapiro discusses a more extended passage on the same theme from the manuscript continuation of the romance in 'Lady Mary Wroth describes a "boy actress" ', *Medieval and Renaissance Drama in England*, vol. 4 (1987), pp. 187–94.
10 *Henslowe's Diary*, ed. R. A. Foakes and R. T. Rickert (Cambridge: Cambridge University Press, 1961), p. 325.

Jonathan Dollimore

Sex and death

In homophobic representations of AIDS, homosexuality and death become inseparable; homoerotic desire is construed as death-driven, death-desiring and death-dealing.

Ellis Hanson reminds us that this association is not new: 'notions of death have been at the heart of nearly every historical construction of same-sex desire.' People living with AIDS, especially gay men, are represented in some quarters of the press as vampire-like, 'the dead who dare to speak and sin and walk abroad, the undead with AIDS'.[1] In another article in the same book, Jeff Nunokawa shows that this connection between homosexuality and death isn't just something projected on to gay culture by a homophobic dominant culture; within gay culture also, homosexuality has been regarded fatalistically, morbidly, and as somehow doomed of its very nature. Nunokawa identifies texts as different as Oscar Wilde's *Dorian Gray*, Randy Shilts's *And the Band Played On*, and James Merrill's in *The Inner Room*, as inclined to 'cultivate the confusion of gay identity with a death-driven narrative', and representing 'doom as the specific fate of gay men'.[2]

There are other, more recent, and perhaps more disturbing examples. Hugo, the protagonist of Oscar Moore's 1991 novel *A Matter of Life and Sex*, initially promises to be the horny adolescent at a premium in gay culture – the 'sassy street urchin who knew what he wanted and wanted it now'; the 'flouting, flaunting rudeboy', who doesn't come into tissues, preferring instead 'to see his sperm fly'.[3] But in this narrative he is also the boy for whom sex and death come together; who eventually dies of AIDS. In the midst of anarchic sexual yearning in a Parisian bathhouse, death is calmly courted: 'with sex choking his throat and thumping against his chest' Hugo throws himself

into the clinch of sex with the smile of one preparing his last fix.

Textual Practice **9**:1, 1995, 27–53   © 1995 Routledge   0950–236X

There, in the stream of sweat and hallucination of amyl ... as the man's penis swelled and loomed ... and Hugo's mouth and eyes drooled in one gasping hunger, a quiet voice whispered – this could be the boy that kills you. And a quiet voice answered back – so then, this is the way to die.[4]

Compare that with a reviewer of James Miller's controversial 1993 biography of Michel Foucault:

In the autumn of 1983, after he had already collapsed and less than a year before his own death, [Foucault] could still be found in the baths and bars. He laughed at talk of 'safe-sex' and reportedly said [to D. A. Miller] 'to die for the love of boys: what could be more beautiful?'[5]

Miller takes this as evidence of Foucault's attraction to death, and suicide especially, and reminds us that, in the *History of Sexuality*, Foucault speaks of 'the individual driven, in spite of himself, by the sombre madness of sex'.[6] For his part, Miller's reviewer remarks solemnly that Foucault 'remained a glutton for sexual danger and excess'.[7]

To die for the love of boys is one thing. But what about actively contributing to their death? In 1983 a rumour was circulating alleging that Foucault, in James Miller's words, 'knowing he was dying of AIDS ... deliberately tried to infect other people with the disease'.[8] This too has a parallel in Moore's novel[9] where, some one hundred pages on, we read of the same or another Parisian bathhouse in which Hugo 'fucked a man in the backroom ... and released jets of poisoned spunk into his bowels'.[10]

In Moore's novel, sex and death, desire and disease, weld together in lurid death-bed dreams which are familiar in the sense of having cultural and, in particular, a literary, precedent: not so much the romantic *angst* of dying in Venice; more the Jacobean obsession with death as the motor of life; death energizes and disintegrates life almost indistinguishably, almost in the one motion, and never more so than when in the guise of desire: 'in this light people changed all the time. One moment they were pristine youth, the next a skull peered through the dark and cavities replaced the eyes.'[11] Death is always already there, which is why age is read back into youth, and why future death, and the decline that leads ineluctably to it, are vividly imaged as the truth of the here and now:

The dark was never dark enough in the bathhouse. Light played tricks, switching the pretty boy of one minute into a skeleton the next, the lissom youth suddenly chomping toothlessly on his dick, a body muscled and rippling in the spotlight that sagged and collapsed in the harsher light of the showers. . . . He didn't know anymore whether he was standing or lying, whether this was sex or death.[12]

But this is not a text from the moral right; in *A Matter of Life and Sex*, AIDS is not God's punishment for promiscuity, the wages of sin, and while the narrator is undoubtedly disenchanted with homosexual experience, especially anal intercourse, it's in an avowedly non-moralistic way; in places AIDS is 'used' as just another brutal material proof of how the interests of death inhabit desire: perversely, lethally, ecstatically, fatalistically. As such, some have found it almost as offensive as the rantings of the moral right.

Moore exploits a death/desire paradox which perhaps finds its most extreme statement in the Jacobean period, but which is endemic to western culture. Initially made very far back, it has been affirmed, explored, perverted, transcended, disavowed, ever since.[13] Denis de Rougemont, in an influential study,[14] dates the modern form of this preoccupation to the twelfth century, and follows it forward in almost exclusively heterosexual terms, neglecting the fact that the age-old anxieties generated by the thought that death somehow inhabits desire have notoriously been concentrated on male homosexuality, and never more so than now, the furore over Foucault being just one case in point. Though definitely not in conditions of our own choosing, gay men are currently confronting these displaced anxieties in all their repressed and overt violence.

Promiscuity

The fatal catalyst that supposedly welds homosexuality and death is promiscuity – Hugo in the Parisian bathhouses, Foucault in the Californian ones. This is not just a construction of the tabloid enemies of gay men in relation to AIDS; compare James Baldwin's account of the New York homosexual underworld which he knew in his teens:

Sometimes, eventually, inevitably, I would find myself in bed with one of these men, a despairing and dreadful conjunction, since their need was as relentless as quicksand and as impersonal, and sexual rumour concerning blacks had preceded me. As for sexual roles, these were created by the imagination and limited only by one's stamina.

At bottom what I had learned was that the male desire for

a male roams everywhere, avid, desperate, unimaginably lonely, culminating often in drugs, piety, madness or death. It was also dreadfully like watching myself at the end of a long, slow-moving line: Soon I would be next. All of this was very frightening. It was lonely, and impersonal and demeaning. I could not believe – after all, I was only nineteen – that I could have been driven to the lonesome place where these men and I met each other so soon, to stay.[15]

Whereas for Baldwin death was one possible outcome of homosexual alienation, for Rupert Haselden it would seem to be homosexual desire's desperate objective. Haselden, writing in 1991[16] in the British left/liberal newspaper, *The Guardian*, and self-identified as gay, effectively reworks Baldwin's sense of homosexual desire, now with an AIDS-inflected fatalism. He asks why the London cruise bars are filling up again, despite AIDS. He concludes:

There is an inbuilt fatalism to being gay. Biologically maladaptive, unable to reproduce, our futures are limited to individual existence and what the individual makes of it. Without the continuity of children we are self-destructive, living for today because we have no tomorrow.

So, continues Haselden, we turn to casual promiscuous sex, hoping to escape from a hostile world into the bars and clubs. At their most self-indulgent gay men exemplify the futility of existence, reminding others of their own mortality. As regards AIDS, which 'dangles like a flashing neon sign in the bars and clubs', fear has given way to acceptance: 'we are coming to see it as our fate'; AIDS has become an excuse for a *carpe diem* attitude to life, intensified by the thrill of 'dicing with death, of tempting fate'. And, according to this same writer, the same thing is happening all round the world in the dangerously promiscuous scenarios of gay culture.[17]

Revolution and redemption

Not long ago, and for a short time only, the promiscuous homosexual encounter inspired an utterly different vision full of revolutionary aspiration; that encounter became, potentially, the new spearhead of an already existing sexual radicalism:

Promiscuous homosexuals (outlaws with dual identities ...) are the shock troops of the sexual revolution. The streets are the battleground, the revolution is the sexhunt, [and] a radical statement is made each time a man has sex with another on a street.

A radicalism promising life, or orgasm, instead of death:

> Cum instead of blood. Satisfied bodies instead of dead ones. Death versus orgasm. Would they bust everyone? With cum-smeared tanks would they crush all?[18]

But even as Rechy was writing, the wild space of the promiscuous encounter was narrowing (from underworld to bar to bathhouse), with the sexual practices becoming sometimes more transgressive (sado-masochism and fist-fucking) but presumably less revolutionary; the wildness of a once vaguely defined illicit sexuality became in a sense even wilder, yet now *precisely* defined and ritualized. Not inappropriately, Foucault called the bathhouses 'laboratories of sexual experimentation'.[19] It is this urban confinement of homosexual transgression that is most striking in post-war gay culture. Where once the homosexual exile wandered abroad, sometimes literally across seas and continents, in search of the liberation of the foreign and the exotic, now he might haunt the confining, claustrophobic spaces of the bathhouse. Even there we hear echoes of those earlier times. Thus, after an unsuccessful sexual encounter, the narrator of Michael Rumaker's *A Day and Night at the Baths* laments: 'I have always felt myself a person in exile, anonymous in the cities, inconspicuous in the windowless cubicles of baths such as this; banned from the rural places. . . .'

In Rumaker's text, contemporary with Rechy's *Sexual Outlaw* (1977), sexual revolution is already only an ironic half-hope, half-joke: 'if this secret gets out, it'll revolutionize the world' whispers a boy whom the narrator has just blown. Rumaker affirms instead a view of deviant sex as benignly redemptive rather than tragically redemptive (Baldwin) or violently revolutionary (Rechy). His narrator is cautious, domesticated and very much on the side of ordinary life, taking with him to the baths not drugs but a packed lunch of health food. While there he's careful to stub out his cigarettes in the right places to avoid fire hazard; he regrets having forgotten his skin moisturizer, and is careful about hygiene.

If revolution is unrealistic, Rumaker is hugely optimistic about the democracy of the bathhouse; this place of the most un-American activities is also the last refuge of the American dream; here 'without estrangements of class or money or position, or false distinctions of any kind . . . was the possibility to be nourished and enlivened in the blood-heat and heartbeat of others, regardless of who or what we were. Nurturing others we nurture ourselves.' In this vision, where homosexuality = health = life, nothing, apparently, could be further away from the pathological version of the same (homosexuality = disease = death). Arguably though, this vision remains overdetermined by precisely the same conservative values which produce the pathologized version. Even the American family is invoked: having had sex with an old man the narrator says afterwards, 'Gay father . . . thank you.'[20] From such experiences the narrator envisions, albeit briefly, a US-style utopia world where gay sex is free, benign and healing, and sufficiently sanitized to be reincorporated in civic society;[21] in great green parks people engage in 'mutually consenting and courteous erotic play'. Then, says the narrator, gay children will live again, the mental hospitals will empty and the prison population be depleted.

When the narrator gets fucked in group sex, gender divisions are effortlessly transcended: 'Now I am a woman, and now I am a man, there's no confusion. The false selves slide away in my nakedness.' Still being fucked, he is possessed by revelation, as in the mystery rites 'subsumed in the will and drive of eros . . . taken down and down into the nameless, faceless, anonymous dark of the flesh. . . . To know it is all *a beauty of beginning, of the sane and healthy lust that makes us all.*' Here, ecstasy is a 'revelation . . . that will keep me sane and whole'.[22]

By way of prefiguring what follows, compare Rumaker's allegorical appropriation of 'primitive' sexual ritual with that in Thomas Mann's *Death in Venice*. The difference couldn't be greater. For Rumaker the connection with a primitive past is all about a therapeutic recovery of a lost wholeness, of being freed from the 'false selves' of sexual difference, of being put back in touch with the 'sane and healthy lust that makes us all'. For Mann's Aschenbach it's exactly the opposite; the primitive sexual ritual of which he dreams does indeed hold out the possibility of a liberation of the self, but one inseparable from an anarchic, violent annihilation of the self. Aschenbach dreams his own death in 'fear and desire, with a shuddering curiosity'. The dream is wracked with ambivalence: he hears the music of the 'cruellest sweetness' bewitching not only the mind but 'his very entrails'. The ritual is anarchic, violent, bestial and stinks of 'wounds, uncleanness, and disease'. The 'uttermost surrender', the 'whirling lust' that Aschenbach desires yet fears, and most acutely when confronted with 'the obscene symbol of the godhead', is a masochistic, penetrative ecstasy whose climax is death.[23] Not much room here for packed lunches and the safety-conscious.

Except that the safety-consciousness of Rumaker's narrator turns out to be that safest of narrative ruses, a retrospective premonition; the book concludes with a dedication to the victims of an actual fire in the very bathhouse which is its subject. Now a puritanical or fundamentalist perspective might construe the fire as providential intervention, a divine punishment for sexual evil. Even a gay identi-fied perspective, while obviously and vigorously dissenting from *that* view, might see the fire as having more resonant implications, be they symbolic or socio-political. But not Rumaker: even that fire can be subsumed into a benign narrative:

And, out of the ashes and ruin of all despair,
and in spite of it,
to the spirit of the rainbow gay and lesbian phoenix,
rising.

Impossibilities of desire

Rechy's and Rumaker's respective visions seem worlds away from the AIDS-related fatalism of Moore and Haselden, for both of whom gay desire (all desire?) courts death because it is regarded as essen-tially *impossible*. By that I mean they share an acute sense that desire is driven by a lack inherently incapable of satisfaction; that what prevents the fulfilment of desire is not just that its object is contin-gently unobtainable, but that desire is rooted in a self-destructive contradiction. In short the very nature of desire is what prevents its fulfilment. Thus Hugo in *A Matter of Life and Sex* is helplessly 'pinioned by lust', yet unable to achieve ecstasy. His sexual life 'was a future whose past was always more exciting ... a future with loneliness sewn into the seam and death woven into the fabric, unseen until too late, a single sinister thread'. Sometimes he strains 'for the relief of an orgasm which, when it came, was only a spasm without the shudder, an anti-climax that offered no feeling of relief. Just a small grey wave of depression.'[24] Hugo's sexual compulsiveness suggests an inner futility or impossibility to desire, obscurely but profoundly linked to a sense of loss; a link which binds death into desire.

For Rupert Haselden the death/desire connection is paramount, and premised on a similar sense of futility. Homosexuality is intrinsi-cally self-destructive, death-desiring *and* death-dealing, qualities epitomized in its allegedly compulsive promiscuity – indeed for him qualities almost synonymous with promiscuity and his belief that homosexuals are 'Biologically maladaptive, unable to reproduce'.

To find the sex/death paradox in so-called 'post-AIDS' writers like these for whom, in different ways, desire is impossible, compulsive or doomed, is perhaps predictable. In fact the same paradox haunts Rechy's revolutionary view of desire, and Rumaker's redemptive view of the same, and in ways which reveal the pre/post AIDS categorization to be facile and misleading.

Sometimes, Rechy tells an interviewer, 'after a night of hustling and dark cruising alleys, I think of suicide'; to another interviewer he says: 'Finally, that's the only freedom you have ... the freedom to die.'[25] For Rechy, for most of the time, the alienation which precipitated such suicidal lows can mainly be laid at the door of social oppression. But his entire revolutionary take on sexual deviance remains haunted by an older aesthetic/theological vision as articulated by Baldwin, above: 'the male desire for a male roams everywhere, avid, desperate, unimaginably lonely, culminating often in drugs, piety, madness or death.'

Returning to Rumaker's vision, one wonders how sex – any kind of sex – can be so completely colonized by the language of saneness, health, wholeness and optimism – everything *but* death. In short, how can sex be made simultaneously to redeem and repress so much? If the exiles prowling 'the litter and stink of this hidden-away bathhouse' are seeking 'the miracle of a barely imagined paradise ... a tiny glint of the shy and elusive flower that enfolds the secret and the meaning', aren't they searching for nothing less than the redemption of self *and* world? Can sex, even deviant sex, ever deliver that? And when it does fail to deliver, as it must, then the quest for redemption so often becomes death-haunted. Such is the case even with Rumaker's text. Actually it begins with death: on his way to the baths the narrator encounters the aftermath of a suicide who had leaped from the Empire State Building. 'Intimate with suicide among us', he wonders if the victim was gay and, so tormented by 'traditional ignorance ... the hostility around him, and, finally, his own', that he flings himself 'with unutterable relief' from the eighty-fifth floor. A little later we encounter the desperate pathetic desire of those close to death, and the aggressive behaviour of those who remind the narrator of the sexually brutal men he had searched out in the past, 'unconsciously seeking my own internalized need for punishment and death'. Then there is the youth, aged maybe 15 or 16, who is already old and trapped by desire for the rest of his days in one of these bathhouse cubicles,

> his desire gone meaningless, only the spasms of habit remaining, returning him again and again to this spot; someone damned to

haunt these hallways forever, even long after the building collapsed in decay and dust or burned ... the aborted and beaten spirit of him prowling always.

Such desperation is concealed by a flat expression or bored, indifferent eyes.

Of course all this misery can be attributed to social oppression, which is to say that, in the better society which it is in our power to achieve, it will disappear. And, for the narrator, even as we are waiting for that social transformation to occur, the negative sexual scenario can resolve itself into the benignly redemptive one; just as in the midst of clap and syphilis there is always penicillin, free VD examinations, and the Gay Men's Health Project in Greenwich Village, so the desperation can end in good sex. Except that in this ('pre AIDS') text there is a residual fear of disease that can't be eradicated, and a connection of desire with such disease. This connection is literal, but also works as a metaphor for the helpless self-destructiveness of desire: the narrator imagines the beautiful arse to be 'rampant with hepatitis, the penises that flamed with passion flaming with spirochetes as well'; he also imagines sailors carrying all manner of disease from all parts of the globe to this one place – 'carrying here centuries-old infections of the fathers'. And the 'gay sons' driven by desire to risk these infections, 'driven to this contagious harbor again and again', there being 'no ports free of the contaminating fathers'.

So as the narrator explores this misery there is the sense that it might not be so easy. He remarks, poignantly, the 'love-scrawls of KY-sticky fingers' on the cubicle walls, 'graffiti tracks of passion' evoking 'the cries and breaths and urgencies of all who had ever come in secret yearning to this cubicle'. On the one hand those scrawls are the definitive traces of urban transcience and anonymity inside of which the most memorable of all fleeting experiences may occur; on the other, they document the endlessly, 'eternally' repeated sexual encounter in which nothing changes, least of all the loneliness of desire, a loneliness invulnerable even to redemptive sex: 'So many of us frightened here ... *so many faces that passed me with the look of urgent and perilous need that seemed to have nothing to do with sex.*'[26]

So Nunokawa is right, the death–sex connection is very much inside gay culture. But it's one thing to disarticulate the lethal connections between death and homosexuality made by, say, the moral right, quite another to censor or disavow insightful gay writing about the death/desire paradox; to see it as always as the result of internalized homophobia, to be countered with consciousness raising and positive self-images. This is normalizing of a particularly insidious kind, not least because it implicitly concedes much ground to the enemies of gay culture. There is something else: out of a respect for, even an identification with, those who have died, who are dying or who are ill, there is a wish, even an urgent need, to repudiate a seemingly irresponsible and offensive use of death as metaphor. But as D. A. Miller suggests in relation to Susan Sontag's writing on illness, in trying to cleanse our discourse of insidious metaphors, we often only leave the unseen, unregarded and equally damaging ones in place.[27]

Homosexual desire has been regarded in diverse ways by gay people themselves – as revolutionary, as redemptive, as self-shattering, as normal, as death-driven, to name but some, and some of whose metaphors even now test the nerve of gay studies, even the avowedly non-politically correct nerve of queer theory. And not surprisingly: on the one hand this connection of homosexual desire and death is made by those who want homosexuals literally to die, and would actually kill them or behave in ways which contribute to their literal death, given the chance. On the other hand this death/desire connection is part of our history, as of theirs, albeit differently: the sexually dissident have always tended to know more about it, confronting and exploring what the sexually conventional typically disavow, in particular the fact that the strange dynamic which, in western culture, binds death into desire, cannot be dismissed as pathological or marginal, because it happens to be crucial in the formation of the western subject, and in its (our) gendering, and its (our) fantasy life. In suggesting as much it's not my intention to offer a robust redefinition of the radical agenda. Just now, just for the moment, my interest is in those aspects of sexual longing usually effaced by such agendas and the sexual politics which they serve; those nuances of the history of desire which disappear in the wake of those furious grim struggles which necessarily inflect the relationship between the sexually dominant and the sexually deviant, and which increasingly define sexual politics itself.

Is the rectum a grave?

In a provocative article, 'Is the rectum a grave?', Leo Bersani criticizes uncompromisingly that normalizing vision of gay desire which has figured as one aspect of gay liberation and which is epitomized in Rumaker's text. First because it is 'unnecessarily and even dangerously tame'; second because it is disingenuous about the revulsion which homosexual behaviour inspires, and third because it wants to dilute the menace which homosexuality holds for a homophobic society:

> The revulsion it turns out is all a big mistake: what we're really up to is pluralism and diversity, and getting buggered is just one moment in the practice of those laudable humanistic virtues.

Bersani goes on to argue that phallocentrism is not primarily the denial of power to women but rather the denial of the value of powerlessness in both men and women. By powerlessness he means not gentleness, non-aggressiveness, or even passivity, but rather the positive potential for a 'radical disintegration and humiliation of the self'. This is masochism in the sense of a sexual pleasure that crosses a threshold, and shatters psychic organization; in which 'the self is exuberantly discarded' and there occurs 'the terrifying appeal of a loss of the ego, of a self-debasement'. A kind of death.

This means that the problematic aspects of sexuality cannot be seen to derive simply or only from social oppression or bad social relations. On the contrary, for Bersani, 'the social structures from which it is often said that the eroticizing of mastery and subordination derive are perhaps themselves derivations (and sublimations) of the indissociable nature of sexual pleasure and the exercise or loss of power.' The terrifying appeal of a loss of the ego is, he continues, why men doing 'passive' anal sex are demonized. He points to the anthropological evidence which suggests a widespread condemnation of such sex even in cultures that have not regarded sex between men as unnatural or sinful. Even or especially for the Athenians, to be penetrated was to abdicate power. Bersani concludes, in what has become a controversial passage: 'if the rectum is the grave in which the masculine ideal (an ideal shared – differently – by men *and* women) of proud subjectivity is buried, then it should be celebrated for its very potential for death.' He adds, in a passage less frequently cited:

> Tragically, AIDS has literalized that potential as the certainty of biological death, and has therefore reinforced the heterosexual association of anal sex with a self-annihilation originally and primarily identified with the fantasmatic mystery of an insatiable, unstoppable female sexuality. It may, finally, be in the gay man's rectum that he demolishes his own perhaps otherwise uncontrollable identification with a murderous judgment against him.

Bersani also wonders whether we should say, not that so-called passive sex is 'demeaning', but rather that *'the value of sexuality itself is to demean the seriousness of efforts to redeem it'*.[28]

The homoerotically perverse encounter with the death/desire paradox enacts a dangerous knowledge. 'Enacts' because the challenge of deviant desire lies in its potential for acting out awkward, provocative, ambivalent versions of what otherwise remains culturally and psychically disavowed. Another instance of this is Bersani's description of (some) gay men's relationship to masculinity. Against the congenial political line that gay machismo is straightforwardly a parodic subversion of masculinity, Bersani contends that it includes a worshipful tribute to, a '*yearning* toward' the straight machismo style and behaviour it defiles. And if, in Jeffrey Weeks's phrase, gay men 'gnaw at the roots of a male heterosexual identity', this is because, 'from within their nearly mad identification with it, *they never cease to feel the appeal of its being violated*'.[29]

Ecstasy and self-annihilation

So, in the place of the fatalistic narrative of those like Haselden, the revolutionary narrative of those like Rechy, the redemptive normalizing of Rumaker's vision, or the straightforward identity politics which would resist oppression in the name of what we truly and healthily are, given the social space to breathe – instead of all those, Bersani suggests this other scenario wherein identity is conflicted by desire, fantasy, and ambivalent identification, and potentially, strangely, annihilated in the process of being affirmed. Perhaps Foucault, in his famous essay 'Preface to transgression', was imagining something similar in relation to transgression more generally. In transgression of the limit, he says, the limit is suddenly 'fulfilled by this alien plenitude which invades it to the core of its being'.[30]

Explored here is an attitude to loss fundamentally different from that encountered so far. No longer is there a struggle to redeem or transcend loss; rather loss becomes paradoxically liberating but always dangerous, at once self-shatteringly and self-renewing because transvalued: 'not a *desire* for something [but] a desire *to be* with an intensity that cannot be contained – held in or defined – by a self'.[31] Speaking broadly, Bersani and Foucault are identifying with a perspective which includes Bataille, Lacan, Deleuze, and Barthes – just some of those French thinkers who in turn have been influential in the Anglo-American context, though hardly ever in what they have had to say about desire's strange relation to death. And beyond them all, are Nietzsche and the Marquis de Sade. Bataille alone may serve to illustrate this longer, diverse perspective. In his book on eroticism, subtitled 'Death and Sensuality', he claimed, or rather fantasized, eroticism as a violation of our very being – 'a violation bordering on death, bordering on murder':

> Eroticism opens the way to death, Death opens the way to the denial of our individual lives. Without doing violence to our inner selves, are we able to bear a negation that carries us to the farthest bounds of possibility?
>
> (p. 24)

When people experience sexual ecstasy their unity is shattered, the personality dies.[32] And obscenity is the name we give to the unease which disrupts 'the possession of a recognised and stable individuality'.[33]

Foucault was influenced by Bataille, and, for someone otherwise so reticent about himself, he was forthcoming about his own personal take on desire and death, albeit facetiously. In 1982, hinting at desire's impossibility, he declared:

> I would like and I hope I'll die of an overdose [*laughter*] of pleasure of any kind. Because I think it's really difficult and I always have this feeling that I do not feel *the* pleasure, the complete, total pleasure and, for me, it's related to death ... the kind of pleasure I would consider as *the* real pleasure would be so deep, so intense, so overwhelming that I couldn't survive it. I would die.

Once when high on opium, he was hit by a car. As he lay in the street, for a few seconds 'I had the impression that I was dying and it was really a very, very intense pleasure. . . . It was, it still is now, one of my best memories.'[34] Having apparently made one or more suicide attempts himself when younger, Foucault defended people's right to kill themselves; in fact he celebrated suicide. No conduct, he said in 1982, 'is more beautiful or, consequently, more worthy of careful thought than suicide. One should work on one's suicide throughout one's life.'[35] However these remarks were meant to be taken, the fact remains that Foucault's concern with the death/desire dynamic, and its connection with the negation of the self, recur through his writing, and in ways which are both fascinating and disturbing.

Crucially, anti-essentialism or anti-humanism was for Foucault (as for most gay intellectuals) much more than showing that western concepts of 'man' or of the individual are philosophical errors; when he spoke or wrote of the death of the author, the death of man, the death of humanism, the death of the subject, he really wanted to subvert these normalizing, repressive ways of thinking, being, and desiring. Behind all this is a utopian ideal of release at once psychic and social; in place of so-called 'man', what must be produced 'is something that absolutely does not exist, about which we know nothing ... the creation of something totally different.'[36] Later he suggested that homosexuality, especially the extreme scenarios of sado-masochism, could provide something like this; here it was possible to 'invent oneself' polymorphously, especially with the help of drugs. More generally, his vision for gay culture was that it would invent new ways of living.[37] Not surprisingly he too was against identity politics, and gay essentializing: this remark, with which many have since identified, is from 1969:

> Do not ask me who I am, and do not ask me to stay the same: leave it to our bureaucrats and our police to see that our papers are in order. At least spare us their morality when we write.[38]

Such self-disidentification also led him eventually to renounce the very idea of desire, speaking instead of pleasure. For Foucault – and here he seems to have been distancing himself from Deleuze and Guattari – desire is a notion already imbued with oppression; to desire is already to be the deep subject of enlightenment discourse: ' "Tell me what your desire is and I will tell you who you are, whether you are normal or not, and then I can specify or disqualify your desire." ' By contrast 'there is no pathology of pleasure, no "abnormal" pleasure. It is an event "outside the subject" or on the edge of the subject.'[39]

To reiterate: for Foucault the *disidentification of self*, which in turn involved a fascination with death itself, was at once political, historical and subjective. Only then does it become an intellectual imperative. In the introduction to *The Use of Pleasure* (1984) he said that it was curiosity that motivated him to write. He goes on to say (in a passage read at his funeral by Deleuze) that this is not the curiosity which seeks confirmation of what one wants to hear, but the kind of curiosity which 'enables one to get free of oneself', the curiosity for a knowledge that finds 'the knower straying afield of himself'. Curiosity finds its way to death, that (until recently) ignored aspect of this philosopher's thought.[40]

Foucault on death

Currently, the 'theorizing' of what I have called desire's impossibility is almost exclusively associated with psychoanalysis, and especially with Jacques Lacan who claimed to find in the most desperate affirmation of life the purest form of the death drive; who declared that it is from death that existence takes on all the meaning it has; who theorized desire as lack, absence and impossibility – in short, desire as death.[41] But, as I indicated earlier, we can also find the association in many other western writers, including Foucault. Throughout his work there are cryptic, lyrical, paradoxical speculations on how we *live* death – how, that is, its changing face organizes our identity, language, sexuality and our future.

In *The Birth of the Clinic* he argues that, whereas in the Renaissance death was the great leveller, in modern culture (from the nineteenth century) death becomes constitutive of singularity; it is in the perception of death that the individual finds him or herself. Death gives to life 'a face that cannot be exchanged. Death left its old tragic heaven and became the lyrical core of man: his invisible truth, his visible secret.'[42] Towards the end of *The Order of Things* Foucault remarks that if death – 'the Death that is at work in [man's] suffering' – is the precondition of knowledge, and if desire – 'the Desire that has lost its object' – is what remains 'always *unthought* at the heart of thought', then death and desire are already in a paradoxical enabling proximity within and for our culture.[43] Language especially is organized by this proximity:

It is quite likely that the approach of death – its sovereign gesture, its prominence within human memory – hollows out in the present and in existence the void toward which and from which we speak. . . .

Perhaps there exists in speech an essential affinity between death, endless striving, and the self-representation of language. . . . In this sense death is undoubtedly the most essential of the accidents of language (its limit and its centre): from the day that men began to speak toward death and against it, in order to grasp and imprison it, something was born, a murmering which repeats, recounts, and redoubles itself endlessly, which has undergone an uncanny process of amplification and thickening, in which our language is today lodged and hidden.[44]

Many were, and still are, disturbed by Foucault's anti-humanism, and not surprisingly since he was uncompromising about its implications. In the conclusion of *The Archeology of Knowledge* he affects sympathy with humanist aspirations but rehearses them only to relish their demise, reinstating death at the centre of the illusions of the timid post-Christian attempts to preserve immortality. The humanist, says Foucault, wants to discern in discourse 'the gentle, silent, intimate consciousness' of its author, and, through that, 'the murmur . . . of insubstantial immortalities'. But what the humanist must realize is that in speaking or writing 'I am not banishing my death, but actually establishing it; or rather I am abolishing all interiority in that exterior that is so indifferent to my life, and so *neutral*, that it makes no distinction between my life and my death.'[45]

In later work he wants to show how death is strangely at work in the power/sexuality dynamic. We are familiar with Foucault's argument that sex is constitutive of identity – 'it is through sex . . . that each individual has to pass in order to have access to his own intelligibility', but there is a further turn to this argument:

> The Faustian pact, whose temptation has been instilled in us by the deployment of sexuality, is now as follows: to exchange life in its entirety for sex itself, for the truth and sovereignty of sex. Sex is worth dying for. It is in this (strictly historical) sense that sex is indeed imbued with the death instinct. When a long while ago the West discovered love, it bestowed on it a value high enough to make death acceptable; nowadays it is sex that claims this equivalence.[46]

Against psychoanalysis Foucault here indicates the historical ground not only of the death drive, but also of desire's impossibility, which now, at least partly, derives from the fact that 'we expect our intelligibility to come from what was for many centuries thought of as a madness [i.e. sex].'[47] But if the death drive is in this sense an effect of power working through sexuality, death (like desire) thereby also has the potential to elude power, especially through suicide; death becomes the 'ultimate' instance of what Foucault elsewhere calls a reverse-discourse: 'Death is power's limit, the moment that escapes it; death becomes the most secret aspect of existence, the most "private".'[48]

Foucault cruising

'Sex is worth dying for': that is what those like James Miller attribute to the Foucault who cruised the bathhouses of San Francisco in the early 1980s. The rumour that Foucault deliberately tried to infect others is discounted; although circulating for almost a decade, Miller finds no evidence for it. It was true that Foucault was deeply sceptical about AIDS. But so were many others in 1982–3, and *at the time* with reason; certainly they were right to discredit the idea of a 'gay cancer' as it was then called. As D. A. Miller says: 'it wasn't as if people didn't know about AIDS, but everyone was unwilling to believe it would attack you because you were gay.'[49]

But Foucault did, apparently, say to D. A. Miller: 'To die for the love of boys: What could be more beautiful?' This is so conventional as to be consciously attitudinizing, but that does not preclude it being a 'sincere' expression of desire. On the contrary gay culture often inscribes the sincere within the insincere by way of simultaneously saying something truthful about desire, and undermining 'sincerity' as one of its most oppressive manifestations. ('In matters of grave importance style, not sincerity, is the vital thing' – Wilde.) It's precisely this sensibility of the in/sincere, the light, second-nature assumption of irony, the intuitive, self-expressive self-effacement of the gay affect, its rhetorical vengefulness – all of which involves yet another kind of self-disidentification – which those like James Miller fail to see. What they imagine is a fatally crude connection between Foucault's writing and his alleged sexual practices:

> the crux of what is most original and challenging about Foucault's way of thinking ... is his unrelenting, deeply ambiguous and profoundly problematic preoccupation with death, which he explored not only in ... his writing, but also, and I believe critically, in ... sado-masochistic eroticism.[50]

According to Miller, the anonymous sexual encounter, perhaps also in an S and M context, offered Foucault the prospect of being liberated into something different – a 'limit experience'. AIDS became another limit experience, and now a fatal one, leading Foucault into

> potentially suicidal acts of passion with consenting partners, most of them likely to be infected already; deliberately throwing caution to the wind, Foucault and these men were wagering their lives together.[51]

To act out self-annihilating fantasies sexually is hardly unknown. Whether Foucault did or not I do not know, and hardly care either way if only because I cannot see how we could know. More importantly, those like Miller who speculate not only that he did, but that the fantasies were actualized in life-threatening ways, reproduce a tendentious conflation between death, AIDS, promiscuity and sadomasochism. Ironically, what Foucault had to say on death was largely ignored until it could be revisited as 'evidence' for this supposed erotic, suicidal and/or murderous obsession with the subject. Perhaps what compels this 'biographical' quest are fantasies of the antihumanist Foucault – he who had dared to declare the death of the author, of the subject, of man and of humanism – fucking others to death, or, better still, being fucked to death himself.

Certainly, the same biographical quest obliterates the very sensibility it purports to reveal, and – the cultural context which informs that sensibility – the nuances of a homosexual history at once, and inseparably, aesthetic, psychic, social and political. I've briefly connected Foucault's philosophy of self-disidentification with one such past going back through Bataille. In the rest of this essay I want to locate Foucault's 'promiscuity' in another kind of gay history, again trying to be faithful to those same nuances.

The wonder of the pleasure

Renaud Camus's *Tricks* is a narrative of twenty-five 'promiscuous' homosexual encounters graphic enough to have merited the charge of obscenity. 'Sexual practices', says Roland Barthes in the preface to this book, 'are banal, impoverished, doomed to repetition, and [in] this . . . disproportionate to the wonder of the pleasure they afford.'[52] Note how Barthes hints at – has in mind – the self-destructive impossibility of desire: these practices are banal, impoverished, *doomed to repetition*. Hovering beyond or within that impossibility is a sense of death-in-life, desire as a frenzied, compulsive, negative, quest for an impossible gratification. And yet, insists Barthes, sexual acts are also the source of pleasure. But I've already misrepresented him and missed precisely what's significant: if Barthes invokes the impossibility of desire in order to circumvent it, this isn't because he speaks simply of the *pleasure* of sex; that would be banal. He speaks rather of *the wonder* of this pleasure.

The sense of the trick that we find in Renaud Camus and Roland Barthes is quite different from the doomed, self-destructive promiscuity of Haselden and Moore, or Rechy's revolutionary fuck, or Rumaker's benignly redemptive one, or even Bersani's perspective of desire as self-shattering. This is Barthes' memorable description of it:

> *Trick* – the encounter which takes place only once: more than cruising, less than love: an intensity, which passes without regret. Consequently, for me, *Trick* becomes the metaphor for many adventures which are not sexual; the encounter of a glance, a gaze, an idea, an image, ephemeral and forceful association, which consents to dissolve so lightly, a faithless benevolence: a way of

not getting stuck in desire, though without evading it; all in all, a kind of wisdom.

(*Tricks*, p. 10)

'A way of not getting stuck in desire' – far from being an expression of desire's impossibility, the trick here becomes a way of evading it, without thereby evading desire itself. Once again the difference involves a fundamentally different attitude to loss. Also, desire as 'a kind of wisdom': that which is typically thought to be thrown to the wind in cruising (wisdom), is rediscovered within it. Just as the poet C. P. Cavafy literally derived creative impetus, in fact an entire literary aesthetic, from the promiscuous encounter, so Barthes further de-alienates the trick by making it a metaphor for the eroticizing of non-sexual cultural practices; as in his own cultural and literary theory, wherein *draguer* – to cruise, seduce, loiter, follow, to engage with anonymously/publicly – becomes central not only for a gay aesthetic, but, more generally, for the urban, modernist, literary aesthetic to which Barthes contributed so significantly. And once again self-disidentification is crucial. In relation to Stendhal he speaks of the 'amorous plural', a pleasure 'analogous to that enjoyed today by someone "cruising"', and involving an *'irregular discontinuity ...* simultaneously aesthetic, psychological, and metaphysical'.[53] As with homosexuals before him, for Barthes the casual sexual encounter has the potential not so much for a discovery of his true self, as a liberation *from* self, from a self-oppressive identity – especially the subordinated identity:

> What society will not tolerate is that ... the something I am should be openly expressed as provisional ... insignificant, ines-sential, in a word irrelevant. Just say 'I am' and you will be socially saved.[54]

Anti-essentialism as a theoretical statement about identity is mislead-ing to the point of being useless. Which is why, according to Jeffrey Weeks and others, the essentialist/anti-essentialist debate has become sterile. What has contributed to this sterility is first, trying to resolve it theoretically rather than exploring it historically; second, and consequently, the disregard of experience – not experience essential-ized, but the experiential dimension of anti-essentialism. And that is found most significantly in gay culture. A secondary purpose of my remarks on erotic self-disidentification in gay history is to keep the debate alive in ways which matter. Certainly for Barthes (as for Wilde and others before him) anti-essentialism was felt experientially; in his aesthetic, a marginal decentred sexuality informs a deviant sensibility which emerges into visibility as a philosophy of the self and of the social wherein the self is disidentified, and prescriptive, essentialist sexual norms are provoked into disarray.[55]

To those who regard this as just a precious Parisian aesthetic with nothing to say to hard-core sexual politicians, I suggest that what we learn from Barthes (as from Foucault and Wilde, albeit differently in each case) is that oppression inheres in the subjected *as* their, or our, identity, and must be eventually experienced and contested there. This is never truer than when this subjection of identity so directly involves the subjection of desire. Identity for the homosexual is always conflicted: at once ascribed, proscribed and internalized, it is in terms of identities that we have experienced self-hatred, violence, mutilation and death. Conversely, identity is also that in the name of which liberation is fiercely fought for. Not surprisingly then, this very self-realization has always been strangely bound up with a defiant refusal of self. Historically and aesthetically, the promiscuous encounter focuses this, enacting the possibility of a simultaneous identification/disidentification in which I cease to be the fixed, tyrannized subject and become – become what? One hesitates here only because *what* one becomes is never secure, never as certain as what the euphoria of self-discovery promises. One becomes something other for sure, yet, equally surely, never the abstract free-floating subject of the postmodern; and this is because, for the gay person, what remains in place is *always at risk*: psychically, socially, sexually, legally, and in other ways, and probably all at once, inseparably. But still, remarkably, desire enables a self-realization which is also a defiant refusal of self. Still, now: as a gay poet writes in 1991, in a poem called 'Our Shadows', also about cruising and the anonymous sexual encounter:

You were the emptiness I sought,
The escape from thought . . .

There was truth & trust wrapped in the swift embrace
Of strangers who could vanish without trace.[56]

For this poet 'truth and trust' derive not from a fullness of subjective being, not from the authentic encounter between self and other, nor even from the completion of me in another, but from the other as 'the emptiness I sought, / The escape from thought', and the possibility of both vanishing 'without trace'. The word 'strangers' equalizes the you and I: fantasy and identification circulate because, and not in spite of, anonymity.

Once, while taking drugs, Foucault apparently said: 'Contact with a strange body *affords an experience of the truth* similar to what I am experiencing now.'[57] 'An experience of the truth': what might such a philosophically reckless remark, uttered by one sceptical of both 'experience' and 'truth', mean in this context? Perhaps that, in the anonymous yet intensely subjective encounter with the absolute uniqueness of the 'anybody', the divide between reality and fantasy momentarily shifts and even dissolves, and other divisions too, including those between public and private, self and other. Or rather, that this is an encounter which presupposes, which only occurs because of, these divisions, even as it momentarily suspends them, in fantasy and actually. In short, an encounter in which deviant desire is experienced as at once an effect and a refusal of history. Which means that such encounters are where history and agency, reality and fantasy, despair and idealism, sameness and difference, may converge in highly charged ways. So, for sure, such encounters can be compulsive, desperate and driven in the way Baldwin describes, but also be the occasion of identification and empathy across differences of many kinds, including those of class, age, and race. Differences that are sometimes registered in casual intimacy like slight, ecstatic shocks; discerned as a reticence, or maybe a confidence, the poise of the body, a curiosity about what precisely is desired, and how; in the anonymous, elusive but always individual gesture or expression, what Cavafy once called, perfectly, 'the beauty of *anomalous* charm'.

That our desires are saturated with our histories, including the histories of our distress, and our loss, is true; it's true also that this can make desire very blind. But the blindness of desire remains matched by a mobility of desire, and, sometimes, a deviant kind of knowledge, both of which may become entangled with that blindness without ever being quite contained by it. Another cruising poem:

breathing the strong smell of each other
I want it to last forever
it is never enough
warm in the coldness of the heart

we stood holding each other
two men locking eyes and lips
then your mind cut the flow
and it was abruptly over

yet I felt curiously healed
as if life were about to begin[58]

Again the impossibility of desire is invoked in the impossible drive for completion in the 'forever'; in the realization that desire 'is never enough'; in the regret at the other's cutting of 'the flow'. And yet, despite all that, the poet feels *'curiously* healed' (as ever, the pensive qualifiers are crucial), feeling as if life were beginning or – again, precise qualification – 'about' to begin. In this last qualification is perhaps the recognition that gratification only ever suspends the experience of incompletion; that the ecstatic moment is already its own loss, ecstasy only existing in, through, and as, a loss which is the occasion of both regret and freedom. Which means these alternative narratives cannot be celebrated as simply antithetical to those pre-occupied with death. There are connections between the two if only because, as Foucault has suggested, death has come to inhabit the two most crucial attributes of identity: knowledge and desire, haunting desire as loss, and remaining 'always *unthought* at the heart of thought'. It's in this way that death, having left its old tragic heaven, now helps constitute modern individuality – 'the lyrical core of man: his invisible truth, his visible secret'. Ecstatic self-disidentification may have as its obverse a desire for death, or at least find within itself the shadow of such a desire. Again, there is a history inside such desires. A certain kind of desire – romantic, deviant – experiences this history as a tension. On the one hand is the yearning to compensate for the loss which haunts desire, to overcome or redeem a loss experienced as unwelcome, unbearable, yet seemingly unavoidable (the Aristophanes myth). This is the drive towards unity. On the other hand there is the yearning to become lost; to annihilate the self in ecstasy; to render oblivious the self riven by, constituted by, loss. This is the drive to undifferentiation (Schopenhauer, Freud, Bataille). *Now* an attempt to flee that sense of separation and incompleteness, a wish for difference without pain, for unity, identity, and selfhood, through union with the other; *now* a desired, even a willed loss of identity in which death is metaphor for, or fantasized or the literal event guaranteeing, the transcendence of desire. And dying in ecstacy might be fantasized as the supreme pleasure because it is a fulfilment which is also the permanent and not merely the temporary extinction of desire. In short, the drive to undifferentiation has become a drive to death but also a drive for transcendence, and metaphysical unity and entropic dispersal have come to resemble each other. It is not strange that the two drives seem now experientially opposed, now indistinguishable; nor is it surprising to discern within that instability an idealism which resists both drives – in Bersani's words – not a desire *for* something, but a desire *to be* uncontainable within self-hood.

To disavow homosexual writing about all this in the name of a progressive politics is only to concede almost everything to a

reactionary politics. Instead we should recognize that writing as arguably the most insightful account of something central to western
culture; writing which explores the complexity of the death/desire
dynamic in (at the very least) an implicit or direct repudiation of
the clichéd, hysterical, and moralistic representations of it by the
reactionary politics which currently dominate our culture, and for
which homosexuality equals death.

*

To be dying, to see a lover or friend die, is to encounter an immense
gulf between desire and death, even or especially in their proximity.
Today gay writers are of necessity living both the proximity and the
gulf, which is also to experience desire itself as a kind of grieving. In
his memorable recent collection, *The Man with Night Sweats*, Thom
Gunn writes:

My thoughts are crowded with death
and it draws so oddly on the sexual
that I am confused
confused to be attracted
by, in effect, my own annihilation.

In the same collection he describes an encounter:

Once when you went to see
Another with a fever
In a like hospital bed . . .

You climbed in there beside him
And hugged him plain in view,
Though you were sick enough,
And had your own fears too.[59]

*

Barthes wrote wisely of the potential, the paradoxical wisdom of the
casual sexual encounter; sufficiently so for me to risk the very repetition which the trick ideally foregoes:

> *Trick* – the encounter which takes place only once: more than
> cruising, less than love: an intensity, which passes without
> regret. . . . *Trick* becomes the metaphor for many adventures which
> are not sexual; the encounter of a glance, a gaze, an idea, an image,
> ephemeral and forceful association, which consents to dissolve so
> lightly, a faithless benevolence: a way of not getting stuck in
> desire, though without evading it; all in all a kind of wisdom.

University of Sussex

Notes

My thanks to Rachel Bowlby, Ben Gove, Alan Sinfield and Lindsay Smith for thoughts on an earlier draft of this piece.

1 Ellis Hanson, 'Undead', in D. Fuss (ed.), *Inside/Out: Lesbian Theories, Gay Theories* (London and New York: Routledge, 1991), pp. 324–5).
2 ibid., p. 317.
3 Oscar Moore, *A Matter of Life and Sex* (London: Penguin Books, 1992), pp. 29, 39, 49, 116. This novel was first published in 1991 under the pseudonym Alec F. Moran by Paper Drum.
4 ibid., p.146.
5 Mark Lilla, 'A taste for pain' (a review of James Miller, *The Passion of Michel Foucault* and Didier Eribon, *Michel Foucault*), *Times Literary Supplement*, 26 March 1993, pp. 3–4 (this quotation p. 4).
6 Michel Foucault, *History of Sexuality, 1: An Introduction* (New York: Vintage Books (1978), 1980) p. 39.
7 Lilla, op. cit., p. 4.
8 James Miller, *The Passion of Michel Foucault* (New York: Simon & Schuster, 1993), p. 375.
9 Or Cyril Collard's autobiographical novel, *Savage Nights*, trans. William Rodarmor (London: Quartet Books (1989), 1993), which became the basis of a controversial film of the same name with Collard as lead and director.
10 op. cit., p.255.
11 ibid., p. 137.
12 ibid., pp. 304–5. Compare, from a decade earlier, Andrew Holleran's *Dancer From the Dance*: 'five feet away from the corpse, people lay taking the sun and admiring a man who had just given the kiss of life to a young boy. Death and desire, death and desire' (p. 30–1).
13 See Jonathan Dollimore, 'Desire is death', in *Material Culture in the Early Modern Period*, ed. Margreta de Grazia *et al.* (Cambridge: Cambridge University Press, 1995).
14 Denis de Rougemont, *Love in the Western World*, revised and augmented edition (1956) (New York: Fawcett, 1966).
15 James Baldwin, 'Here be dragons', in *The Price of the Ticket: Collected Non-Fiction 1948–1985* (London: Joseph, 1985), p. 683.
16 This article originally appeared in *Impact* (Autumn 1991), pp. 14–15, a magazine published by the *Guardian* newspaper. Later it was reprinted in the *Weekend Guardian* (7–8 September 1991, pp. 20–1) and became the subject of intense controversy.
17 Haselden, pp. 14–15. Douglas Crimp insists on a contrary account of gay promiscuity: 'Our promiscuity taught us many things, not only about the pleasures of sex, but about the great multiplicity of those pleasures. It is that psychic preparation, that experimentation, that conscious work on our own sexualities that has allowed many of us to change our sexual behaviors.' So, against the claim that promiscuity will destroy the gay community, Crimp insists 'in fact *it is our promiscuity that will save us*'. Further: 'all those who contend that gay male promiscuity is merely sexual *compulsion* resulting from fear of intimacy are now faced with very strong evidence against their prejudices. For if compulsion were so easily overcome or redirected, it would hardly deserve the name' ('How

to have promiscuity in an epidemic', in D. Crimp (ed.), *AIDS: Cultural Analysis, Cultural Activism* (Cambridge, Mass.: MIT Press, 1988) p. 253).

18 John Rechy, *The Sexual Outlaw* (London: W. H. Allen (1977), 1978), p. 301.

19 Cited in David Macey, *The Lives of Michel Foucault* (London: Hutchinson, 1993), p. 369.

20 Michael Rumaker, *A Day and a Night at the Baths* (California: Grey Fox Press (1977), 1979), pp. 27, 32, 17, 63, 55; cf. p. 17.

21 And, again, the family: every hometown in America will have a free public bath in which 'purified mothers and other women teach the girl-children and purified fathers and other men teach the boy-children, in gentle massage, in merry bubble-winking strokes of beginning awareness ... in encouraging right and clean and courteous ways ... and then none can ever be unkind to another' (Rumaker, p. 47).

22 ibid., pp. 47, 71–2, my emphasis.

23 Thomas Mann, *Death in Venice* (1912), trans. H. T. Lowe-Porter (Harmondsworth: Penguin Books, 1971), pp. 70–3. Compare Guy Hocquenghem: 'Homosexual desire is neither on the side of death nor on the side of life; it is the killer of civilised egos' (*Homosexual Desire*, p. 136).

24 Moore, op. cit., pp. 255, 144, 39.

25 Rechy, op. cit., pp. 71, 48.

26 Rumaker, op. cit., pp. 2, 19–20, 59, 27, 39, 28, 23, 45, my emphasis.

27 D. A. Miller, 'Sontag's Urbanity', in *The Lesbian and Gay Studies Reader*, ed. Henry Abelove *et al.* (London and New York: Routledge, 1993), p. 217.

28 Leo Bersani, 'Is the rectum a grave', in D. Crimp (ed.), *AIDS: Cultural Analysis, Cultural Activism*, pp. 218–19, 217, 218, 220, 216, 222.

29 ibid., p. 209.

30 Michel Foucault, 'A preface to transgression', in *Language, Counter-Memory, Practice: Selected Essays and Interviews*, ed. with intro. by D. F. Bouchard and Sherry Simon (Oxford: Basil Blackwell, 1977), p. 34.

31 Leo Bersani, *The Culture of Redemption* (Cambridge, Mass.: Harvard University Press, 1990, pp. 100–1).

32 Georges Bataille, *Erotism: Death and Sensuality*, trans. Mary Dalwood (San Francisco: City Light Books (1962), 1986), pp. 16–17, 24, 105–6. Compare Bersani's more searching account of sexual excitement 'as both a turning away from other and a dying to the self. The appeal of that dying – the desire to be shattered out of coherence – is perhaps what psychoanalysis has sought most urgently to repress' (*The Culture of Redemption*, p. 45).

33 pp. 17–18; cf. p. 59: 'repugnance and horror are the mainsprings of my desire [which is] only aroused as long as its object causes a chasm no less deep than death to yawn within me ... this desire originates in its opposite, horror.'

34 *Michel Foucault: Politics, Philosophy, Culture: Interviews and Other Writings 1977–84*, trans. Alan Sheridan and others, ed. with introduction by Lawrence D. Kritzman (London and New York: Routledge, 1988), p. 12.

35 James Miller, op. cit., p. 351.

36 James Miller, op. cit., p. 336.

37 David Macey, op. cit., pp. 365, 371, 367.

38 Michel Foucault, *The Archeology of Knowledge*, trans. A. M. Sheridan Smith (London: Tavistock (1969), 1972), p. 17.
39 Cited in Macey, op. cit., p. 365.
40 Michel Foucault, *The Use of Pleasure*, trans. Robert Hurley (London: Penguin Books, 1985), p. 8.
41 See especially Jacques Lacan, *The Ethics of Psychoanalysis 1959–1960: the Seminar of Jacques Lacan*, Book VII, ed. Jacques-Alain Miller, trans. Dennis Porter (London: Routledge, 1992), and Richard Boothby, *Death and Desire: Psychoanalytic Theory in Lacan's Return to Freud* (New York and London: Routledge, 1991).
42 Michel Foucault, *The Birth of the Clinc: An Archaeological of Medical Perception* (London: Tavistock, 1973), p. 170; cf. p. 197: 'the experience of individuality in modern culture is bound up with that of death: from Hölderlin's Empedocles to Nietzsche's Zarathustra, and on to Freudian man, an obstinate relation to death prescribes the universal its singular face, and lends to each individual the power of being heard forever; the individual owes to death a meaning which does not cease with him. The division that it traces and the finitude whose mark it imposes link, paradoxically, the universality of language and the precarious, irreplaceable form of the individual.'
43 Michel Foucault, *The Order of Things: An Archeology of the Human Sciences* (London: Tavistock (1966), 1974), p. 376.
44 *Language, Counter-Memory*, pp. 53, 55; cf. pp. 54–5: 'Headed toward death, language turns back upon itself; it encounters something like a mirror; and to stop this death which would stop it, it possesses but a single power: that of giving birth to its own image in a play of mirrors that has no limits. From the depths of the mirror where it sets out to arrive anew at the point where it started (at death), but so as finally to escape death, another language can be heard – the image of actual language, but as a miniscule, interior, and virtual model; it is the song of the bard who has already sung of Ulysses before the *Odyssey* and before Ulysses himself (since Ulysses hears the song), but who will also sing of him endlessly after his death (since, for the bard, Ulysses is already as good as dead); and Ulysses, who is alive, receives this song as a wife receives her slain husband.'
45 Michel Foucault, *The Archeology of Knowledge*, trans. A. M. Sheridan Smith (London: Tavistock (1969), 1972), p. 210.
46 op. cit., pp. 155, 156.
47 ibid., p. 156.
48 *History*, pp. 138 and 101.
49 Cited in James Miller, op. cit., p. 349.
50 Miller, op. cit., p.7.
51 ibid., p.381.
52 Roland Barthes, Preface to Renaud Camus, *Tricks: 25 Encounters* (1979), trans. Richard Howard (New York: Saint Martin's Press, 1981), p. viii.
53 Roland Barthes, *The Rustle of Language*, trans. Richard Howard (Oxford: Basil Blackwell), p. 298.
54 ibid., pp. 291–2.
55 Dollimore, *Sexual Dissidence*, Part 3.
56 Alan Brayne, 'Our shadows' in Peter Daniels (ed.), *Take Any Train: A Book of Gay Men's Poetry* (London: The Oscars Press, 1991).

57 Cited by James Miller, op. cit., p. 251.

58 Harold Norse, 'Breathing the Strong Smell', in *The Penguin Book of Homosexual Verse*, ed. Stephen Coote (Harmondsworth: Penguin Books, 1983).

59 Thom Gunn, 'In Time of Plague' and 'Memory Unsettled', in *The Man with Night Sweats* (London: Faber, 1992). Reprinted with permission.

Lynda Hart

Blood, piss, and tears: the queer real

We are at the Performance Space in Sydney. It's the 16th of July 1994, and I know we really are here because I can't stop shaking. There is no heat in this building. I am freezing in this 'mildest of all' Australian winters and I bet they say that to all the girls. I could have hallucinated the scene; I can't remember much about what people said. The whole thing could have been phantasmatic. But I was cold. So I remember it as real.

I'm on a panel called 'Performing Sexualities' with Anna Munster. I've just finished reading a collection of her essays, most of them published over the years in *Wicked Women*, the Australian lesbian s/m magazine, and I'm thinking of her as 'the real thing'. Not just because she really 'does it', as opposed to just spectating – 'I am not a horrified onlooker'[1] she reminds us – but because of some undefinable, uncapturable quality in her writing that makes me 'believe' her, which is to say, I identify with her. So I guess that means that *I'm* the one who, for me, is really the *real thing*. My narcissism is alive and up and running, I see. I am very pleased when I read my paper after she finishes hers and though the audience has nothing to say to us at all, we survive the interminable 30–second post-presentation silence and begin cheerfully chatting with each other about blood, piss, and tears. I am happy about this mutual recognition. It makes me think that she thinks I'm real too. That's nice.

A story Anna tells stays with me all these months later. She had staged a performance at a Sex Subculture party in an ongoing series of queer theatrics at dance parties. Anna played a psychologically precarious female patient who is catheterized by a 'slightly disturbed male doctor'.[2] The catheterization was a simulation. The empty catheter bag was swapped for a full one, *out of sight of the audience*, then the bag was ripped open and its liquid poured out over the audience. Classical mimesis – the 'most naïve form of representation'[3]

Textual Practice 9:1, 1995, 55–66

– produced in the spectators a quite naïve reaction. Munster reported that for weeks after the performance she heard *nothing* but criticism for failing to perform 'safe sex' in a queer venue. Of course, Munster *had* in fact filled the bag with Lucozade. So the performance was '*safe*', *but was it sex*? The audience was not, as they believed, doused in piss. But as Munster said, they 'bought the theatrical illusion'.[4]

It's a curious thing to have bought in a contemporary queer site-specific space. Even my undergraduates laugh when I tell them about the spectator who rushed on stage to replace Hamlet's hat because it was a cold night out there waiting for his father's ghost. They think it's hilarious that anyone could be so silly as to try to save Desdemona from Othello's strangling embrace. And they don't blame Mr Garrick one bit for banishing the audience from the stage of Drury Lane in 1763 in order to put a stop to such interruptions as the one made by a gentleman who, evidently overcome with pity, stepped from behind the scenes during a performance of *King Lear* and threw his arms around Mrs Woffington as she played Cordelia.[5]

And yet, when I teach Tim Miller's *My Queer Body*, these same students become obsessed with wanting to know if the man in the audience whose lap received Miller's naked body was forewarned, i.e. *staged*. They thought it was fine for Miller to plant his naked butt on a guy as long as it was a performance. What if it were 'the real thing', I asked them. That was easy for them to answer: then it was invasive, by which they meant immoral.

Then there is the case of Ron Athey in the US and the latest NEA brouhaha. In much the same way that the work of the 'NEA Four' performance artists was ludicrously sensationalized, Athey stood accused of dripping HIV-positive blood – real blood not stage blood – on to his audience's heads. Weeks after Athey performed 'Excerpted Rites Transformation' at Minneapolis's Walker Art Center, a writer for the Minneapolis *Star Tribune*, who had never seen the show (shades of Karen Finley and the *Washington Post*) reported that spectators were stampeding out of the theatre to avoid being contaminated by HIV-positive blood dripping from bloody towels that were sent 'winging above the audience on revolving clothes-lines'.[6] What Athey actually does is part ordeal art, part purification ritual, part sado-masochistic enactment. Some of those purported 'bloody towels' are now installed in a Soho gallery in New York.[7] They are prints on paper made from blotting the blood of Darryl Carlton, an artist who performs with Athey. Athey makes twelve cuts into Carlton's back, reopening already existing scars, in a stair-step formation which is a traditional African tribal pattern, and a triangle to symbolize queer. Assistants blot the blood with paper towels, hang them from a clothes-line, and wind them out over the audience. The prints are bagged in plastic immediately after this section of the performance. Carlton is HIV-negative anyway. If it matters, which it shouldn't, but evidently it does.

The controversy about Athey's performance has this in common with Munster's catheterization scene: both aroused very strong responses that had to do with the 'realness' of the performance. In Munster's case, artifice was mistaken for the real. In Athey's case, the blood was real, but the terror was phantasmatic. By switching the catheter bag *offstage*, Munster deliberately played to a credulous audience that may have been duped precisely because they were *not* expecting 'realism' in a queer/s/m performance venue. Athey, on the other hand, insists quite emphatically on the 'realness' of his performance. He says: 'my work is based on physically, dynamically altering the body. I cannot fake cutting. My theater is controlled actual experience.'[8] Athey's spectators are with him in regard to this realness. Mark Russell, director of New York's P.S.122, describes Athey's work as 'a rite of passage, a cleansing trial', in which 'artifice would not be appropriate.'[9] This is not true only of his 'blood work'. When he presides over a dyke wedding ritual, a member of the audience just has to know if Julie and Pigpen, the celebrants, are lovers in real life. Athey tells 'true' stories of his boyhood; the piercings he performs on himself and others are real. C. Carr reports that a spectator behind her at Athey's performance shouted: 'It's not entertainment. It's something more.'[10] And Athey describes his own work, his 'blood work' in particular, as 'the loudest form of expression, for when you're beyond words'.[11] Getting beyond words seems to be the thing, the point, the 'real thing'. As Elaine Scarry has written, that place *beyond* words is a place we call pain.[12] Scarry's study is quite emphatically about *physical* pain, as is Athey's piercing/ cutting 'blood work' and as is sado-masochism.

If, as Scarry has argued, pain *is* the place where language leaves us; or, to put it slightly differently, if the leaving of language is what we call pain, then my question is this: Why are these queer artists carrying the place of the inexpressible, the place of pain, in perform-ances that have elicited an uncommon concern and unselfconscious new naïveté about representation? What is this purchase on/of the 'Real' in queer performances about? Munster has this to say: 'queer performance is literally saturated by a desire to understand and pose the body as raw material, the body unmediated by the form and consumption of spectacle.'[13] She links this desire with the complicity of a drive that permeates gay and lesbian identity politics – the drive toward *visibility*. Maybe we all know by now in the global academic discourse that 'the screen is not simply a field for display but is simultaneously a device which eradicates, which screens out what is not fit for public consumption',[14] but there is still an overwhelming urge (is it indeed a 'drive', something like an instinct?) to mark a stationary place, to appeal to a referent, to have recourse to a/the 'real thing'. What are the implications of that mark, that referent, becoming located on queer performative bodies?

It strikes me as particularly interesting, and relatively unnoticed, that these performances, which have become so vexed for their 'realness' (real or presumed!) are both firmly within the parameters of a vast discourse that is none the less recognizable as queer sado-masochism (in my mind not redundant, though some would say that s/m is always already queer, I think that it can be quite straight(forward)). In other words, we are talking about 'scenes that have either been taken *for* real, with the artist's complicity (Athey) or have been assumed to be real (Munster).

First, it is odd enough when one stops to think of it, that *only* s/m sexuality is absolutely permeated by theatrical rhetoric. One (two, three, or more) people *do 'scenes'*. They do not 'have sex' like 'normal' people. Non-kinky heterosexual sex acts rarely if ever are described as *doing scenes*. Although one can easily imagine a straight man referring to sex with a prostitute as a scene. It seems that the 'anti-theatrical prejudice', which has been functional and pervasive at least since Plato, is an operative paradox in s/m performance. For, on the one hand, by virtue of the very 'fact' of their theatricality, these practices occupy a denigrated space in our cultural imaginary. On the other hand, practitioners of s/m sexuality have found some means of defence against the onslaught of both the New Right and some feminists by appealing precisely to that theatricality that is otherwise demeaned. Depending then on the context, s/m performers may find themselves saying something like this: 'it's not real, it's *only* a performance', in an appeal for tolerance.

Sado-masochistic sexuality is about *doing*. Whereas 'straight' sex (whatever the preference of the people involved) is about *having*. Now this is an obvious but, I think, crucial and fascinating difference. For, the notion of 'having sex' signifies at once that 'sex' is something one can own, and that it (sex) was there *prior to the performance*. The s/m sensualist, quite contrarily, in *doing* a scene, *makes* sex in the performance. Unless, of course, the scene is a realistic one, in which case there is an illusion of reality constructed, which is. to say that the scene makes possible the fantasy of a referent – a truth or reality prior to the performance. Even this naïve realism, however, is *performative*. If straight sex (by which I mean not necessarily het sex but any sexual acts that make a claim to the natural) has been presumed to be the 'real thing', then what are we to make of this tendency toward *denial* of performativity in work like Munster's and Athey's?

These two recent queer performance encounters with the 'real' lead me back to the controversies within feminism about the place of lesbian s/m. What strikes me as missing from these ongoing debates is a consideration of them in terms of *performativity*. Here I do not have space to take up the issue of what these debates, in themselves, *rhetorically* perform. What I would like to do in the space that I have is to consider how one might read the controversies about lesbian s/m differently, and hence push past an impasse that has been fortified by over two decades of very repetitive arguments, by asking not whether s/m is real or role-playing, but rather take as a given that we are always already on stage whether or not we are recognizing its edge, and ask what *kind* of performance lesbian s/m might be.

It is my contention that sado-masochism is the site of such highly charged controversies among feminists not because of the 'violence' that it purportedly perpetuates and condones, but because it is comprised of a group of sexual acts in which the eroticism is evoked precisely in the ambiguity between the 'real' and the 'performed'.

Changing the scene (again)

Tracking 'universals of performance', Herbert Blau does so in the service of pursuing

> the thing which appears in that subjunctive moment when whatever was there before becomes a performance. Or, as far as it is imaginable, that which in performance is other than that which is *not* performance, the cipher which marks it off from, shall we say life? or shall we say death?[15]

While performative discourse has come to include everything that was once referred to as everyday activities, and the distinction between 'doing' and 'acting' is so murky as to be nearly indecipherable, there is, none the less, as Blau points out, a 'crucial particle of difference ... between just breathing eating sleeping loving and *performing* those functions of just living; that is, with more or less deliberation.'[16]

Feminist positions both for and against s/m sexual practices seem to be in pursuit of the moment when something presumably *authentic* occurs. But lesbian sado-masochists seek that moment *within* the performance. Accepting that we are always already in representation, even when we are enacting our most private experience, the lesbian sado-masochist is aroused by the dialectic of appearance/disappearance and the pleasurable suffering that constitutes the persistent failure to master its implacable necessity.

The cipher that marks off the distinction between performance and 'life or death' figures in sado-masochism in the 'becoming nothing' that the ritual enacts. The body of the bottom is the place where this marking is inscribed. Tops facilitate this passage and serve as the guarantee of returnings. Lesbian sado-masochistic sexual practices, as described and defined by practitioners, consummately enact Blau's first, and most important, 'universal' of performance – the *consciousness* of performance. Minimally, any act that can rightly be called a performance contains cues, what Blau calls 'marks of punctuation which are inflections ... of *consciousness*'.[17] Although all 'acts' are performances, in a *performative act* the participants must be aware of themselves as actors in the very moment that they are performing. In contradistinction to the realistic method in which the actor strives to disappear into the character she is performing, the s/m performer takes up a position in relation to her 'self' and the role she plays that is much more akin to the Brechtian *gestus*. Thus, being somewhat alienated from oneself is a precondition for s/m performance.

The vacillation between forgetting and remembering one's self in performance is the measure whereby we determine what kind of performance is being enacted. There is something, however, in between forgetting and remembering that haunts all performance. Blau calls it '*theater*, the truth of illusion, which haunts *all* performance whether or not it occurs in the theater'.[18]

It is this *theater* that I think is the ghost in the machinery of feminist debates concerning sado-masochism. Although it encompasses a wide range of practices, the movement of sado-masochistic sexuality is toward a delicate, precarious borderline where testing and transgressing the line between the real and the phantasmic deeply troubles a feminist movement invested in consciousness and clarity.

The abundance of theatrical metaphors in s/m testimony and theory is not casual. The 'scene' or 'scenario' is a staple concept repetitively evoked in s/m rhetoric. In Theodor Reik's massive study of the etiology of masochism, he persistently returns to performance metaphors. Reik's 'demonstrative' feature in masochism is the 'showing or wanting-to-be seen ... a means to invite the sexually gratifying punishment'.[19] Masochism, he argues, must have a public: 'in most cases it has the character of a performance and frequently it does not dispense with a certain theatrical flavor.'[20]

As his analysis develops, we see that Reik conceives of masochism as theatrical because he is thinking of the male submissive's desire for suffering at the hands of a dominant female as a disfigured, or distorted, enactment of his unconscious desire to change places with her. Hence the male masochist, 'whatever he does represents a performance, a kind of enacted scene.'[21] For Reik, masochism is symptomatic of desires that are repressed. He cites one example that indicates the masochistic acting out as a way to preclude the 'real' fantasy: when the masochistic 'reversal was undone,' ... 'he nourished the fantasy "that he was a lust-murderer on the lookout for his female victims." '[22] Reik thus believes in masochism as a symptom that conceals the 'original' wish, which might be the 'homosexual-feminine attitude toward the fathers ... behind the façade', although he dismisses this possibility as having no decisive importance.[23] If male masochism is the symptomatic expression of femininity, as Freud suggested, Reik argues that as such it 'has the meaning of a performance'.[24]

Thus we can see in Reik's analysis of masochism a belief in the truth concealed by the illusion. His search is geared toward locating a 'hidden aim'; his etiological analysis presumes a model from which all the manifestations of masochism emanate through detours. Like the anti-s/m feminists then, Reik's rhetoric is haunted by the truth/model *behind* the illusion. Reik rescues masochism from the 'real' *by* theatricalizing it: 'it is in accordance with the theatrical element in masochism that it seldom becomes a matter of "deadly earnest" as with the sadistic perversion.'[25] The masochistic desire must then, however, remain in the realm of fantasy (theatre), for if it emerges into the 'real' (practice), the masochist would perhaps not be in 'deadly earnest', but he would be in deadly danger, since the sadistic perversion is *not* theatricalized. The fantasy of masochism, for Reik, is classical theatre – a dialectic between concealment and display in which the wanting to be seen is in tension with the desire to be hidden.

It is this truth *behind* the illusion that the anti-s/m feminists wish to expose and contain when they insist that acting out the fantasy is both self-destructive for the participants and potentially harmful for all women. While acknowledging the pervasiveness of both sadistic but, especially, masochistic fantasies among women, they will insist that realizing these fantasies is giving in to internalized misogyny.[26] Trapped in a reproductive model, these feminists cannot imagine that repetitions might be transformative. Acting is necessarily an 'acting out' that merely duplicates the original. Their logic leads to efforts to maintain rigid boundaries between fantasy and practice, failing to recognize that there is no illusion as naïve as the illusion of unmediated experience.

Lesbian sado-masochists are themselves, however, sometimes inclined to describe their practices as 'pure theater'. Susan Farr, for example, says that 'what is going on is a drama where two principals . . . act at being master and slave, play at being fearsome and fearful.'[27] She cites the clues to the drama in the fact that the roles are interchangeable, and that the dialogue tends to be repetitive and scripted. And yet she acknowledges that much of it is 'pure improvisation'. This dialectic between the scriptural and the spontaneous is prevalent in pro-s/m accounts. On the one hand, there is the insistence that the scene is rigidly controlled, with a decided emphasis on the bottom's mastery of the limits. On the other hand, the eroticism depends on the anticipation that the limits will be pushed to the breaking point, that the 'scene' will cross over into the 'real'. This ambivalence and the inability to resolve it captures what I think is constitutive of the eroticism of s/m – the manipulation of boundaries between the 'real' and the performed. The scene is played out in the space where what was 'theatre' strains to approach 'life', whatever it is that we believe was there *before or beyond* theatricality.

The pleasurable suffering that is enacted in lesbian sado-masochism is much more than the paradoxical desire for pleasure detoured through pain. These narratives also enact the pathos of the impossibility of love, the conflict between desiring-fantasy's shattering of the self and the necessity for returning to a coherent self in order to take one's place in the symbolic order, and the persistent fantasy of something that exists beyond language. Or, to shift to another register, the constancy of a belief in something that is before or other than performance. Linguistically, this would be the persistence of a belief in the constative even as the performative devours any effort to hold on to a commensurability between the speech act and a referent that is not constituted in the performative.

S/m sexuality pushes hard against the referent that feminism needs to make its truth claims. But s/m also longs for a referent, for something that provides an anchor, or ground, *beyond* representation. As Artaud wanted a theatre that 'to the degree that life is unrepresentable [was] meant to be the *equal* of life',[28] I think that lesbian sado-masochism is a performance that yearns for an experience that is beyond the closure of representation, and it seeks that beyond through the apparently paradoxical method of discipline, regulation, prescription. Artaud's visionary theatre of cruelty would have banished mimesis and returned the theatre to something that was prior to or beyond imitation. He theorized the effective annihilation of theatre, in the *name of theatre*, to create a theatre that would be the equal of life. More than any other theoretician of performance, Artaud sought the 'thing in itself'.

Derrida describes Artaud's longing in a way that would complement a feminist agenda:

> Artaud desired the impossibility of theater, wanted to erase the stage, no longer wanted to see what transpires in a locality always inhabited by or haunted by the father and subjected to the repetition of murder.[29]

Most feminists, I think, would share this desire for a scene not haunted by the law of the father, a way out of the endlessly repetitive oedipal drama. But the way out, if there is a way out, is not through accumulating testimonials about the 'truth' of our illusions. Rather, it must be through performing the illusions, producing, multiplying and traversing them. Those who are watching the performance of sado-masochism and condemning it are like the spectators at a play who think they are outside the spectacle. The appeal to 'natural' expressions of sexuality is like the illusion of the spectator who believes that she is merely 'living'. The struggle is not to avoid repetition, but to repeat with differences that are transformative.

Whether we are spectators or performers, time is of the essence. That is to say, our temporalities indeed define whether we are conscious of ourselves as inside or outside the performance. The flight forward is both an *overtaking* and overcoming of the anxiety that had been pursuing the masochist. If anticipation is the dominating mode of the suspense, here we are still in a linear temporality. The leap into the perverse scene, however, constitutes a bridge across the gap between the past and the future. It is a leap that can always be only one of faith. The scene takes place in what appears to be the 'present', but if it is a present indicative it is a performative one in which the 'I' is *ek-static* – a being put out of its place.

But this time is not to be confused with the willful forgetting of classical theatre. If the performative time of s/m is understood as psychoanalytic, the bliss that is an ek-stasis is more like Nietzsche's 'oblivion', an active forgetting. Nietzsche's oblivion is 'not merely a *vis inertiae* . . . but an active screening device' without which there can 'be no happiness, no serenity, no hope, no pride, no *present*'.[30] Active forgetting 'represents a power, a form of strong health'.[31]

Oblivion, Nietzsche argues, is a faculty designed to solve the problem and the paradox of promising. In claiming to anticipate the future, the promise tries to make the future present, or past – as if it had already been. Promising thus always takes place in psychoanalytic time – the future that is already. And hence what one promises is the impossible. The promise of love, Shoshana Felman argues, is *'par excellence* the promise that can't be kept' and ' "I promise" is the *performative* utterance *par excellence.'*[32] If the one who promises is the seducer, she tricks the one whom she seduces into thinking that the performative is constative. That is, seduction is a 'trap', which consists in 'producing a referential illusion through an utterance that is self-referential', the 'illusion of a *real* or extralinguistic act of commitment created by an utterance that refers only to itself.'[33] The promise produces a belief in the constative – the order of meaning/truth.

Deleuze claims that Lewis Carroll's surfaces cannot communicate with Artaud's depths. Yet Deleuze has himself located in his own commentary a moment when these two worlds coincide. Brief, precious, infinitely worth waiting for, and endlessly repeatable, it is that moment when 'the little girl skirts the surface of the water, like Alice in the pool of her own tears.'[34] For it is in this moment that she is neither surface nor depth. Her body still partially submerged but her head breaking through the pool of tears, Alice inhabits the borderline for a split second. This breaking of the waters is the breach in language, where one catches a glimpse of full speech.

The top does not merely wait on the shore, dispassionately observing the descent and resurgence of the bottom. Nor does she simply facilitate that movement. She takes and is taken there by and goes and comes there *with* the bottom. Neither anticipation nor recollection, it is not waiting for what could be, nor remembering what has been. Neither real nor phantasmic, but a sexuality that is self-conscious about the ways in which fantasy constructs the real *by* posing the *illusion of authenticity*, s/m strives to hold, while forever failing to capture, lovers mingled in that tense more impossible even than the future anterior – the present, where they are suspended together.

University of Pennsylvania

Notes

1 Anna Munster, 'Towards a theatre of queer operations', paper presented at 'Performing Sexualities', The Performance Space, Sydney, Australia, 16 July 1994, p. 1. A portion of this paper is published in *Kink* (Sydney, Australia: Wicked Women Publications, 1993).
2 ibid.
3 Jacques Derrida, 'The theater of cruelty and the closure of representation', in *Writing and Difference*, trans. Alan Bass (Chicago: University of Chicago Press, 1978), p. 234.
4 Munster, 'Queer operations'.
5 Theatrical history is rife with such anecdotes. For the Garrick/Woffington one see: Donald Sinden, *The Everyman Book of Theatrical Anecdotes* (London and Melbourne: J. M. Dent, 1987), p. 32.
6 Cited by C. Carr, 'Washed in the blood', *The Village Voice* (5 July 1994), p. 16.
7 TZ'Art and Co., 28 Wooster Street, New York, NY. As part of the installation 'Sanctuary (moth to the flame),' 21 July–26 August 1994.
8 Ron Athey quoted in *LA Weekly*, 8 July–14 July 1994, p. 24.
9 ibid.
10 All in C. Carr, 'Washed in the blood'.
11 ibid.
12 Elaine Scarry, *The Body in Pain: The Making and Unmaking of the World* (New York: Oxford University Press, 1985).
13 Munster, 'Queer operations'.
14 ibid.
15 Herbert Blau, *The Eye of Prey: Subversions of the Postmodern* (Bloomington, Indiana: Indiana University Press, 1987), p. 180.
16 Blau, p. 161.
17 Blau, p. 162.
18 Blau, pp. 164–5.
19 Theodor Reik, *Masochism in Modern Man*, trans. Margaret H. Beigel and Gertrud M. Kurth (New York: Farrar, Straus & Co., 1941), p. 73.
20 Reik, p. 78.
21 Reik, p. 199.
22 Reik, p. 203.
23 Reik, p. 207.
24 Reik, p. 203.
25 Reik, p. 49.
26 Such arguments are ubiquitous in anti-porn, anti-s/m feminist rhetoric. Two anthologies represent these positions well: Robin Ruth Linden *et al.*, *Against Sadomasochism: A Radical Feminist Analysis* (East Palo Alto, Cal.: Frog in the Well Press, 1982), and Irene Reti (ed.),*Unleashing Feminism: Critiquing Lesbian Sadomasochism in the Gay Nineties* (Santa Cruz, Cal.: HerBooks, 1993). I am not engaging directly with these arguments here because they detract from the focus of this essay. I do address them in my book-in-progress, *Between the Body and the Flesh: Performing Lesbian Sadomasochism* (forthcoming from Columbia University Press).
27 Samois (eds), *Coming to Power: Writings and Graphics on Lesbian S/M* (Boston: Alyson Publications, 1982), p. 38.
28 Blau, p. 166.

29 Derrida, p. 249.
30 Friedrich Nietzsche, *The Genealogy of Morals*, trans. Francis Golffing (New York: Doubleday, 1956), p. 189.
31 ibid.
32 Shoshana Felman, *The Literary Speech Act*, trans. Catherine Porter (Ithaca: Cornell University Press, 1983), pp. 12 and 30.
33 Felman, p. 31.
34 Gilles Deleuze, *The Logic of Sense*, trans. Mark Lester (New York: Columbia University Press, 1990), p. 93.

Margreta de Grazia

Soliloquies and wages in the age of emergent consciousness

A penny for your thoughts

Suppose the Christian world had started counting time from the Crucifixion rather than the Nativity. On the traditional assumption that Christ was 33 when crucified, every date ('year of our Lord') would have to be set back 33 years. Consider the twentieth century: it would lose to the nineteenth no less than the First World War, Proust, the Russian Revolution, Cubism, silent films, modernism itself, though there is as yet no knowing what the first 33 years of the next century might hold in compensatory store. The focus of this essay – sixteenth-century England – would also look quite different. While losing the better part of the Reformation and Humanism – Luther, Erasmus, and More – it would extend its poetic canon to include Donne, Herbert, Drayton, Greville, most of Jonson, a stellar roster of women – Aemilia Lanyer, Mary Wroth, Mary Sidney – and most conveniently: the entire Shakespeare corpus. At the turn of the century, marking the epochal break would be not *Hamlet*, but Ford's *Broken Heart*, or perhaps Milton's *Comus*. The *fin de siècle* economic crisis of the 1590s would be pre-empted by the conflicts of the Thirty Years War abroad and between Calvinists and Arminians at home, both religious struggles charged with newly appropriate millenarianist fervour. And what a dramatic turn of the century it would now be, Parliament dissolved and England on the brink of civil war!

This opening exercise is intended to emphasize the artificiality of the temporal units by which history is divided.[1] Change the starting-point and offset the whole chronological sequence. As it turns out, there is historical precedent for this particular adjustment: time was actually counted from the Crucifixion in the early centuries of the Christian era before it became standard practice to begin with the Nativity. It is not, however, the beginning of the Christian era that will be of concern here, but rather the beginning of another era: the

Textual Practice 9:1, 1995, 67–92

TP

modern. Although sometimes located elsewhere (in the Enlightenment, in Romanticism, in the Industrial Revolution), a long and solid tradition identifies that beginning with the Renaissance. Since the nineteenth century when Hegel pressed history into the service of World History, the Renaissance has been assigned the function of setting the modern in motion.[2] Why was Renaissance made synonymous with Early Modern? Why was the period whose very name suggests recuperative re-birth (of the ancient) identified with innovative birth (of the modern)?[3]

This essay begins with an attempt to address these questions. It then continues with a consideration of how consequential this assignment has been to our hermeneutic and empirical approaches to the period. It does so by examining two records from seventeenth-century England: one literary (an early Shakespearean quarto), registering mental activity; the other documentary (early printing-house records), registering manual activity. The first contains the thought of Hamlet, the consummate early modern consciousness; the second records the work of journeyman printers, typical early modern wage-earners. The essay begins with massive generalizations involving huge tracts of time and vast conceptual schemes; but it continues with modest minutiae from literary sources and trade documents. The extremes of the two parts suggest how mighty historical schema bear down on slight particulars. My contention is that the imperative to see the Renaissance as precipitating the modern has pressured these details into looking modern before their time.

I Early modern

[T]he fact that the world becomes picture at all is what distinguishes the essence of the modern age.

Heidegger

In an important essay entitled 'The age of the world picture', Heidegger asks 'Does every period of history have its world picture?'[4] His answer: No. Only the modern period. The possession of a world view is in fact what makes the period modern; it is its 'regulative idea', to use Kant's term, or 'cultural dominant', to use Jameson's. By 'world picture' Heidegger means the way we represent the world to ourselves: how we set it before ourselves to be seen and known (indeed it is only when so 'enframed' that it becomes visible and intelligible). While this metaphysical way of knowing dates from Descartes' *cogito*, it is not until the late eighteenth century that it is turned into a way of looking at history, of viewing the world, so that a phrase is needed to designate it, *Weltanschauung*. The concept has become so pervasive that it is assumed that historical divisions were always integral and complete, like a picture. Yet a *period* of history, like an *epoch*, at one time indicated an intervening break or turn rather than a durational term or span.[5]

While the Renaissance has certainly been imagined as a world picture – the Elizabethan one, for example – it certainly did not itself divide historical time into such discrete and coherent units. This is not to say that it had no way of periodizing the past. The theological divisions of the Middle Ages are still much in evidence: the four empires of the Book of Daniel, the three Pauline *tempora* (before the law, under the law, and in the time of grace); the Joachimite three ages of the Father, the Son, and the Holy Ghost; and most widespread of all, the six ages corresponding to the six days of God's Creation. The tripartite division of Polydore Vergil's *Historica Anglicae* derives from Paul, only Vergil curves it around again so that England's life is cyclically renewed after the Norman Conquest. Reigns of monarchs are used to organize English history, especially in recording legal precedents. Attempts were made to align regnal years with biblical schema as is illustrated by John Foxe's *Acts and Monuments*. In Protestant answer to Papist history, England's past is divided into five eras of struggle between Christ and Anti-Christ, beginning with Constantine and culminating apocalyptically in the revelational sixth era of Elizabeth's reign.

It is significant that the temporal unit free of these political and religious valences – the century – was not available in the Renaissance. Until the eighteenth century, a *century* was a collective noun, like a dozen, referring to 100 similar things of any kind. It could designate a military unit, like the subdivision of a Roman legion. But its primary use was to classify textual materials: there are *centuries* of ballads, prayers, stories, poems, adages.[6] There are also *decades* and *chiliades*: Henry Constable's *Diana* is divided into seven decades or units of ten sonnets. Erasmus' *Adages* consisted of *chiliades* or units of 1,000 adages subdivided into *centuries*. Only rarely did a century refer to 100 years, as in the case of the influential Protestant history known as the *Magdeburg Centuries* (1560–74), though the 100-year divisions did not begin with the century.[7]

That *century* did not specify *century of years* until the eighteenth century, lends support to Daniel Milo's remarkable theory that the division of the past into centuries is a relatively recent innovation dating from the French Revolution.[8] Through an examination of book titles before and after the French Revolution, he demonstrates that '*le siècle*' became the standard historical unit only after the 1790s.

History had to suffer as decisive (and rending) a break with the past as the Revolution before the past could be isolated as a self-contained unit – the *ancien régime* – subject to division into discrete centurial units. The past then became a closed book, as it were, divisible into 100-year chapters. As calendrical time was reformed on a decimal base (a ten-month year, a ten-day week, a ten-hour day, a hundred-minute hour, a hundred-second minute), so too historical time was rearranged according to centurial units, and space was simultaneously decimalized by the metric system. Like these units of measurement, the century provided a *secular* unit of division – one without taint of monarchy or divinity.[9]

And yet no sooner had time been demonarchized and desacralized than Hegel undertook to mystify it anew, infusing it, animating it with Spirit or Consciousness. The neutrality of the arithmetic century was inflected with purpose, even intent, motivated to express itself through world-historical peoples and events. History was imagined as consciousness moving strenuously and relentlessly forward, away from constraining nature and toward absolute self-consciousness or freedom. It is not until the Hegelian nineteenth century that periods come to possess the diachronic and synchronic features we now assume: both a static cultural coherence (spanning across time) as well as a dynamic teleological thrust (driving through time). It may be, as many have sensed and argued, that Hegel's teleological drive toward full consciousness is simply a replay of the Christian eschatological push toward New Heaven and New Earth; that all narratives of progress, development and evolution are what Blumemberg calls secularized *reoccupations* of Christian eschatology.[10] But what has no Christian precedent is Hegel's representation of that movement in terms of a developing consciousness, in terms precisely of that singularly human aptitude for consciousness which, in Hegel's words, 'makes the individual comprehend himself as a person, in his uniqueness as a universal in himself'.[11]

Once Hegel brought historical time to consciousness, periods started to assume a strikingly anthropological flair – possessing moods, temperaments, character, feelings, personalities. Indeed Marx repeatedly refers to Hegel's history of dialectically developing consciousness as an upside-down man – standing on his airy ideational head – who needs to be set right on solid substantial feet.[12] In response to this anthropomorphism, even the centurial unit seems to lose its neutrality, converted now to a 100-year lifespan, a superannuated human lifespan.[13] At the end of the nineteenth century, Hegelian consciousness and the Enlightenment century come together at the first opportunity: at *fin de siècle*. Consciousness takes the form of consciousness-of-being-at-the-end, something it could only feel if it were at one with the centurial figure. It is a strange and fallacious pathos – a sympathetic identification with a purely arithmetic division, an equation of personal mood with a temporal modality, registered in one of the earliest (1886) definitions of the malady: 'to be *fin de siècle* ... is to languish with one's century, to decay along with it.'[14]

This is not to say that there was nothing anthropological about epochal time before Hegel's animation. From the Church Fathers onward, the ages of the world and ages of man have been set in correspondence – as in the frequent tripartite progression from infancy to adolescence to maturity that could be superimposed on the various trinitarian divisions, or in the Six-Ages-of-the-World scheme that ended in an indeterminate period of senescence: 'You are surprised that the world grows old?' asks Augustine in 410. 'Man is born, grows up, ages. ... If a man grows old he is full of tribulations, if the world grows old it is full of disasters.'[15] What makes possible this identification of the human with the historical is their subjection to fallen decay, to mortality's organic rundown. But Hegel exempts History from his decline by splitting it off from Nature: assigning different trajectories to each – that of nature, moving smoothly and directly ('undialectically'); that of History, moving through dialectical conflict raising it to ever higher planes: 'Development, which in Nature is a quiet unfolding, is in Spirit a hard, infinite struggle against itself.'[16] After Hegel, historical time transforms from a natural to a conscious being, conflicted with itself rather than slipping into organic decay and death (and occasionally cyclical rejuvenation).[17]

It would be entertaining, perhaps even instructive, to do a chronological line-up of all the humanoid manifestations historical periods have taken – from ageing senescent ages, to ages with feeling, ages with personality or character, ages with features or physiognomy. And then, around the *fin de siècle*, to track the tendency for ages to grow increasingly psychological, even psychotic – so that *fin de siècle*'s nervous disorder, a neurosis just short of hysteria, has developed in recent diagnoses (what Fredric Jameson discusses as attempts at 'taking the temperature of the age')[18] into psychic disorder, suggesting that it is not just *we* who keep up with the *times* but the *times* that keep up with *us*, incorporating (assimilating) the latest historical and psychological theories, advancing from Hegelian continuities to Foucaultian ruptures, from Freudian hysteria to Deleuzian schizophrenia.

I've pushed this analogy between the human (particularly the psychological) and the temporal in order to stress their tight association, reflected not only in our imagining periods (as moods, temperaments, minds, etc.) but also in our imagining individuals as epitomizing periods (Chaucer, for example, or Voltaire, or Napoleon). As Blumemberg has noted, an epoch needs an embodiment of an epoch, 'a widely visible and effective boundary figure' like Columbus, Luther, Copernicus or Descartes.[19] Shakespeare often plays that role for the English Renaissance; sometimes his own career is seen to straddle the boundary, conveniently reaching mid-point at the century's turning-point, with the epochal *Hamlet*. Not only does he embody the age – the Age of Shakespeare – but in Dowden's Hegelian account, he embodies all of world history: his life and works divided into four imposing Epochs or Eras (with *Hamlet* marking the midway point).[20] There seems to be an innate affinity between historical periods and great men, geniuses, heroes, as if one were custom-made to suit the other. Indeed, for Heidegger, the two are coextensive: 'That the world becomes picture is one and the same event with the event of man's becoming *subiectum*.'[21]

This rapport lends credence to Foucault's great insight in the *Archaeology of Knowledge*, that the two, *consciousness* ('sovereignty of consciousness' or the 'sovereign subject') and *continuous periods* are bound together. The two comprise 'the two sides of the same system of thought'.[22] The 'subject of consciousness' needs continuous periods in order to secure its primacy by extending its sway backwards and forwards on the temporal continuum. In the nineteenth century, consciousness suffered damaging assaults from what Foucault calls decentring discourses – psychoanalysis, Marxist economics, ethnography – all disciplines that threw his privileged position into question. It became imperative then for consciousness to seek 'shelter' in a history of continuous periods, what Foucault terms 'the old citadel of history' – to ensconce and entrench itself there in the hope of a future reinstatement and restitution. Foucault's discourses of knowledge and power would unseat consciousness as the subject of history, his archaeologies would disrupt the continuities of periodization: both in the hope of deploying a method of historical analysis 'purged of all anthropomorphism'.

There is more, however, to the anthropological 'system of thought' than consciousness and continuous periods: like subject and narrative, they need a place to go – a *telos*. This is the other requirement of 'history proper' which Foucault decries – the chiliastic discourse that links together 'sex, the revelation of truth, the overturning of global laws, the proclamation of a new day to come, and the promise of a certain felicity.'[23] And to move toward an end, even an open-ended end, an *origin* must be posited: a starting-point from which that continuous history of consciousness can move toward its liberating *telos*. It is to satisfy this imperative that the Renaissance is brought into the picture as the point of origin from which the modern can get purposefully under way. And with that move the entire history of consciousness is stretched back (two to three hundred years) onto the Renaissance to complete the formation: a subject, a narrative, an end – and a beginning.

It might then be said that the Renaissance was invented in the nineteenth century to provide the starting-point for the modern: a way-back-then to set off an ever-receding-now. Indeed, there is little else on which its earliest formulations agree. (Not even a common name is shared – Hegel and Marx never use the name 'Renaissance' – only Burckhardt, and uneasily – distancing himself from the term by putting it in quotes and frequently preferring the designation 'beginning of the modern age'.[24]) There is no agreement on the time or the place: for Hegel it is early sixteenth-century Germany, for Burckhardt it is quattrocento Italy, for Marx it is, in its classical form, sixteenth-century England.[25] Nor is there agreement on the cause, though an escape from the tenebrous and somnolent blackout of the Middle Ages is always presupposed – an escape from Nature, from Church, from Necessity. Thus, for Hegel, it is Luther's pull inwards away from Catholic super-sensuousness; for Burckhardt, it is the lax laws and mores of the independent city states; for Marx, it is the primitive accumulation of capital. And yet for all three, however at variance about time, place, and cause: the period just after the great fault of the Middle Ages begins the modern. All three cases – Hegel's spiritual, Burckhardt's cultural, or Marx's economic – require the emergence of consciousness – whether in the form of Hegel's 'pure inwardness' or 'meditative introversion of the soul upon itself'; or Burckhardt's self-recognizing *'individual'* capable of looking both objectively outward and subjectively inward; or the consciousness entailed by a new economic structure, in which the labourer ceases to be slave, serf, or bondman to another, to become a freeseller of his labour power entering into new social relations of production.[26]

II Soliloquies

Imagine people who could only think aloud. (As there are people who can only read aloud.)

Wittgenstein, *Philosophical Investigations*

In the earliest text of Shakespeare's *Hamlet* (Q1, 1603), there is a stage direction that tradition has chosen to ignore. It requires that

Hamlet enter reading a book at a particularly critical point: just before he delivers the most famous speech in the language, 'To be or not to be.'[27] The stage direction occurs in Claudius's comment to Polonius as Hamlet enters, 'see where hee comes, poring uppon a booke.'[28] The question I wish to raise is, what does Hamlet do with the book once he starts speaking? Perhaps he shuts it, indicating the switch from reading to himself to talking to himself. But suppose he keeps the book open as he speaks, his eyes remaining fixed ('poring') upon it still? Would that mean that he is continuing the same activity: still reading, though now not silently but aloud? Is it possible that Hamlet's, Shakespeare's, the culture's most celebrated soliloquy: is read from a book?

Classified as a 'Bad Quarto' because of its highly mediated relation to Shakespeare, generally considered an abominable corruption and mutilation of Shakespeare's play, the 1603 *Hamlet* has enjoyed, it must be said, little authority.[29] Except in one regard. Because Bad Quartos are believed to be transcriptions of performances, their stage directions are considered valid indices to the early stagings of the plays. Many modern editions and performances of *Hamlet*, for example, adopt the following stage directions on the sole authority of the Bad Quarto: 'Enter the ghost in his night gowne', 'Enter Ofelia playing on a Lute, and her haire downe singing', and 'the Queene falles down and dies'.[30] Why then has this particular one been slighted? Is it unthinkable that Hamlet is reading 'To be or not to be' from a book?

The question answers itself: Hamlet is giving a soliloquy, not a recitation; speaking from within, not reading off a book. Alone on stage, with no motive to dissemble or conceal, he speaks his mind or thinks aloud. The occasion is of supreme value to the audience, for it offers what all characters within the play desire (and one dies for): a chance to glimpse Hamlet's inner being, his mystery, that within which passeth show. In this respect, the soliloquy compensates for the representational limitations of the dramatic form. By disclosing what goes on inside a character, the soliloquy substitutes for the narrative voice which in the novel, for example, routinely describes what characters feel and think. The soliloquy, it might be said, turns up the volume on thought. In a theatre aspiring to any degree of naturalism, it is an awkward solution to be sure: speaking is asked to give the illusion of non-speaking,[31] a particular strain on verisimilitude when, as is not infrequently the case in Elizabethan and Jacobean drama, such spoken non-speech is overheard.[32] The problem remains until film introduces the technique of voice-over, most spectacularly in Olivier's 1948 psychoanalytic *Hamlet* in which the camera seems to be boring into the back of his skull, drawing the viewer through an x-ray image of cerebral grey matter before passing into the resounding chambers of his brain.[33]

If a soliloquy represents a character's inner being, it cannot by definition be read from a book. It amplifies what Hamlet has in mind not in hand, what he is thinking not holding, what is deep within him not lifted off a page, private cogitation not generic publication. But where do such convictions come from?[34] Certainly not from the Shakespearean texts themselves, which never use the word. The early texts do have ways of directing a character to appear alone on stage, for example with stage directions (*Exeunt. Manet Hamlet* (F1, I.ii.128)), or with instructions within the text itself ('Now I am alone' (Q2, F1, II.ii.543); 'Leaue me friends' (Q2, F1, III.ii.377))).[35] What is to be understood by these specifications? Are we right in assuming that Hamlet *solus* is talking to himself or thinking aloud? Is he like Descartes, left alone with his thoughts – 'I have retired by myself' – conducting an interior monologue with himself – 'I will discourse with myself alone' – in order to demonstrate consciousness? Is the soliloquy a dramatized *cogito*?[36]

According to Raymond Williams, there could be no such thing as a character talking to himself on the Shakespearean stage for the simple reason that it was physically impossible to produce the illusion that a character was alone.[37] Situated around the platform stage, the audience in looking at the performance also looked at itself. An omnibus *Exeunt* might clear the stage, but not the theatre. When Hamlet says, 'Now I am alone' (II.ii.543) what is understood is that he is alone before the audience. Not until the advent of the recessed proscenium stage enclosed (on three sides) by walls rather than surrounded by an audience could the illusion that the actor was alone be produced. The audience, so conspicuous around the platform stage, was set apart (pushed out of the picture) by the new conventions of space, seating, and eventually lighting.[38] An actor could give the illusion of being 'alone' precisely because it was if the audience were not there.

As Williams also shows, it was not until the Restoration that *soliloquy* became a dramatic term for what only then seems to have been recognized as an exceptional kind of speaking.[39] Prior to this, the word's uses in English derived from Augustine's coinage to describe a new and complex discourse: 'I asked myself questions and I replied to myself, as if we were two, reason and I, whereas I was of course just one. As a result I called the work *Soliloquies*.'[40] Though a Latinization of *monologue*, the work takes the form of a dialogue between Augustine and Reason. Translated into Old English by King Alfred in the ninth century, *Soliloquies* were widely influential in religious meditational treatises for which the word became a synonym. At the same time, the word retained its conversational tie, so that Cawdrey's 1613 dictionary defined *soliloquie* as 'private talk', suggesting confidential and confessional exchanges, not conducted in public.[41] Around the time of the first *Hamlet* texts, then, soliloquies might have designated confidential dialogues, like those between Hamlet and Ophelia or Gertrude (in closets) or Horatio.[42] According to Williams's surprising statistics, it is this kind of secluded talking – not talk to himself – that distinguishes Hamlet from other dramatic speakers.[43]

But even if we imagine Shakespeare transcending both the stage for which he wrote and the language in which he wrote – there is some question as to whether 'To be or not to be' could satisfy latter-day criteria for inner speech: deep subjectivity, profound self-revelation, intense introspection. To begin with, the soliloquy has no particular relation at all to Hamlet. Unlike his other (six) soliloquies, this one avoids the egocentric marker 'I' – first through infinitive propositions which require no subject and then through the use of a generalized and impersonal 'we' and 'us'. As there is no marker for Hamlet, so there are no deictics fastening the content to his experience – no spatial 'heres', temporal 'nows', or personal 'hes' or 'shes'.[44] In other words, the soliloquy is *generic* rather than *reflexive*.[45] Those who have looked there for Hamlet's experience have been disappointed, finding, for example, instead of a ghostly revenant, a reference to death as the country from which 'No traveller returns' (III.ii.79–80). As one recent editor concludes, the speech contains no individuating insights, but rather 'what would occur to any well-read Renaissance man meditating upon death'.[46]

The speech is as little linked to the play *Hamlet* as to the character. As its textual history bears out, it could drift from one position to another. In Q1, Hamlet delivers it after the ghost's injunction. In Q2 and F, Hamlet gives it after he has encountered the players and devised a trap to determine Claudius's guilt. In either position, it functions to break dramatic momentum, casting pale thought in the way of swift action.[47] As such it could be interchanged with any of the soliloquies – or slipped in at any number of other places: after, for example, Hamlet returns from England or contemplates Yorick's skull or enjoins Horatio to survive him. As it could appear here or there, so too it could disappear altogether.[48]

It is because the speech is semantically and formally self-contained that it is, like an inset, transferable. As has been demonstrated, it is a rhetorical set-piece, a model of humanist composition, focused on the topos death, richly and deftly varied through both affinity and opposition.[49] Autonomous and detachable, it has all the makings of what it soon becomes: an anthology piece which, like a proverb, is fit for reproducing and recontextualizing, lifting and resituating. That it can migrate out of *Hamlet* into later texts, opens up the possibility that it has migrated into *Hamlet* from earlier ones. Scholars have long noted how this speech echoes a number of other works, classical and Christian. The dilemma of whether to remain alive in misery or to face the uncertainties of unknown death and the comparison of death to a sleep (with or without dreams), turn out to be, not unexpectedly, highly traditional topoi. The following works have been proposed as possible sources: Plutarch's *Moralia*, Cicero's *Tusculan Disputations*, Augustine's *De Libero Arbitrio*, Cardan's *De Consolatione*, Montaigne's *Essays*, Charron's *Of Wisdome*, the Homily given regularly in Anglican services, *Against the Fear of Death*.[50]

Suppose that, one day, out of the dusty archive a verbatim source for the soliloquy were discovered. Would it mean acknowledging that Shakespeare cribbed his soliloquy from the book of another, that the early rumours about his appropriative tendencies ('borrowed plumes') were true? Or would the critical tradition be at fault for not having recognized that the book in Hamlet's hands was intended to function like quotation marks, flagging the work of another? The embarrassment would then be not his, but ours for having mistaken an obvious citation for Shakespeare's representation of Hamlet's unique consciousness.

It would be a different matter, however, if the book were written not by another but by Hamlet himself, so that the book *held* in his hand would be also *written* in his hand. Suppose it were the very book he mentions after the Ghost's visitation, the commonplace book he whips out and wipes out in order to record the Ghost's commandment, 'My tables. Meet it is I set it down' (I.v.107). His tables (newly replenished in the interim) might contain entries from one or any number of the texts listed above. It might also contain the 'Words, words, words' he reads at Polonius, the 'matter' or 'Slanders' written by the 'satirical rogue' (Juvenal? Guazzo? Erasmus?) (II.ii.192ff.). Hamlet could then be carrying the same commonplace book on all three occasions, indeed on *all* occasions, as a *vademecum* requires.[51]

The theory of the tablebook helps account for 'To be not to be's' formal features – its universality, self-containment, rhetorical polish, philosophical eclecticism. (It also explains why Hamlet tends to speak so sententiously.) It only complicates, however, the attempt to understand what a soliloquy is. What relation can commonplaces have to Hamlet's own thoughts? Are they *his*, if they originate in the words of others? Can the proper articulate itself through the common? The unique express itself through citation? Could consciousness be structured like a collection of *sententiae*? Would this mean that thinking and remembering were interconnected: 'thoughts and remembrance fitted' (IV.v.176–7)?

Mallarmé wrote of Hamlet, 'He walks about, and the book he reads is himself.'[52] Mallarmé intends this, of course, metaphorically: Hamlet is so inwardly turned (self-reflective, introspective, solipsistic) that it is as if he were at once the subject reading and the object being read. Let us, however, be literal-minded and slip a real book in his hands: his tablebook. Does it make any sense at all to say that 'the tablebook he reads is himself?' as if on its pages were inscribed his very being? Even the most personal kinds of writing – a diary, say, or an autobiography – fall short of that kind of commensurability. How could a tablebook have any such aspirations when its contents are consensual? If a modern editor could be convinced that Hamlet were reading words of another (a BIG if), he or she would enclose those words in quotation marks to indicate that they belonged to someone else. If an early modern transcriber inserted quotation marks, however, they would signify the reverse: that the material was not private but generally (even universally) applicable and deployable.[53] Until the eighteenth century, quoting involved issues not of property but of authority. Without custom, rule, or law to arbitrate the *meum* and *suum* of discourse, is it normative to think and speak in words of others? If we were to discover that 'Conscience does makes cowards of us all' is a quotation from Augustine, would it be less proper to Hamlet? or Shakespeare? Does mediation render thought and speech inauthentic?

The practice of quoting raises another matter. To *quote* in Shakespeare's period is not to borrow the words of someone else, but to *note* or *mark* them, either actually (by making a note or mark on paper – recording) or mentally (by mentally noting or marking – remembering). This same ambiguity pertains to Hamlet's tablebook. Without stage direction, there is no knowing whether Hamlet is jotting the Ghost's 'Remember me' (I.v.91) on a note pad or making a mental note of it, writing on an outer 'book and volume' or remembering within the 'book and volume of the brain' (103).[54] To raise the problem to philosophical heights: is the tablebook *mind* or *matter*?[55] The problem also crops up when Polonius instructs his son, 'And these few precepts in thy memory / Look thou character' (I.ii.58–9). If Laertes were to oblige, would he put them in his table (as memo) or merely keep them in mind (as memory)?[56]

This fuss over the status of memory tables recalls the controversy over another table, the commemorative table that superseded the tablets of Moses – the Eucharistic table ('Do this in remembrance of me'). 'God be at your table' (IV.v.44), says the distracted Ophelia, one of the play's many allusions to the controversy which, as Stephen Greenblatt has recently argued, shadows over this play.[57] The Reformation's substitution of plain *table* for mystical *altar* is in itself a consequence of this controversy.[58] Splitting the church was the key issue of whether Christ's sacrifice was to be remembered in the body or in the mind: was the bread and wine really Christ's body or just symbolically so? As one Reformer put it, the identification of bread and wine with body and blood involved one of two things: a material change or a turn of phrase – 'either transubstantiation or a trope'.[59]

The same uncertainty arises over the status of another object in *Hamlet*: Ophelia's flowers. 'I a bin gathering of flouers', she says in Q1, and once again the early texts do not indicate whether she enters with them in hand or in mind, as prop or trope. Either way, Ophelia tells us what the flowers stand for: 'There's rosemary, that's for remembrance ... And there is pansies [pensees], that's for thoughts' (IV.v.173–5). Each flower bears a motto, gathered together they form a *posy* (compare Isabella Whitney's *A sweet Nosegay, or pleasant Posye*, 1573) – a gathering of flowers to be read and said, a *florilegium* or *anthologia*. Like Hamlet's tablebook, her flowerbook is a collection of wise sayings or *sententiae* which she distributes and recites.[60] Its content is quite predictable: her father's and brother's 'prescripts' on how to protect her virginity – advice to keep 'Out of the shot and danger of desire' (I.iii.35) lest she lend too credent ear to vows made 'When the blood burns' (116) and her 'chaste treasure open' (31). In her 'memory lock'd' (85), such prescripts are meant to function as lock and key to her 'chaste treasure'. Flowers on how to avoid being de-flowered: 'Best safety lies in fear' (43).

Ophelia's posy has come un-gathered, however. As her strewing of both 'conjectures' (IV.v.15) and flowers indicates, both mind and posy are torn apart, 'distract' (3). Her copy of Hamlet's 'book and volume of the brain' reads, therefore, like 'a document in madness' (176), containing disjoint and scattered pieces of ballads, refrains, folk tables, and riddles. She chants these 'snatches' (IV.vii.176) even while drowning, the last of them a 'melodious lay' (181). There is only one thing to keep such common bits and pieces from finding their way into a maiden's florilegium – their vulgarity. For her 'distracted' flowers concern violated chastity, telling of green girls who did not know their 'true love' (IV.v.23), believed burning vows ('Quoth she, "Before you tumbled me, / You promis'd me to wed" (62–3), and "dupp'd the chamber door" ' (53)). No longer virgins, they are now either salacious like the baker's daughter (42) or despoiled like the master's daughter abducted by the steward (171). With uncouth 'country matters' for subject matter, Ophelia's flowers are themselves uncultivated: wildflowers or rank and gross weeds.

It is out of noxious wildflowers and obscene weeds that Ophelia weaves together another posy, a fantastic garland – a 'crownet (Coronet, F)' of weeds (IV.vii.171) – 'weedy trophies' of unweeded tropes, lewd turns of phrase. Among the wild flowers are 'long purples' which 'cold maids do dead men's fingers call' (170). Drawn or printed in the margins of early modern books, pointing index fingers appeared interchangeably with flowers to mark venerable and authoritative passages ('saws of books', I.v.100), to be 'quoted' or culled into the reader's own posy.[61] Dead men's fingers, testicle-like tubers, like the pointing 'indices' or 'fists' directing attention from the margins of scripted and printed pages, indecently pointing at prescripts ('old man's sawe[s]', Q1) to keep cold maids cold. Pointing happens to be Polonius's characteristic gesture – and he only has one point to make: that Hamlet is driven mad by desire for his daughter – 'Mark the encounter' (II.ii.164) and 'Oh ho! do you mark that' (III.ii.109). This is the desire that he insists Ophelia mark too, by giving her prescripts and teaching her to construe Hamlet's behaviour accordingly. In her final scene, she may have picked up his sententious habit of pointing, twice bidding the court to mark her words, her father's words come true – 'Pray you mark' (IV.v.28,35) – a marginal pointing purple flower, a violet dead man's finger.

It is in the attempt to hang her weedy posy between the forked branches of the tree that Ophelia falls into the brook and drowns.[62] The graphics are crude (indeed pornographic), but doesn't a coronet between limbs, an O between sticks, approximate that deceptively virginal 'face between ... forks' imagined by Lear?[63]

OPH. I think nothing, my lord.
HAM. That's a fair thought to lie between maids' legs.

(III.ii.116–17)[64]

The maid's lap and head are anatomically superimposed to represent *maidenhead*, an easy overlap since both take the form of Ophelia's first initial: *nothing* between the legs and *nothing* in mind ('I do not know, my lord, what I should think' (I.iii.104); 'My lord, I do not know' (II.i.85); 'I think nothing, my lord'). Ophelia attempts to hang a pathetic and grotesque effigy of herself as unweeded posy, made up of naughty sayings – the vulgar 'lays' of laid girls she chants when she is alone (or has the illusion of being alone). 'Thoughts and remembrances' spoken aloud: a soliloquy then?

Since the end of the nineteenth century, *Hamlet* has been hailed as Shakespeare's most modern play, as the play that itself breaks out of the medieval and into the modern. Hamlet's consciousness, it is said, as dramatized primarily through his soliloquies, is what makes it so precocious. And yet, there is something decidedly *un*modern about the way the play frames mind (memory and thought) as table and posy. What sense would it make to frame modern consciousness that way? Even a metaphorical use – a figuring of immaterial and exclusive consciousness as material and discursive tablebook and flowerbook – would seem catachrestical. For mind as table and posy puzzles the distinctions upheld by consciousness. It blurs the dispensations of *meum* and *suum*: as if my thoughts could be the prescripts and sayings of others. It defies the metaphysics of mind and matter: as if mind could be held in hand. It collapses the distinction between inner and outer: as if thinking aloud were a form of talking. In other words, table and posy are hardly the stuff of soliloquy – at least if imagined as Hamlet's consciousness externalized.

III Wages

> If workers were asked: 'How much are your wages?' ... they would mention different sums of money which they receive ... for the performance of a particular piece of work, for example, weaving a yard of linen or type-setting a printed sheet.
>
> Marx, *Wage Labour and Capital*

We shift now from a dramatic convention for representing thought to an economic structure for compensating work. In doing so we follow the precedent of Marx who pre-empted Hegel's history of consciousness with a materialist history of production. He preserved, however, Hegel's linear dialectic of progress, including the key juncture at the sixteenth century to mark the transition from not faith to consciousness but feudalism to capitalism. Like its ideational counterpart and antithesis, the economic has since been under pressure to look modern: to look like the beginning of capitalism. In turning to a typical early modern work-place, the printing-house, we will once again focus on materials that have been largely overlooked, indeed buried in an archive.[65] They are the late seventeenth-century records from Cambridge University Press recently retrieved and examined by D. F. McKenzie.[66] Though from a later date and another town, these documents reflect the printing-house conditions already prevalent at the beginning of the century in London, the time and place of *Hamlet*'s first printing.

With the documents that will concern us here – receipts of wages paid to compositors and pressmen for their output – McKenzie has exposed some rather startling errors in how scholars had imagined printing-house production. In attempting to calculate output, bibliographers had previously assumed that printers regularly worked to maximum capacity. This meant that if one compositor could set 1,000 ens or letters an hour and one full press crew could press 250 impressions in the same time, daily production would total these sums multiplied by 12, the number of hours in a workday: 12,000 ens and 3,000 impressions. As McKenzie demonstrated, however, these calculations were based on two erroneous assumptions: that there was a uniform rate of production and that workmen worked to maximum capacity. The records revealed instead both that there were great fluctuations in output from worker to worker (and even for a single worker from day to day) and that the figures were far lower than had been conjectured.

McKenzie found an explanation for these incongruities in historical change. Scholars had anachronistically been positing a typical post-Industrial workman, regularly working to earn as much as possible so that he might purchase goods beyond his needs. But the pre-Industrial workman, McKenzie argues, worked only until he earned enough for subsistence; once bare needs were satisfied, he sought relief from toil rather than additional wages. The desire to make holiday prevailed over any incentive to increase wages. (Indeed, it took a more developed market to create such incentives.)

McKenzie is certainly right in insisting that these seventeenth-century printers were 'men whose attitudes to work were quite different from ours'.[67] The difference, however, may be more than a matter of attitude. Here the vouchers themselves mislead in suggesting that wages were the only form of compensation. They give the impression that a printer worked only for a certain sum of money which, according to McKenzie, was the variable amount needed to meet subsistence. But a journeyman was also given board at his master's house; he might be remembered in his will (and receive occasional gifts). Furthermore, the two years' experience he acquired in his master's shop entitled him to guild membership, to that identity which would qualify him for the privileges of citizenship including the right to own his own shop: 'The journeyman of today became the master of tomorrow.'[68] What the vouchers do not register, then, are a range of non-monetary, domestic and civic benefits (and the social relations they entail). The printing-house combined two systems of remuneration generally kept distinct, as by Hobbes: 'REWARD, is either of *gift*, or by *contract*. When by contract, it is called *salary*, and *wages*.'[69]

To assume compensation in terms exclusively of wages is to

assume a worker who is thus compensated.[70] It assumes, in fact, a worker who can be drawn into the equation stated by Marx's typical workman in the epigraph above. On any given day, the workman nets a sum of money equal to the value of what he produces. In the epigraph, the presence of the typesetter as an alternate for the cloth-maker – the printed sheet for the yard of linen – enables us to add the printer's product on to *Capital's* well-known formula of commodity exchange: '20 yards of linen = 1 coat' = *20 sheets of printed paper.*[71] Because commodification has the capacity to convert everything into its own terms, the list could be extended indefinitely, to include, notoriously, the worker himself, '20 yards of linen. . .' = *1 day's labour.* The monetary value of his labour power transforms the pro-ducer into the same system of values as the product. Thus wages are a worker's ticket into the system, just as price tags function to admit products. Like a magic that can turn heterogeneous entities into the same substance, the process of equivalent exchange elides differences, transforming linen, coat, printed paper, and human activity into the same monetary form. The magic, for Marx, is an historical effect, though it passes itself off as a natural one – one limited, to return to our concern with periodization, to the mode of production defining the modern.

Wages, then, are crucial to the capitalist system of equivalences. Non-monetary compensation would disrupt the equation, for how could a journeyman's relation to his master's family or to the guild corporation be quantified? One might want to go further than McKenzie, then, and say that workers working regularly for maximum wages imply not only a different attitude from that of early modern printers, but a different economic system altogether.

Another assumption, ostensibly unrelated, was also disproven by the vouchers. Bibliographers had generally assumed that printers worked on one book at a time: one typesetter and one printer running off consecutively the sheets to be gathered into a single book. But the records unearthed by McKenzie demonstrate that it was routine printing-house practice to set and print several books concurrently rather than consecutively. This means that a typesetter was commonly setting pages of several different books at a time.

The vouchers seem to require nothing less than a reconceptualiz-ing of both wages and jobs in the early modern printing-house. Indeed the misconstrual of one seems to have entailed the miscon-strual of the other. The paying-out of individual wages assumes the performance of a discrete job. Now it might be possible to identify such a job if a compositor had remained within the confines of a single page or even of a single book. Its margins or covers would demarcate the job, cordon it off, packaging it into quadrilateral units which could be readily identified as the compositor's own job for which he alone was to be compensated. But if several hands routinely set type on a single page, as the documentary evidence indicates, how could such units be determined? (This is what has vexed another bibliographic project – the painstaking attempt to individuate compositorial hands on given pages.)[72]

As several hands worked on one page, so a single hand worked on numerous pages – and of multiple books. The job, then, was no more commodified than the worker; nor was the system of equivalences in place that would later require that they be so. This is not to say that efficiency was less of a premium for these early presses, but that it was sought not through the commodifying forms of specialization and division but rather through a more flexible co-ordination of activities. Calculating total output would involve more a calculus of differentials than a sum of units. A single typesetter's work would have been dispersed throughout the printing-house rather than concentrated on a page or book. Where then was his work to be located? Not in the page, not in the book ... in nothing less than the total output of the printing-house then?

As it turns out, in something greater still. For the several books a single typesetter worked on concurrently might include books to be published by other printing-houses than that of his master. Peter W. M. Blayney has demonstrated that all of the twenty-one printing-houses in London in the late sixteenth and early seventeenth century commonly – 'one might even say habitually – shared books with one another'.[73] Thus Blayney's study of a single book, the 1608 Quarto of *King Lear*, by a single printer, Nicholas Okes, must include not only all of the books being printed concurrently in Okes' shop but also all of the books being printed at the same time by other London printers. (In a fifteen-year span, Okes shared printing with eighteen of the twenty-one printing-houses.) Hardly self-contained, an individual worker's labour sprawls over a range of books, beyond the confines of the page and of the book, beyond the confines of the walls of the printing-house which employed him. Ascertaining his complete output might involve looking through not only books with his master's imprint but any number of books printed by the entire cartel of London printing-houses.[74]

These scholarly assumptions regarding printing practices seem to stem from the same eagerness to precipitate the modern that we observed in treatments of *Hamlet*. In this instance, the journeyman has been pushed into the ranks of the wage-earner. This would draw him into that new population of men free and willing to exchange their labour for pay, created in England by land enclosure and the disbanding of retainers. There is a connection, to be sure, for the journeyman's release from master and land freed him to hire himself out for pay – himself determining whom to serve, for how much and how long.[75] It should be remembered, however, that a seven-year apprenticeship was the prerequisite for such a freedom. As long as the printing trade remained under the regulation of the Stationers' Company, the journeyman remained under its at once restrictive and protective auspices.

So too did the master, for the number of presses he owned, apprentices he kept, copies of books he printed were all mandated by Company ordinances. As the journeyman was no wage-earner, so the master was no capitalist. One of the effects of the guilds was to keep merchants' capital away from the master, for only members of the company were permitted to invest money in the trade. By excluding both the newly available free labourers and the newly accumulated merchants' capital, the guilds worked to forestall the dynamic encounter to which Marx attributes the rise of capitalist production: the encounter between wage-earner and capital.[76] As he also stresses, the guilds and capitalism were distinct and incompatible economic systems, 'As a rule, the whole guild system declines and falls, both master and journeyman, where the capitalist and worker arise.'[77]

Why then the big rush to see a later economic structure in early printing-house production?[78] Bibliographers are well aware, certainly, that the Stationers' Company was chartered to govern the book trade, that their regulations were upheld both by statute and by the customs of the company itself. So why imagine early modern guilds as would-be modern industries?

It is not insignificant that with the exception of the archival work of McKenzie and Blayney, these conclusions have been reached by analysing one book, arguably the most important in the language: the 1623 Shakespeare Folio. The tremendous amount of bibliographic scholarship invested in this book has primarily been directed to determining the relation of the printed book to the imagined authorial holograph behind it – and ultimately to the Shakespearean consciousness behind that. It is because of this aim that McKenzie's trade documents were previously ignored, for the Book itself was considered a complete repository for the history of its own making, 'in isolation from the work on hand *as though the Folio contained in itself all the evidence of its production* [emphasis added].'[79]

Is it a coincidence that manual work should be assigned the same monadic form as Shakespearean consciousness? that analyses of

how the bibliographic monolith was made should be based on atom-
ized units of production? that as creation is imagined emanating from
a single mind so too production is envisioned as issuing from single
hands?

Returning to the subject of the previous section, it is startling
to note how closely capitalist handwork conforms to Cartesian head-
work: both isolating soliloquy and estranging wages share the same
circumscribing autonomy. Thought and work are both imagined
within privatized spheres that become, paradoxically, the ground for
expression and production – the two modes through which the subject extends itself into the world. (As if the subject sealed off could
all the better reach out.) Yet as our focus on soliloquies and wages
has suggested, it is precisely the relation to world that gets lost in
both processes. The words of others get subsumed into Hamlet's
original thought; social networks are assimilated into wages. So too
the material world falls away: mind removes itself from its felt sur-
roundings in order to think; products lose their relation to producers
in order to circulate as commodities. Dichotimized as they are, Cartesian solipsism and capitalist commodification turn out, surprisingly,
to exact the same high cost: the human relation to other subjects
and to objects.

By looking for consciousness in Hamlet's 'soliloquy' and for commodification in early printing-house 'wages', this essay has suggested
that our understanding of both thought and work in this period has
been skewed by the desire to see them as anticipatory of the modern.
Thought is understood as a private process in mind; work is envisioned as a private activity of body. Each capacity excludes the other
and both exclude objective and subjective others. This is not to
recommend that time be rolled back, that the Renaissance be sent
back to the middle ages. The erection of the first public theatre in
1576 and the chartering of the printers' guild in 1556 are in themselves sufficient to mark a new cultural and economic era. Nor is it
to recommend a return to earlier materialities and collectivities.
Hamlet and Ophelia are damaged by that table and posy that are not
consciousness; human energies and financial resources are thwarted
by those discriminatory and exclusionary guilds that are not capitalist. Finally, it is not to recommend that the designation 'early modern'
be discarded as a misleading misnomer. That name guarantees a vital
connection between the remote then and the urgent now, a connection that runs through early modern and modern and late modern
and postmodern and all attenuations of the modern to-be. But this
essay does urge that we resist the impulse to make the early modern

look modern before its time: that we instead slow down and fan out its streamlined drive.

Notes

1 In opening with this exercise, I follow the example of Daniel Milo's stimulating book on historical divisions of time, *Trahir Le Temps (Histoire)* (Paris: Les Belles Lettres, 1991), pp. 17–19.

2 It should be pointed out that in the first part of this century especially, numerous studies pulled the Renaissance back into the Middle Ages in order to protect it from the crisis of modernity, thereby exempting it from the dissociation of sensibility, the shattering of the cosmos, Cartesian dualism, secularization.

3 On the nineteenth-century construction of the Renaissance, see Wallace K. Ferguson, *The Renaissance in Historical Thought: Five Centuries of Interpretation* (New York: Columbia University Press, 1948), pp. 133–94 and William Kerrigan and Gordon Braden, *The Idea of the Renaissance* (Baltimore and London: Johns Hopkins University Press, 1989), pp. 9–10.

4 See *The Question Concerning Technology and Other Essays*, trans. William Lovitt (New York: Harper & Row, 1977), p. 128.

5 See Hans Blumemberg's 'The epochs of the concept of an epoch', in *The Legitimacy of the Modern Age*, trans. Robert M. Wallace (Cambridge, Mass.: MIT Press, 1983), pp. 457–81, esp. p. 459. On the similar semantic history of 'revolution', see Reinhart Koselleck, 'Historical criteria of the modern concept of revolution', in *Futures Past: On the Semantics of Historical Time*, trans. Keith Tribe (Cambridge, Mass. and London: MIT Press, 1985), pp. 38–54.

6 Susan Stewart discusses (and herself follows) the seventeenth-century tradition of writing meditations in units of 100 in 'Traherne's centuries', in *Centuries' Ends, Narrative Means*, ed. Robert Newman (Stanford: Stanford University Press, forthcoming).

7 On the Magdeburg Centuriators, see Hillel Schwartz, *Century's End: A Cultural History of Fin de Siècle From the 990s Through the 1990s* (New York: Doubleday, 1991), p. 93.

8 See '. . . et la Révolution "créa" le siècle', *Trahir Le Temps*, pp. 30–62.

9 On the semantic history of 'secular', see Blumemberg, pp. 18–26. For the anachronistic search for a sixteenth-century *fin de siècle* see Margreta de Grazia, '*Fin de Siècle* Renaissance England', in *Fins de Siecle*, ed. Elaine Searry (Baltimore, Md.: Johns Hopkins University Press, 1994).

10 On the controversy centring on this key concept, see Robert M. Wallace's Introduction to Blumemberg, *Legitimacy*, pp. xi–xxxi.

11 *Reason in History*, trans. Robert S. Hartman (New York: Macmillan, 1953), p. 86.

12 On Hegel's topsy-turviness, see *The Marx–Engels Reader*, 2nd edn, ed. Robert C. Tucker (New York and London: W. W. Norton, 1978), pp. 302, 698.

13 For Marx on Hegel's anthropomorphism, see *The German Ideology, Reader*, pp. 172, 175.

14 Quoted by Schwartz, *Century's Ends*, p. 93.

15 Quoted by Santo Mazzarino in *The End of the Ancient World*, trans. George Holmes (New York: Alfred Knopf, 1966), p. 69.

16 *Reason in History*, p. 69.

17 Consider, however, the continuation of ancient and biblical cyclical cosmologies in Toynbee and Spengler, inspired by Nietzsche's 'eternal recurrence'.

18 See *Postmodernism, or, The Cultural Logic of Late Capitalism* (Durham, NC: Duke University Press, 1991), p. xi.

19 *Legitimacy*, p. 470.

20 See *Shakspere: A Critical Study of his Mind and Art* (1874) (London: Routledge & Kegan Paul, 1967).

21 *Question*, p. 132.

22 *The Archaeology of Knowledge and The Discourse on Language*, trans. A. M. Sheridan (New York: Pantheon Books, 1972), p. 12. For Heidegger too, periodization implies an *anthropological* and *humanistic* focus; see *Question*, p. 133 and Appendix 10, p. 153.

23 *The History of Sexuality, An Introduction*, trans. Robert Hurley (New York: Vintage, 1990), p. 7.

24 See Felix Gilbert, *History: Politics or Culture? Reflections of Ranke and Burckhardt* (Princeton: Princeton University Press, 1990), p. 61.

25 *The Civilization of the Renaissance in Italy*, trans. S. G. C. Middlemore, 2 vols (New York: Harper Torchbooks, 1959); Hegel, *The Philosophy of History*, trans. J. Sibree (New York: Dover Publications, 1956), pp. 412–27; Marx, *Capital, Reader*, pp. 433–4.

26 Hegel, *Philosophy*, p. 421; Burckhardt,*Civilization*, vol. 2, p. 303; Marx, *Capital, Reader*, p. 437.

27 In the 1623 Folio (F), a similar stage direction is specified in an earlier scene ('*Enter Hamlet, reading on a book*') and is implied in both F and the 1604 Quarto (Q2) in Gertrude's remark, 'But look where sadly the poor wretch comes reading' (II.ii.168). When not from Q1, Q2, or F, quotations from *Hamlet* are from Harold Jenkins's Arden edition (London and New York: Methuen, 1982).

28 *The Tragicall Historie of Hamlet Prince of Denmarke* (London, 1603), Ev. All passages from Q1 are taken from the facsimile reproduced in *Shakespeare's Plays in Quarto*, ed. Richard J. B. Allen and Kenneth Muir (Berkeley and Los Angeles: University of California Press, 1981).

29 For an example of the intricate theories that have been devised to account for Q1's idiosyncracies, see Kathleen Irace's computer-assisted analysis with charts and diagrams, 'Origins and Agents of Q1 *Hamlet*, in *The "Hamlet" First Published (Q1, 1603)*,' ed. Thomas Clayton (Newark: University of Delaware Press and London and Toronto: Associated University Presses, 1992), pp. 90–122.

30 G3ᵛ, Hᵛ, I[4]ᵛ.

31 On this speech's success in giving the illusion of the non-spoken, see Morris Leroy Arnold, *The Soliloquies of Shakespeare: A Study in Technic* (New York: Columbia University Press, 1911), p. 21.

32 James Hirsh argues that until the mid-seventeenth century, soliloquies were routinely overheard by other characters on stage. See 'The "To be or not to be" scene and the convention of Shakespearean drama', *Modern Language Quarterly*, 42 (1981), pp. 115–36.

33 See Mary Z. Maher's description in *Modern Hamlets and Their Soliloquies* (Iowa City: University of Iowa Press, 1992), p. 28.

34 For a recent examination of the *Hamlet* soliloquies as 'an intense dramatization of the human mind as the innermost realm of consciousness', see Alex Newell, *The Soliloquies in 'Hamlet': The Structural Design* (Rutherford, Madison, Teaneck: Farleigh Dickinson University Press; and London and Toronto: Associated University Press, 1991), p. 18.

35 See the entries for 'alone', '*solus*', and '*manet*' in *Concordance to Stage Directions and Speech Prefixes*, in Marvin Spevack, *A Complete and Systematic Concordance of the Works of Shakespeare*, vol. VII (Hildesberg and New York: Georg Olms Verlag, 1975). See also 'aside', 'prologue', and 'epilogue'.

36 *Meditations on First Philosophy*, in *Descartes, Philosophical Writings*, trans. and ed. Elizabeth Anscombe and Peter Thomas Geach (Wokingham: Van Nostrand Reinhold, 1986), pp. 61, 76.

37 Raymond Williams, 'On dramatic dialogue and monologue (particularly in Shakespeare)', in *Writing in Society* (London: Verso, n.d.), pp. 31–74. The effect on the soliloquy of the transition from platform to proscenium stage is also discussed by Harley Granville-Barker, *Prefaces to Shakespeare*, vol. 1 (Princeton: Princeton University Press, 1946), pp. 16–17. See also Catherine Belsey, *The Subject of Tragedy: Identity and Difference in Renaissance Drama* (London and New York: Methuen, 1985), pp. 23–6.

38 For a discussion of how poses of self-absorption and reverie similarly excluded the spectator in French Enlightenment painting, see Michael Fried, *Absorption and Theatricality* (Baltimore: Johns Hopkins University Press, 1980).

39 Williams, 'On dialogue', pp. 41–3.

40 Quoted from Augustine's *Retractationes* in *Soliloquies and Immortality of the Soul*, with introduction, translation and commentary by Gerard Watson (Warminster: Aris & Phillips, 1990), p. iv.

41 Robert Cawdrey, *A Table Alphabeticall* (1613).

42 On the spying out of secrets in *Hamlet* and its juridical, epistemological, and political counterparts in early modern England, see Patricia Parker, 'Dilations, spying and the "sunset place" of women', *Representations* 44 (Fall, 1993) 60–95.

43 Williams, 'On dialogue', pp. 57–60.

44 On the relationship of deixis to subjectivity, see Emile Benveniste, 'Relationships of person in the verb', 'The nature of pronouns', and 'Subjectivity in language', in *Problems in General Linguistics*, trans. M. E. Meek (Coral Gables, Fla.: University of Miami Press, 1971).

45 Williams, 'On dialogue', pp. 48–50.

46 For a summary of the critical response to this apparent contradiction, see Jenkins, *Hamlet*, p. 491.

47 Compare James L. Calderwood's observation that the 'greatest retardation comes by means of Hamlet's soliloquies', in *To Be or Not to Be: Negation and Meditation in 'Hamlet'* (New York: Columbia University Press, 1983), p. 154.

48 Because soliloquies, like *sententiae*, are self-contained semantic units, they are particularly suited for cutting and adding. Hamlet's final soliloquy, 'How all occasions do inform against me', appears in Q2 but not in Q1 or F.

49 For an analysis of the soliloquy according to Erasmian principles of composition, see Marion Trousdale, *Shakespeare and the Rhetoricians* (Chapel Hill, N.C.: University of North Carolina Press, 1982), pp. 58–61.

50 For the numerous humanist and Reformation discussions of suicide, see Michael MacDonald and Terence R. Murphy, *Sleepless Souls: Suicide in Early Modern England* (Oxford: Clarendon Press, 1990), esp. pp. 86–95. For an attempt to identify Hamlet's book in Q1, see Hardin Craig, 'Hamlet's Book', *Huntington Library Bulletin* 6 (November 1934), pp. 17–37.

51 Max Thomas examines the forms, uses, and importance of commonplace books in *The Practice of Poetry in Early Modern England*, forthcoming.

52 'Hamlet et Fortinbras', in *La Revue blanche* (1896) quoted by Philip Edwards in *Hamlet, Prince of Denmark* (Cambridge: Cambridge University Press, 1993), p. 35.

53 On the absence of any diacritical marking for 'lifted' passages in the early modern period and on the reversal in the function of quotation marks from flagging commonplaces to cordoning off private expression, see Margreta de Grazia, 'Shakespeare in quotation', in *The Appropriation of Shakespeare*, ed. Jean I. Marsden (London: Harvester-Wheatsheaf, 1991), pp. 57–71. For a richly comprehensive study of the relation of first-hand (original) and second-hand (derivative) writing, see François Compagnon, *La Seconde Main, ou, la travail de la citation* (Paris: Seuil, 1979). On the animating force of quotations and epigraphs particularly in modern poetry, see Gabriel Josipovici, ' "Ego non dixit sed Democritus" ', in *Writing and the Body* (Princeton: Princeton University Press, 1982), pp. 64–99. For a taxonomy of the 'genre of sententiousness, see Geoffrey Bennington, 'Approaching sententiousness', *Sententiousness and the Novel: Laying Down the Law in Eighteenth-Century French Fiction* (Cambridge: Cambridge University Press, 1985), pp. 3–63.

54 There is no stage direction specifying that Hamlet *writes* until Nicholas Rowe's 1709 edition. On the ambiguity of both the 'tables' of Shakespeare's Sonnet 122 and Hamlet's tables, see Jonathan Goldberg, *Voice Terminal Echo: Postmodernism and English Renaissance Texts* (London and New York: Methuen, 1986), pp. 92–100.

55 In distinguishing mind from matter, Descartes intriguingly chooses as representative of matter a variant of Hamlet's tablet: wax, the wax used to seal letters and receive the imprint of the seal, a miniature wax tablet. See Neil Herz, 'Dr. Johnson's forgetfulness, Descartes' piece of wax', in *Eighteenth Century Life*, vol. 16, no. 34 (November 1992), pp. 175–8. For bringing this essay to my attention, I thank Peter Stallybrass.

56 In his discussions of Freud's 'A note upon the "Mystic Writing-Pad" ', Derrida criticizes Freud for upholding the Platonic distinction between memory and mnemic device, presence and trace. See 'Freud and the scene or writing', in *Writing and Difference*, trans. Alan Bass (London: Routledge, 1993), pp. 196–231, esp. p. 227. For the relation of Hamlet's tables to the mystic pad see Goldberg, *Voice*, pp. 96–8, and Marjorie Garber, *Shakespeare's Ghost Writers' Literature as Uncanny Causality* (New York and London: Methuen, 1987), pp. 149–53.

57 On the importance of the Eucharistic controversy to the period's preoccupation with linguistic signs, particularly figuration, see Stephen Greenblatt, 'Remnants of the sacred in early modern England', in *Object and*

Subject: Reconstructing Renaissance Culture, eds Margreta de Grazia, Maureen Quilligan, and Peter Stallybrass (Cambridge: Cambridge University Press, forthcoming).

58 On Elizabeth's Injunctions of 1559 ordering the removal of altars and substituting the table for the altar at communion, see Eamon Duffy, *The Stripping of the Altars: Traditional Religion in England c.1400–c.1580* (New Haven and London: Yale University Press, 1992), p. 568.

59 Quoted by Greenblatt, 'Remnants', from Jaroslav Pelikan, *Reformation of Church and Dogma (1300–1700)*, in *The Christian Tradition: A History of the Development of Doctrine*, 5 vols (Chicago and London: University of Chicago Press, 1983), vol. 4, p. 201.

60 On 'gnomic pointing,' see G. K. Hunter, 'The marking of *sententiae* in Elizabethan plays, poems, and romances', *The Library*, Series 5, 6 (1951), p. 171. On these markings in a seventeenth-century edition of 'Rape of Lucrece', see John Lennard, *But I Digress: The Exploitation of Parentheses in English Printed Verse* (Oxford: Clarendon Press, 1991), pp. 29–31.

61 Compare these 'fists' or 'indices' with the images of disembodied scripting hands in Jonathan Goldberg, 'The violence of the letter', in *Writing Matter: From the Hands of the English Renaissance* (Stanford: Stanford University Press, 1990), pp. 59–107.

62 Compare the emblem decorating Ophelia's sterile willow with the heraldic hatchments on flourishing dynastic trees. See, for example, the engraving of James I's genealogical tree reproduced in *The Riverside Shakespeare*, ed. G. Blakemore Evans (Boston: Houghton Mifflin, 1974), p. 1306.

63 *King Lear* (IV.vi.118), ed. Kenneth Muir (London and New York: Methuen, 1975).

64 The exchange suggests that for the duration of the Mousetrap play, at least, it is Hamlet's head that lies between her legs: 'lady, shall I lie in your lap ... I mean, my head upon your lap' (III.ii.110–13).

65 On the exclusion of trade documents from twentieth-century bibliography, see D. F. McKenzie, 'What's Past is Prologue', The Bibliographic Society Centenary Lecture, 14 July 1992, pp. 8–20.

66 D. F. McKenzie, 'Printers of the mind: some notes on bibliographical theories and printing-house practices', *Studies in Bibliography*, 22 (1969), pp. 1–75.

67 McKenzie, 'Printers of the mind', 10.

68 Friedrich Engels, *Socialism: Utopian and Scientific, Reader*, p. 704.

69 *Leviathan: Or the Matter, Forme and Power of a Commonwealth Ecclesiasticall and Civil*, ed. Michael Oakeshott (New York and London: Collier, 1962), p. 234.

70 On the transition from accessory to full wages, see Engels, *Socialism, Reader*, pp. 700–6.

71 For this formula, see *Capital, Reader*, pp. 308, 313 and 318. On the centrality of cloth and clothing in early modern exchange, see Peter Stallybrass, 'Worn world: clothes and identity on the Renaissance stage', *Reconstructing Renaissance Culture*.

72 For a demonstration of some of the statistical and theoretical problems with this project, see McKenzie, 'Stretching a point: or, the case of the spaced-out comps', *Studies in Bibliography*, 37 (1984), pp. 106–21.

73 'The prevalence of shared printing in the early seventeenth century', *Publications of the Bibliographic Society of America*, 67 (1973), pp. 437–42;

The Texts of 'King Lear' and Their Origins: Nicholas Okes and the First Quarto, vol. I (Cambridge: Cambridge University Press, 1982), pp. 49–50.

74 For the geographical proximity of these shops, see Blayney, *The Bookshops in Paul's Cross Churchyard*, Occasional Papers of the Bibliographical Society, no. 5 (London: The Bibliographic Society, 1990).

75 McKenzie maintains that from as early as 1591, journeymen had individual contracts for which they set the terms, 'Printers of the mind', p. 12.

76 For a discussion of the other precondition for capitalism, see Richard Halpern, *The Poetics of Primitive Accumulation: English Renaissance Culture and the Genealogy of Capital* (Ithaca and London: Cornell University Press, 1991), esp. pp. 61–75.

77 Marx, *Reader*, p. 270.

78 See Marshall McLuhan's influential identification of the printing press with commodity culture, in *The Guttenberg Galaxy: The Making of Typographic Man* (Toronto: University of Toronto Press, 1962), pp. 124–6.

79 McKenzie, 'Printers of the mind', p. 15, n.24.

Graham Holderness, Bryan Loughrey & Andrew Murphy

'What's the matter?' Shakespeare and textual theory

The rapprochement of bibliography and contemporary theory has become so familiar a fact of Shakespeare studies that it is now routinely invoked as a *fait accompli*, and can certainly be seen to have modified the way in which 'mainstream' Shakespeare criticism tends to be conducted.[1] The encounter is, however, to say the least, remarkable. From the early stages of the Oxford/Cambridge polarization between 'scholarship' and 'criticism', bibliography and textual studies have remained on the edge of dominant theoretical and practical developments in criticism. Both American New Criticism and the British *Scrutiny* school shared, in their intimate absorption in the verbal medium of literary texts, a remarkable indifference to the material provenance and historical formation of those texts. In a critical culture partially shaped by that controversy, 'scholarship' has frequently been counterpoised against 'criticism' in a binary opposition dividing academic specialism from collaborative evaluation, setting dry-as-dust textual nit-picking against comprehensive appraisal, differentiating pseudo-scientific minutiae from the organic presence of a fully-lived critical appreciation. Some more recent critical movements such as deconstruction have similarly exhibited little interest in bibliography, being more concerned with the iterability of linguistic signs circulating within a culture than with the historical means by which those signs were originally produced. In this view, a readable text is by nature liberated from any possible enclosing context, even the originating moment of its historical production: the sign possesses the character of being legible even if the originating moment of its production is irrevocably lost. The deconstructionist's eye must therefore be focused on the perpetual motion of those signs in the process of their continual reproduction, rather than on the precise forms in which they were originally fixed by compositor and printing press.

Textual Practice 9:1, 1995, 93–119

The striking penetration of bibliographical preoccupations into theoretical and critical debate has produced a new configuration of critical practices in Shakespeare studies. Although it would probably be true to say that scholarship has held a more powerful position in Shakespeare criticism than is the case in many other fields of study, with many key figures moving between editing and criticism, the basic historical polarization of scholar and critic has even there generally held firm. Suddenly, however, all this has changed. A substantial group of American (or American-based) scholars, critics and theoreticians has gradually and incrementally coalesced to form a new direction in Shakespeare studies, a new wave of scholar-theoreticians already coining new nomenclatures aimed at identifying radically different cultural practices.[2] Some are obviously scholars moving into the territory of theoretical debate, others are practitioners of theoretically inflected criticism beginning to appropriate the principles and methods of textual studies. All share a common interest in new theoretical possibilities generated by an attention to bibliography, and in new cultural practices in editing and publishing facilitated by the impact of contemporary theory.[3]

Ever since the formidable achievements of New Bibliography established in textual studies of Shakespeare a hegemonic school and a dominant methodology, bibliography has evinced (at least until quite recently) considerable stability in its theoretical coherence. Contemporary critical theory, by contrast, has been characterized by much greater internal disagreement – between Marxism and deconstruction, between New Historicism and cultural materialism, between feminism and New Historicism – rendering the theoretical field anything but a stable and unified territory of consensus. Though the theory and practice of bibliography in Shakespeare studies has, again until recently, been fairly easy to characterize – consider, alongside the dominance of New Bibliography, the massive uniformity of traditional editorial practices – to speak of bibliography meeting theory should entail some attempt to identify the theoretical influences at work, and to define the precise nature and effects of the interaction between textual and theoretical activities. This essay aspires in a very modest way to initiate such an undertaking by offering a critique of some of the terms and concepts in play across that wide and diversified range of scholarly and critical practices we prefer to term simply 'textual theory'.

I

One key term running through the whole sequence of debated positions currently emerging within the field of textual studies is 'materialism'. The concept of the text as a 'material object' was given particular currency by Margreta de Grazia's article, 'The essential Shakespeare and the material book', published in 1988 in *Textual Practice*. This essay, a preliminary exposition of the argument developed at length in de Grazia's *Shakespeare Verbatim*, provides a theoretical critique of New Bibliography on the grounds that its claim to a 'materialist' methodology was in reality bogus. For all their preoccupation with the book as a physical object, with the 'material' processes of book-production, with the specific mechanisms and labour-processes by means of which books were produced, published and circulated, the New Bibliographers were ultimately dedicated to the thoroughly idealist aim of reconstructing, by inference from the evidence of surviving printed texts, the form and contents of Shakespeare's lost manuscripts.

W. W. Greg actually used the term 'material' to describe the method pioneered by New Bibliography, a method that

> lays stress upon the *material processes* of book-production, concerning itself primarily with the fortunes of the actual pieces of paper on which the texts were written or printed.
>
> Bibliographers have in fact brought criticism down from . . . the height of aesthetic and philosophical speculation to the *concrete familiarities* of the theatre, the scrivener's shop, and the printing house.[4]

(Our emphases)

The 'materialism' invoked here rests on the philosophical certainties of nineteenth-century positivism: both the physicality of the 'actual pieces of paper' and the 'concrete familiarities' of the processes of textual production are unproblematical categories, posited on a familiar (though in this case decidedly odd) mind/body dualism, in which theatres, bookshops and printing-houses somehow managed to exist on a separate plane quite distinct from 'aesthetic and philosophical speculations'. The claim advanced here is of course nothing less than a bid on behalf of New Bibliography for the status of a science, rooted in empiricist particulars and rigidly bound by the exigencies of physical evidence. Both in respect of method (the procedures by which texts are analysed and interpreted) and discourse (the strategies of presentation and argument) New Bibliography sought to arrogate to itself a quasi-scientific status capable of dismissing criticism and theory as mere 'aesthetic and philosophical speculation', self-evidently inferior to the rigours of a scientific textual practice.

The crudity of this positivistic materialism, uncontentious in its day but scarcely adequate for contemporary theoretical purposes, can be amply demonstrated from other key figures in New Bibliography. Both Fredson Bowers and R. B. McKerrow for instance were content to operate with distinctions as positivistic as those between 'objective' fact and 'subjective' judgement, between the 'textual object' and the 'taste and learning' of the editor. Bowers writes

> Indeed, the heart of the method consists in supplying a *mechanical explanation* for all phenomena *mechanically produced* by the printing process whenever such an explanation can be arrived at on the *recoverable evidence*. On occasion such bibliographical evidence limits the number of possibilities open to the finishing touches of *critical explanation*, which must necessarily refer back to *values*, or *opinions*, as the basis for *judgement*.[5]
>
> (Our emphases)[5]

Just as a 'mechanical explanation' of the process of 'mechanical pro-duction' is bound by 'evidence', so the iron discipline of scientific method forces 'values' and 'opinions' into a very tight corner. 'Judge-ment' should be firmly based on such robust 'evidence' rather than on the undisciplined subjectivity of 'values' or 'opinions'.

None the less, this positivist confidence in the reality of the object (e.g. a printed early-modern play-text) co-exists in New Bibliography with a pessimistic conviction that the object in question is actually a mere simulacrum, a copy of something infinitely more authentic, an imitation of a lost ideal form. The mechanistic language of materialism is suddenly illuminated by an efflux of Platonic ideal-ism. 'Reality' does not after all reside in the physical object we can know and explain by reference to mechanical laws, but in the lost manuscript, the unknown from which the known, the surviving physical object, derives. New Bibliographical method thus amounts in the end to a quest, a search for the lost ideal: its ultimate aim being to 'strip the veil of print from a text' to reveal the characteristics of the underlying manuscript.[6] This central metaphor has generally been understood in platonic and in biblical terms. The choice of the verb 'strip', in conjunction with the particular physical processes involved and the quasi-scientific vocabulary deployed, links the image more closely with Salome's dance (or with the removal of wall-paper) than with Plato's cave or the Hebrew temple. Bowers's metaphor thus invokes a binary opposition of genders, and simultaneously discloses and is trapped by the key contradiction in New Bibliography. For Bowers, the manuscript is a version of the female body, elusively erotic and enticing. The printed text interposes an opaque and obstructive 'veil' (or more usually, in platonic thought as in strip-tease, several veils) between the male desire and its object. Through the medium of scientific method, the intellectual inquirer is empowered to ravish the object, violently tearing aside its protective covering to render the female body naked to the male observer's gaze, answerable to the male desire. The printed text is deemed to 'contain' the manuscript as clothing contains the eroticized female body. At the same time, erotic power is also invested fetishistically in the clothing itself, which, once discarded, simultaneously retains and yields up the erotic potency it derives from its ambiguous function of concealment and disclosure. The pleasures of editing are imagined, then, both as a satisfaction of assured surrender, as resistance is stripped away, and as a more perverse fulfilment through violence, as the tearing of clothing approximates to the dismembering of a body whose erotic qualities the clothing shares. In the absence of the authentic body or manuscript, the manipulation of such discarded coverings as the printed texts, though very much a second-order satisfaction, remains a source of sexual or editorial pleasures.

The development of a patriarchical sexualization of the text by Bowers is attended by a concomitant deployment of a religiously charged lexicon.[7] The New Bibliographers posited an authorial text which had been 'corrupted' in the process of entering the printed state. To be born into the post-lapsarian realm of print was in some sense necessarily to carry a stigma of corruption. Thus the 'materialism' of New Bibliography found no difficulty in reconciling a confidence in the reality of matter with an assurance of its eventual transcendence. Having brought criticism down from the divine heights of speculation, and incarnated it in the concrete familiarities of everyday life, the New Bibliographers completed their re-enactment of the Christian myth by arranging for a re-assumption of the incarnated text, not into the realm of mere human 'opinion', but into the heaven of authorial intention. In this ideological problematic the unfallen manuscript stands for the divinity, the printed text is a fallen and corrupted mortal incarnation, and the modernized, emended edition is a restoration of prelapsarian innocence, paradise regained. The historic reluctance to reprint the printed texts in their original forms might even be related, pursuing this metaphor, to their unredeemed condition: 'touch me not, for I am not yet ascended unto the Father'.

At the stage represented by 'The essential Shakespeare and the material book', Margreta de Grazia was content to leave the argument at an exposure of New Bibliography's residual idealism, an 'anti-materialist ... strain in the study of the book as material object'.[8] A possible implication of this critique is that if the materialist substance of New Bibliography could be recovered and freed from its idealist form, the method would provide a sufficiently robust mechanism for understanding the material nature of cultural and textual production. What this interpretative moment actually represents, however, is a revision of traditional bibliography rather than a convergence of bibliography and theory. 'Materialism' in this problematic means much the same as it meant for Bowers in his 'materialist' definition of New Bibliography. An essentially positivist, or (as Marx termed it) 'mechanical' materialism is affirmed as a practicable counter to the residual idealism of traditional textual studies. But so untheorized a philosophical position will inevitably be vulnerable to continual unconscious collapses back into the idealism with which in New Bibliography it coexisted; and de Grazia herself has since, as we shall presently show, taken the argument beyond the self-contradictions of this particular dualism.

II

A similarly unproblematized materialism, on the other hand, characterizes some of the theoretical articulations of the 'New Textualists', particularly those associated with the Oxford Shakespeare enterprise. The general editors of the Oxford project provide, in an intriguing passage in the *Textual Companion*, a metaphorical defence of the Oxford Shakespeare's editorial procedures:

> In a famous passage in Harold Pinter's *The Homecoming*, Lenny the pimp memorably and at length describes his encounter with a woman who was 'falling apart with the pox'. At the end of his story, the listener asks, 'How did you know she was diseased?' Lenny answers, 'I decided she was.' An editor, in emending, decides that a text is diseased; such decisions may be mistaken. But we know that every early printed edition of Shakespeare's plays is more or less diseased; every compositor and every scribe commits errors. Corruption somewhere is certain; where, is uncertain. We also know that Shakespeare's texts were composed on paper by an author before they were composed in type by a compositor. The lost manuscripts of Shakespeare's work are not the fiction of an idealist critic, but particular material objects

which happen at a particular time to have existed, and at another particular time to have been lost, or to have ceased to exist.

Emendation does not seek to construct an ideal text, but rather to restore certain features of a lost material object (that manuscript) by correcting certain apparent deficiencies in a second material object (this printed text) which purports to be a copy of the first. Most readers will find this procedure reasonable enough.[9]

Once again, the text is imagined as a woman, now irredeemably corrupt and diseased. Just as the pimp claims to be able to diagnose by sight the tell-tale symptoms of venereal disease, so the (male) editor guesses at corruptions within the body of the (female) text. The appropriate editoral practice to adopt when confronted with such decadence is suggested by the drift of Lenny's disquisition:

I clumped her one ... and there she was up against this wall – well, just sliding down the wall, following the blow I'd given her. ... So I just gave her another belt in the nose and a couple of turns of the boot and sort of left it at that.[10]

What the female text lacks in purity the male editor will beat into her by the judicious application of violence: an impressive object-lesson, certainly, in how to handle a text.

We cannot, however, simply 'sort of leave it at that'. In the Pinter text, Lenny's statement is a characteristically perverse assertion of macho defiance in the face of a searching interrogation by Ruth, who is in fact something more than a mere 'listener' in the exchange. The statement is a move in an elaborate 'status-game' between man and woman, each vying for discursive power over the other. Ruth's question is not an innocent request for information, but a cutting riposte to Lenny's macho posturings, a sly demonstration that he had, by his own account, no means of knowing that the woman was 'falling apart with the pox'. Lenny's insistence on the incontrovertibility of his assertion is a kind of defensive wilfulness, an arrogant refusal to heed question or entertain doubt. It is certainly a strange basis on which to found a theory of editing! We find ourselves obliged here to take the woman's part, and put the question again: 'How did you know she was diseased?'

On what basis do we assume, with this kind of religious fatalism and social-Darwinist pessimism, that corruption is everywhere, since the only possible measure of such corruption, the authorial manuscript, is not there to be consulted?[11] The imputed 'materialism' of this editorial policy is precisely the same as that of New Bibliography: a materialist methodology devoted towards an idealist end, that of stripping the Platonic 'veil of print' from a text to reveal the eternal form of the underlying manuscript. The object of which we can have direct knowledge, the printed text, is judged to be corrupt by conjectural reference to the object of which we can by definition have no direct knowledge, the uncorrupted (but non-existent) manuscript. The procedure is self-contradictory, since the historical document is being compared with an 'original' that can be speculatively reconstructed only from the evidence of the historical document itself.

III

Thus far, then, the 'New Textualists' have not even succeeded in breaking free from the positivism of New Bibliography, let alone opened bibliography itself up to currents of genuinely new theory. The importance therefore of Margreta de Grazia's latest contribution to the debate, written jointly with Peter Stallybrass, cannot be underestimated. 'The materiality of the Shakespearean text' offers itself both as a summation of the debate, and (in its title alone) as a definition of terms. The essay contains a vigorous recapitulation of the argument advanced in 'The essential Shakespeare and the material book', now, however, elaborated with more detailed reference to the characteristic features of the early printed texts and a stronger indication of their attractiveness to modern theory. The old bibliographic 'materialism' of the New Bibliographers is synthesized with a new cultural 'materialism' to identify a cultural transaction in which the physical materiality of the historical text offers both resistance and opportunity, identity and relationship, text and context.

> The features that modernization and emendation smooth away *remain stubbornly* in place to *block* the illusion of transparency – the impression that there is some ideal 'original' behind the text.
>
> These features are precisely the focus of this essay: old typefaces and spellings, irregular line and scene divisions, title pages and other paratextual matters, and textual cruxes. Discarded or transformed beyond recognition in standard modern editions, they *remain obstinately* on the pages of the early texts, insisting upon being *looked at, not seen through*. Their *refusal to yield* to modern norms bears witness to the *specific history* of the texts they make up.[12]

(Our emphases)

'Materiality' is both a matter of what the New Bibliographers called 'recoverable evidence' – those physical objects that were circulated as books through Elizabethan and Jacobean culture and that have survived for modern observation – and of the way such evidence has interacted with 'values' and 'opinions', the New Bibliographers' code for the modern reading of early modern texts. Texts are both pro-duced – with historical specificity, at an originating moment of production – and reproduced – iterably in an infinite number of cultural situations unforeseen by the witnesses of that originating moment. The element of historical 'originality' confronts the modern reader as a matter of resistance ('refusal to yield'): a physical identity of the text that speaks of historical difference, and resists contempor-ary appropriation. The emphasis here is on the obstinacy of the early modern text's characteristic signage: physical features that 'remain in place' are therefore not available for free-wheeling deconstructionist interpretation; printed signs that 'block' the modern reader's inquiries and 'remain obstinately on the page' are by definition not open to reconfiguration at the observer's behest, at the inquirer/requirer's whim. If historically generated and recorded signs, despite all our sophisticated strategies of reading and reconstruction, remain on the page, to be 'looked at, rather than seen through', then they not only constitute evidence of historical otherness; they also testify to the vital possibility of a cultural or textual identity that cannot be com-mandeered, a self that cannot be assimilated to the other. Where that virtually all-male club the New Bibliographers evidently cherished beneath their respectable tweed jackets a perverse desire to ravish the printed text in order to release the perfect female body enclosed within it; so the new textual theory (featuring within its ranks many female practitioners) includes on its agenda a strategy of resistance, in which the old text declares, like the modern woman: 'no, I will not be what you want me to be.' That 'refusal to yield' attributed to the early modern text sounds a particularly contemporary note, almost comically linking an ancient chivalric vocabulary with a modern politics of resistance.

This approach could be described as a genuinely 'dialectical' materialism, acknowledging both past and present, facilitating trans-actions between an historic evidence and a modern agenda. The dia-lectical approach gives way, however, in the course of the essay, to a conception of the text as no longer an identifiable physical object with its own characteristic structure, but rather as an element in a more general process of cultural production:

> We need, in other words, to rethink Shakespeare in relation to our new knowledge of collaborative writing, collaborative

printing, and the historical contingencies of textual production . . . if there is any single object between us and such a project, it is the sense that the value of Shakespeare lies elsewhere, in the inner regions of the text rather than in the practices recorded on its surfaces, in what Pierre Macherey has termed the *'postulate of depth'*. . . . But if we reject depth as the object of analysis, we will at the same time have to transform our notion of surface. . . . Perhaps a more helpful way of conceptualizing the text is to be found outside metaphysics, in the materials of the physical book itself: in *paper* . . . paper retains the traces of a wide range of labor practices and metamorphoses. . . . The Shakespearean text is thus, like any Renaissance book, a provisional state in the circulation of matter.[13]

Thus that 'specific history' of an early modern text, graspable by a materialist bibliography, is subsumed into an extremely *general* history of early modern cultural process. While materialist bibliography accepts the visual surface of an early text as accurately eloquent of its physical character, and seeks to *read* it, rather than read *through* it, this materialism is then rejected in favour of a deconstructionist or New Historicist emphasis on textual transparency. The textual surface which first 'obstinately block[ed]' and limited the parameters of interpretation suddenly becomes an open window on to the industrial and commercial processes of the early modern printing trade. Visual signs that first speak of identity, refusing to yield to appropriation, now point only outwards towards context and relationship, towards the 'diversity of labors' that constituted the productive process.

IV

The roots of this version of materialism and the theoretical difficulties it entails lie in modern readings of classic Marxism. There can be little doubt that Marxism, albeit often in an obscured and attenuated form, is a major intellectual component of all modern cultural theory. If this assertion seems highly questionable, the explanation might well lie in the oblique directions by which Marxism, as the 'philosophy that dare not speak its name', has penetrated US culture. Marxism underlies American New Historicism as firmly as it underpins British cultural materialism,[14] despite the obvious contrast, in the UK, of overt acknowledgement ('cultural materialism' being directly derived from Marx's 'historical materialism') and in the US, of systematic occlusion (as even the term 'New Historicism' is replaced by Stephen Greenblatt with the anodyne 'Cultural Poetics'[15]). The fortunes of 'materialism' as we can trace them through the history outlined in this essay enact a trajectory from a crude positivistic 'materialism' employed in much the same way as it was by New Bibiliography, to a sophisticated Marxist theory derived from Marx's own discussions of the commodity in its relation to value, exchange and labour.

Marx's analysis of the commodity in *Das Kapital* proposes that an object possesses use-value (utility to others) only in so far as it contains the product of human labour. Uncultivated land for example can bear a price, but has no use-value without the application to it of human labour. When objects as use-values are exchanged, however, they take on the character of commodities and appear to derive their value from that act of exchange rather than from the process of production. Utility thus seems to become a quality of the object, reflected in its price and exchange-value, rather than the result of a productive process:

> A commodity is therefore a mysterious thing, simply because in it the social character of men's labour appears to them as an objective character stamped upon the product of that labour; because the relation of the producers to the sum total of their own labour is presented to them as a social relation, existing not between themselves, but between the products of their labour. This is the reason why the products of labour become commodities, social things whose qualities are at the same time perceptible and imperceptible by the senses.[16]

The real transaction taking place in the exchange of commodities is a social relation between producers and consumers. Yet it is in the nature of the commodity to mystify that relation, and to hypostatize the commodity as an autonomous object:

> It is a definite social relation between men that assumes in their eyes the fantastic form of a relation between things. In order, therefore, to find an analogy, we must have recourse to the mist-enveloped regions of the religious world. In that world the productions of the human brain appear as independent beings endowed with life, and entering into relation both with one another and the human race. So it is in the world of commodities with the product of men's hands. This I call the Fetishism which attaches itself to the products of labour as soon as they are

produced as commodities, and which is therefore inseparable from the production of commodities.[17]

Marx's revolutionizing of classical economics consisted largely of this redefinition of the commodity in terms not of intrinsic utility and value, but of the social and economic relations involved in its production and exchange. Marx thus shifted the focus of economic analysis from the mysterious, apparently autonomous object (the commodity) to the means of production (industry and labour), the relations of production (property and class) and the system of exchange (the market).

The close correspondence between this analytical model and that employed by de Grazia and Stallybrass should be clear. The theoretical method advocated is one in which the text is stripped of its mystery and spurious autonomy, and re-positioned as an element in a material process of production and circulation. The text may appear to possess, in its own right and as immanent qualities, depth, value and meaning. Traditional interpretative methods confront the text as autonomous, single and individuated, the direct utterance of authorial genius. An application of Marxist economic analysis reveals that this apparent autonomy arises from the character of that text as an isolable commodity, the printed book produced for sale on the commercial market. Where traditional bibliography would seek, by relating the text vertically to its authorial provenance, to invest it with the aura and ambience of mystery, materialist bibliography follows Marx (and of course Marxist-influenced poststructuralism), in relating the text horizontally to the historical conditions of its production. The text only *appears* to be autonomous: in reality it should not only be seen as an element in a process of cultural production, but it should be *read* as eloquent only of its own self-dispersal within the continuum of that process.

This theoretical strategy would then appear to be an accurate 'cultural materialist' application of Marx's economic theory. We would argue, however, that what it in fact finally represents, is rather a misapplication and misunderstanding of Marx's theory. The object forming the commodity does not in Marx simply disappear into an undifferentiated process of production. It still exists, identified by the possession both of material objectivity (an irreducible physical being that distinguishes it from other contingent or comparable objects); and even more significantly, it possesses 'use-value', a specific utility or range of capabilities within the cultural apparatus. The fact that a text is also part of a process of production and circulation does not eliminate that text's specific identity. The text that was printed, sold and preserved had a different physical identity and a different relationship to the general process of production than those other textual forms that we have (erroneously) been accustomed, by the theory and practice of modern editing, to identify as analogous elements within a larger whole: the prompt-book, or a manuscript, or the script mobilized in particular performances. This 'identity' of the text arises not from the ascription of a mysterious authorial presence, or of an immanent 'depth' of meaning and value: but precisely from the text's original character as a commodity, with an exchange-value more manifestly marked than its use-value. Hence the particular historical significance of an early printed text consists in its individuation, its self-differentiation from the process of production and exchange of which it was a part. The theatrical performance sold to its spectators exhausts itself in the simultaneous moment of production and consumption: its physical form is concrete, immediate and transitory; its use-value and exchange-value are identical. The manuscript of an early modern play, worthless except as copy, could be converted to printer's waste and recycled as a bookbinding, its use-value and exchange-value parting company as surface and content were duplicated elsewhere, while depth and form were reduced to raw material.

These problems are focused with unusual clarity by the appearance, in a sale of literary material at Sotheby's (21–22 July 1992), of a leaf of 'manuscript' described in the auctioneer's catalogue as a 'fragment of a contemporary manuscript of an unrecorded Elizabethan or Jacobean play containing a scene very similar to one in Shakespeare's *Henry IV, Part One.*' The fragment corresponds to the scene known in modern editions as 2.1 of *1 Henry IV.* The verbal echoes and parallel action certainly make it as convincing an 'analogue' as many other similar identifications. Sotheby's suggested that the unknown play from which the fragment derived might be a source or an adaptation – 'setting aside the tantalising but tenable proposition that Shakespeare might ever have recycled one of his own scenes himself'; and the catalogue prudently avoided direct attribution of authorship by enclosing the bardic name in cautious parentheses. None the less an implicit claim was made for an 'originality' that takes us back beyond the corruptions of print and publication to a pristine authenticity. Certainly the expected price – £10,000 to £12,000 – seemed index-linked to a Shakespearean connection rather than to some unknown and anonymous Elizabethan hack dramatist. The value placed upon such 'primary source' material by modern scholarship (and reflected in the price of the fragment at auction) contrasts starkly with the low estimate in which such a manuscript

was held within the historical conditions governing cultural production in the early modern period. The fragment was found in the
binding of a Geneva edition of Homer's *Odyssey*, printed in 1586
and bound at Oxford around 1600. Evidently the whole play from
which it derives was used by printers as binder's waste – contemporary drama functioning as scrap paper facilitating the publication of
an ancient literary classic. Thus both the performance and the manuscript disappear into the undifferentiated continuum of productive
practices, and are lost to history. The printed text, on the other hand,
survives, to initiate the 'Shakespeare' of the future.

We are faced then with two reciprocally antagonistic propositions. First, we have a conception of the early printed text as an
'original', a 'material book' constituting specific 'historical evidence'.
Second, there is the poststructuralist view that the early printed text
was never more than an undifferentiated element in a process of
production and exchange. In one problematic a text is specific, individual, historic, declaring an irreducible individual identity. In the
other a text is overdetermined, undifferentiated, unfixed, and eloquent
only of the historical process of which it was a part. In de Grazia
and Stallybrass these propositions are at certain points dialectically
interrelated, but at others, mutually cancelling.

We have presented examples of how the unreconstructed 'materialism' of New Bibliography can assume a Marxist gloss without
essentially surrendering its complicity with some traditional method-
ologies and assumptions, as in de Grazia's early formulation in 'The
essential Shakespeare and the material book'. We have presented other
examples of how a genuinely 'dialectical' materialism, such as that
displayed in parts of 'the materiality of the Shakespearean text', could
be developed from these roots, by linking a 'historical materialist'
confidence in the reality of matter with a 'dialectical materialist'
acknowledgement of the social and economic structures within which
matter is both shaped and defined. Both these theoretical positions
need to be distinguished clearly and sharply from a third theoretical
direction, also claiming the title of 'materialism', and displaying some
close correspondences with aspects of Marxist philosophy. This
additional mutation of materialism derives directly from such theoretical fields as poststructuralism, deconstruction and New Historicism. 'Materialism' here parts company with the conviction of textual
identity shared by both the earlier versions, and reconceives the text
as self-dispersing, a 'provisional state in the circulation of matter'.
Other assertions of the latter view, undeflected by any residual
materialism, can be found in the work of Jonathan Goldberg, Stephen
Orgel, and Jerome MacGann:

There never has been, and never can be, an unedited Shakespeare text. Textual criticism and post-structuralism agree therefore: we have no originals, only copies. The historicity of the text means that there is no text itself; it means that the text cannot be fixed in terms of original or final intentions.[18]

The history of realisations of the text ... is the history of the text.[19]

Texts are produced and reproduced under specific social and institutional conditions, and hence ... every text, including those that may appear to be purely private, is a social text. This view entails a corollary understanding, that 'text' is not a 'material thing' but a material event or set of events, a point in time or a moment in space where certain communicative interchanges are being practiced.[20]

Despite the obvious differences, there appears to be an underlying complicity between New Bibliography and the poststructuralist wing of 'New Textualism', which lies in the fact that both regard any individual text, including the original (i.e. initially published) printed text of a Shakespeare play, as a signpost pointing towards something greater and more complete than itself. Whether that larger domain is (for New Bibliography) the authorial manuscript or the author's intentions, or (for poststructuralist 'New Textualism') the continuum of language, the process of history, or the system of cultural production, the method remains strikingly similar. The meaning and value of a text always lie outside and beyond it. It is remarkable how frequently de Grazia and Stallybrass demonstrate their implicit conviction that a 'text' is, even rhetorically, always larger than any individual textualization. 'How many variants between texts of a given play', they ask, 'warrant the reproduction of the play in multiple forms?'[21] Here the primary object is not an individual text but a 'play' that contains several component elements, among which may be a number of printed texts. Or again, 'The process [photography] that appears best suited for duplicating the material text ends up reproducing only one of its multiple forms.'[22] Here the 'material text' possesses a transcendent unity greater than the printed texts that represent its various 'multiple forms'. Ultimately in this poststructuralist 'materialism', the printed text becomes a glass through which the great process of historical and cultural production and circulation can be perceived. Both poststructuralist 'New Textualism' and New Bibliography share, oddly, a suspicious mistrust of what we (as materialist bibliographers) accept as 'primary evidence', the early printed texts. It is as though New Bibliographical materialism, interested in textual surface but committed to spiritual depth, and poststructuralist bibliographic materialism, unable to focus on textual surface as anything other than a transparent window on to the underlying depths of history, encounter one another finally as strange but compatible bedfellows. Both ultimately participate in that deflection of attention – from material text to textual material – earlier identified by Margreta de Grazia: 'When meaning and value are posited outside or beyond the text, its physical properties, even in their most ready form – the precise letters and words on a page – command little attention.'[23] In deconstruction, language points only towards the absence of its referent. In New Bibliography the orphaned text cries for its lost father, the manuscript. But equally in poststructuralist 'New Textualism' the text, facing dissolution in the acid solutions of history and culture, hungers to be reunited with the transcendent completeness of the unity from which it has fallen.

This contradiction arises from the untheorized presence of incompatible theoretical influences; and these incommensurable theoretical perspectives point differentially towards quite different cultural practices.

V

It is to those cultural practices, specifically methods of editing and dissemination, that we now must turn. So far the argument has been conducted on a theoretical level, and is very obviously open to the charge that we are essaying a critique of theoretical eclecticism, in the interests of some rigorous ideological purism. The proof of this particular pudding is, however, as Brecht was fond of saying, very much in the eating. The real impact and effectivity of different textual theories occurs when they initiate and sustain particular kinds of editorial practice.

Margreta de Grazia and Peter Stallybrass indicatively exemplify the practices of 'New Textualism' primarily by reference to two editorial enterprises: the Oxford Shakespeare (1986) and Michael Warren's *The Complete* King Lear *1608–23* (1989). The former printed two separate texts of *King Lear* (1608 Quarto and First Folio); the latter published four separate texts of that title, two Quarto texts and one Folio, in an unbound, loose-leaf format (each individually boxed), together with a bound parallel text of F1 and Q1. Other symptomatic instances cited are Stephen Booth's edition of *Shakespeare's Sonnets* (1977), which sets a facsimile original against a modern edition; and Paul Bertram and Bernice Kliman's *The Three-Text* Hamlet: *Parallel Texts of the First and Second Quartos and First Folio* (1991). Although various differentiating observations are made about these different publishing projects, they are all cited as parties to a 'textual revolution', a revolution practically implemented by those editions that enable, in the place of the traditional conflated or single control-text edition, a *multiplicity* of texts: 'for over two hundred years, *King Lear* was one text; in 1986, with the Oxford Shakespeare, it became two; in 1989, with *The Complete* King Lear *1608–1623*, it became four (at least).' Progress is no longer measured retrospectively, as it was in the editorial culture initiated by the eighteenth-century scholars, and reconfirmed by New Bibliography, as a slow and gradual approximation to the *authorial* original; but in the culture of 'New Textualism' prospectively, by the degree to which the modern edition can be seen splitting into modern textual forms correspondent to the original individually printed texts. The Oxford Shakespeare's acknowledgement of two discrete texts of *King Lear* is posited as the editorial breakthrough; Michael Warren's unbinding of *King Lear* into two discrete Quarto texts and one Folio text is welcomed for its celebration of textual multiplicity. In the latter the resolution of textuality into distinct original constituents is perceived as merely preparatory to a full-blown deconstructionist dispersal of all textual elements – books, pages, lines, words – into raw textual material, wide open to contemporary appropriation, de- and re-construction.

> Facsimiles confer a sanctity upon the particulars of the duplicated text, hypostatising forms that were quite fluidly variable at their publication.... Michael Warren's *The Complete* King Lear *1608–1623* designedly resists this arrest by opening up the textual proliferation that was endemic to early modern printing practices.[24]

Just as in the normal processes of early modern publication such texts were altered in the course of printing and before being finally bound, so the modern deconstructionist reader can freely manipulate the textual elements of the various texts entitled *King Lear* to form any number of differential versions.

This textual revolution is, as de Grazia and Stallybrass admit, an uneven affair. If we unpick the theoretical strands implied by the specific editorial practices here cited and celebrated, we find nothing like the consensus proposed by the term 'New Textualism'. Prominent within the body of theoretical practices they distinguish by that title, and clearly exemplified both by the Oxford Shakespeare and by the work of Michael Warren, is a perspective quite formally anchored to certain editorial traditions, and more appropriately labelled simply 'revisionism'.

Textual Revisionism acknowledges textual multiplicity as a fact, only to reconcile it with the integrity of the author. Shakespeare did not, it is true, write only one *King Lear*; he may have written two, and one is a revision of the other. The texts are different, as two children of different ages and the same parentage may differ: but both issue from the same parental source. For the proponents of the New Bibliography the answer to the problem of the dispersal of a work over several different incarnations was to reduce this multiplicity to uniformity, by privileging one incarnation and subordinating the others to it. From the late 1970s onwards the hegemony of the New Bibliography was systematically challenged by the proponents of revisionism, for whom the conflation of many texts into a single compounded text was anathema. They proposed the separating out of individual textualizations, suggesting that such variations (or, at least some of them) may reflect distinct versions of a given text.

Although, textually, the revisionists have laid great emphasis on multiplicity, the source of this multiplicity has been seen as essentially singular: *King Lear* may have two bodies, but there is only one Shakespeare, the originator of both individual texts. The coherence of that authorial construction is of course guaranteed by cultural and institutional more than by bibliographical conditions. If the differentiation of texts into multiplicity occurs within a cultural project framed by the author-function, then any rediscovered polyvocality will quickly be assimilated to an authorial monotone. The Oxford Shakespeare (with its radically disembodied *Lears*) is partly based on an editorial strategy, derived from a convergence of theatrical influence and textual plurality, that points well beyond the constricting problematic of the institutional context – the 'Oxford Shakespeare' – within which it was developed. Ideological commitment to that totalizing authorial project entails a deprioritizing of the texts as we find them in history: discrete, mutually independent, overdetermined by particular conditions of cultural production – prior to (and also of course subsequent to) the editorial establishment of a canon in 1623. The radical theoretical possibilities released by a recognition of textual plurality, involving the deconstruction of the mainstream editorial tradition and an archaeological excavation of the 'real foundations' of that cultural edifice – the earliest printed texts themselves – become suppressed within the determining framework of an authorial construction. A theoretical move that could potentially

return the texts to history and free them from the ideological constrictions of a canonical reproduction, loses its strategic mobility as
the texts themselves are implicitly re-connected to the patriarchal
source, silently re-inscribed within the ideological problematic of an
authoritarian cultural apparatus. Revision theory, even in its new
theatrically-inflected form of a directorial 'para-text' putatively supplied by Shakespeare, can still reconcile evidence of plurality between
texts within the conceptual stability of an alternative author-function.
Matthew Arnold's serenely detached master of a ready-perfected
poetic speech, is replaced by Wells and Taylor's restlessly-revising,
theatrically-engaged perfectionist playwright.[25]

The Oxford editors have made it clear, by deriving their individual play-texts from single sources, by printing alternative texts of
King Lear, and by confessing to some degree of regret that the
project could not in this respect have been more ambitious, that they
acknowledge a wider applicability for the general principle of textual
plurality. But since that aspiration remains firmly located within the
hypothesis of authorial revision, it points not towards the liberation
of texts from canonical colonization and authorial sovereignty, but
towards the juxtaposition of multiple texts re-inscribed into a
relationship of parallelism and reciprocal interdependence. 'I should
like to see', says Stanley Wells, 'double editions of all other plays
where there are significant differences between the early witnesses to
the texts.'[26] Ideally, then, a reader or theatre worker should be offered
not a multiplicity of *discrete* texts, but an opportunity to compare
an early with a revised version, or an authorial draft with a theatri-
cally adapted script. Texts in this model are related not horizontally
and diachronically to historical conditions of production and contexts
of cultural appropriation, but vertically and synchronically to one
another, and to their 'onlie begetter'.[27]

This problematic clearly acknowledges the influence of other
determining factors, especially those involved in theatrical realization:
but the final explanation of a text's mobility is located not in theatre
or history or cultural context, but in the controlling mastery of
authorial intention. The *Textual Companion* to the Oxford Shakespeare defines the processes of canonization in a biological metaphor
which invokes the operations of nature rather than the constructions
of artifice. A play, like a child, is the product of two parents, 'born of
the fruitful union of a unique author and a unique society'. Careful
to acknowledge the limits of authorial mastery, the editors none the
less elaborate here a metaphorical fantasy which validates a rigid and
exclusive conception of canon as an ideological totality:

> Like children, works of art acquire a being independent of those who conceived them. We may judge and interpret and enjoy a poem or person, without knowing the author or the father. But poems, like persons, come in families.... In this sense a 'Complete Works' is the literary equivalent of a family reunion, the gathering of a clan of siblings.... In recognizing the existence of such literary families, we need not accept any exaggerated theoretical estimate of the power of one parent – the 'author' – to impose successfully and consistently his or her intentions upon the children: we simply accept that each parent had some influence, often unconscious, commonly unpredictable, upon the maturing of each individual creation.[28]

However prudently hedged about with qualifications, the metaphor remains questionable in its privileging of a particular sociological form of the family, one that was indeed in Shakespeare's time only in the process of historical formation. Patrilinear, consanguinous, formed from the creative coupling of a clearly identified father ('Shakespeare') with a vacuous female other ('society'), tightly sealed in its legal definition of membership, a particular ethnocentric conception of family structure is here hypostatized as universal.[29] The metaphor operates to contain an appropriate interest in the diversity of offspring within a set of deeply conservative editorial assumptions – all texts receive their signature of legitimacy from the authorial father; qualifications for membership, based on a community of blood, must be decided by an attestation of legitimate title; bastard offspring (such as 'Bad Quartos') are firmly placed outside the parameters of the family structure.

The textual scholar, who appears here in the guise of a family solicitor or real-estate lawyer, can prosecute his business of determining composition and inheritance, secure in the conviction that the canonical family is a formation of nature, not a construction of art. When Heminge and Condell, dedicating *Mr. William Shakespeares Comedies, Histories, & Tragedies*, offered the plays to the patronage of the Earls of Pembroke and Montgomery – 'We have but collected them, and done an office to the dead, to procure his orphanes, Guardians' – they were invoking, in the same metaphor as the Oxford editors', a somewhat different form of the family.

De Grazia and Stallybrass rightly take the revisionists to task for offering the possibility of textual multiplicity with one hand only to snatch it away again with the other, as this multiplicity is referred back, again and again, to the unifying figure of Shakespeare, as the single authentic source of the texts' polyvocality. As they themselves cogently observe: 'The recognition of multiple texts and variant passages is compromised by a theory of revision that ends up unifying and regulating what it had dispersed and loosened: all intertextual and intratextual variants are claimed in the name of a revising Shakespeare.'[30] Once again, there is a stress here on the materiality of the text, the conditions of its production, and on the displacement of 'Shakespeare' as a unifying force, the guarantor of meaning and coherence. In this call for a rethinking of the texts, de Grazia and Stallybrass appear to set themselves against both the New Bibliographic and the Revisionist positions.

Nevertheless, as we have already noted, in the concluding paragraphs of their article, the authors offer a particular celebration of Michael Warren's *The Complete* King Lear *1608–1623*. Of Warren's project, de Grazia and Stallybrass write:

> The collected facsimiles of Warren's *The Complete* King Lear open up a vastly wider range of textual possibility within the seventeenth century itself, both among different printings and among different formes of the same printing. Its three unbound *Lears* (Q1, Q2, and F1), each succeeded by either uncorrected or corrected pages, allows, indeed coaxes, the reader to assemble any number and combination of pages.[31]

The essay concludes with an affirmation of the bibliographic *jouissance* available from an 'unstitched' reader's enraptured contemplation of infinite textual possibilities:

> Perhaps we should imagine ourselves critically positioned in this great bibliographic divide ... unstitched like Warren's loose pages – in the space of historical difference. It might take our minds off the solitary genius immanent in the text and removed from the means of mechanical and theatrical reproduction. This genius is, after all, an impoverished, ghostly thing compared to the complex social practices that shaped, and still shape, the absorbent surface of the Shakespearean text. Perhaps it is these practices that should be the objects not only of our labors but also of our desires.[32]

There are several points to be noted here. The first is that, while Michael Warren, in *The Complete* King Lear, *packages* his texts in a novel way, the fundamental principle governing the project is little different from the New Bibliographic/Revisionist orthodoxy which de Grazia and Stallybrass attack with such acuity elsewhere in their article. Warren gathers his diverse texts under the rubric of a single entity (the singular *Complete* King Lear), quite literally enclosing them together in a box. The individual texts are thus constellated around a single centre – no longer, perhaps, explicitly the revising author, but still the metacategory of 'the [singular] play', of which each actual published text is merely a part.

Furthermore, while Warren's edition clearly reflects 'the textual proliferation that was endemic to early modern printing practices', Paul Werstine has noted a distinctly contrary tendency in the parallel-text volume which forms part of his box of texts. 'In the parallel-text fascimile', Werstine observes, 'some agent has intervened by altering the photographs of F1 . . . the rules have been stripped from the F1 columns and gray space has been added so that their width seems to match that of the Q1 pages.'

> The visual effect is to stabilize both texts in opposition to each other and thus to endow each with a specious integrity. Consequently the photographs provide a visual analogue to the argumentative strategy of the revisionists, which has been to stabilize the texts by constructing mutually exclusive readings of Q1 and F1 and then logocentrically projecting these readings back onto Shakespeare as his differing but complete intentions for *King Lear*.[33]

In this sense, the textual new order which de Grazia and Stallybrass find in Warren's multiple-singular *Lear* begins to look remarkably like the old order which they castigate elsewhere. In some respects, this version of New Textualism is both New Bibliography and Textual Revisionism, writ large.

The real point of attraction of Warren's presentation of his materials for de Grazia and Stallybrass seems to lie in the fact that within the greater box that is *The Complete* King Lear, there can be found three smaller boxes containing unbound facsimiles of Q1, Q2 and F1. The enclosing walls of the box-within-a-box notwithstanding, the decision to print these texts in a loose-leaf format is taken as indicative of a metaphorical unbinding of the text, an opening up of the text to the free play of assemblage or disassemblage, subverting (in Foucault's terms) the tendency of the authorial principle to impede the 'free circulation, decomposition, and recomposition of fiction'.[34] The loose-leaf format 'allows, indeed coaxes, the reader to assemble any number and combination of pages' – to make and remake, one supposes, his or her own *Lear*(s). Quite how the reader is enabled to construct unilateral textualizations from printed pages – which by virtue of their material technology explicitly resist such manipulation, holding their words, sentences and paragraphs firmly in linear sequence – is not exactly clear.

At the end of an article dedicated to 'The *materiality* of the

Shakespearean *text*', de Grazia and Stallybrass leave us with a glorious vision of a kind of postmodernist self-multiplying *Lear*, the infinitely variable states of which might serve as 'the objects not only of our labors but also of our desires'. Both the 'materiality' alluded to in the article's title and de Grazia and Stallybrass's worthy formulation of the need 'to rethink Shakespeare in relation to our new knowledge of collaborative writing, collaborative printing, and the historical contingencies of textual production'[35] have been (in our view uneasily) linked to a poststructuralist delight in the unbound, the unstitched, the sign in free and unanchored infinite play. The authors leave their own reader faced with a programme advocating both a scholarly engagement with the materiality and material conditions, 'the historical contingencies of textual production', and with an image of the critic cathecting his or her desire to the free play of an indeterminate and decidedly *im*material text. Elizabeth Fox-Genovese's observation in 'Literary criticism and the politics of the New Historicism' seems peculiarly apt in this context: 'contemporary criticism', she writes, 'implicitly, when not explicitly, grants the text a status *sui generis*, as if it somehow defied the laws of time, mortality, history, and politics'.[36] The objective of a true materialist bibliography would surely be to restore the context of just these laws to the texts with which it would engage.

VII

There is no necessary connection, finally, between the various theoretical and editorial strategies congregated beneath the umbrella of 'New Textualism'. Some 'New Textualists' simply replicate the idealism of New Bibliography; while others adopt from poststructuralism a preoccupation with an unstructured process of production in which texts are nothing more than 'a provisional state in the circulation of matter'. Poststructuralist New Textualism may succeed, as de Grazia and Stallybrass momentarily succeed, in gathering the text as a material object into temporary focus: but will inevitably tend to be driven by its theoretical commitment to a deconstructive logic (as in the formulations of McGann, Orgel and Goldberg), to disperse the text into immaterial process. The true logic of a poststructuralist bibliography points in fact not towards the individual textualization recognized as material form, but towards an eclectic embracing of the relationships between texts (whether in the comparative form of a parallel-text edition, or in the loose-leaf carnival of Warren's boxed *King Lears*), and of the interpenetration of texts with one another. It needs to be emphasized that there is then no hindrance to acceptance of the traditional conflated edition as a valid space of textual free play, a desired instance of textual intercourse. Margreta de Grazia and Peter Stallybrass actually go some way in the direction of this curious reversion:

> If, as we have argued, there is no 'original', the later editions cannot be accused of a falling off and away, for there is no fixed point from which such falling could be measured. . . . There is no intrinsic reason *not* to have a modernized, translated, rewritten 'Shakespeare'. In an important sense, that is all we *can* have, because the material signs of early modern quartos and folios will themselves necessarily mean differently when read within new systems of textual production.[37]

The poststructuralist truism that there is no possibility of recovering original meaning (because the sign derives its signifying capability entirely from the structural context of its contemporary reading), is here expanded to a concession that the material signs themselves might just as well be manipulated, translated, modernized, since the end result of either process – the modern reading or the modern manipulation of the ancient text – will in any case be a contemporary appropriation. If 'the history of readings of the text is the history of the text', then why prefer an original form to a modern permutation? Employing, in the course of a critique of the Oxford Shakespeare, very similar deconstructionist terms and concepts, Brian Parker has inferred from the same theoretical premises a preference for the traditional conflated edition, which by providing the reader with a geological formation of overlapping textual variants, offers a complete packaged experience of textual multiplicity: 'it seems to me that a conflated edition, that makes no claims to authority and questions its own readings in adjacent footnotes, can come much closer to the exhilaration of postmodernist "bricolage" '.[38]

The debate has by this point shifted far enough from the principles and methods of materialist bibliography to suggest the need for some recuperative action. As theoretical speculation mutates into the endorsement of particular cultural practices, it emerges that for poststructuralist 'New Textualism' there is no essential difference between one kind of textualization and another. The theatrical performance, based on a provisional script; the printed pages of an early modern text, in production incessantly modified by the practice of 'continuous copy'; the conflated modern edition; the parallel-text version; the 'Shakespeare Unbound' of *The Complete* King Lear . . . each enacts its own particular and variant contribution to the metanarrative of cultural production, the great carnival of paper. All the more important then is the welcome summons from Margreta de Grazia and Peter Stallybrass to focus on the 'historical contingencies of textual production', a perspective which would necessarily facilitate a thorough decomposition of those strange compilations of separate texts, the modern editions, that pass under such generic titles as 'King Lear' or 'Hamlet' into the various discrete and to some degree incommensurable textualizations produced by historical contingency, and indiscriminately merged in most modern editorial practices. We need, in short, a general recovery of such textualizations, as they existed before their colonization by the modern edition; and once recovered we need, to quote de Grazia and Stallybrass again, to look *at* rather than *through* them, if we are to distinguish and discriminate each text's particular capability for the production of meaning.

Notes

1 See, for instance, among many recent examples, R. A. Foakes, *Hamlet vs Lear: Cultural Politics and Shakespeare's Art* (Cambridge: Cambridge University Press, 1993), and Howard Mills, *Working with Shakespeare* (Hemel Hempstead: Harvester-Wheatsheaf, 1993), two general critical studies each of which devotes a long chapter to matters of textual theory.

2 For example, 'a social theory of texts' – the name applied to Jerome McGann's efforts to focus attention on the institutional and collaborative aspects of textual production (see, in particular, McGann's own *Critique of Modern Textual Editing* (Charlottesville: University of Virginia Press, 1992; first published University of Chicago Press, 1983) or 'the New Textualism', coined by Margreta de Grazia and Peter Stallybrass to identify a range of editorial projects and theoretical interventions among those scholars listed in note 3 below – see their article 'The materiality of the Shakespearean text', in *Shakespeare Quarterly*, 44 (Fall 1993), pp. 255–83.

3 The roll-call of significant contributors consists of (in alphabetical order): Jonathan Goldberg, see, for example, 'Textual properties' in *Shakespeare Quarterly*, 37 (Summer 1986), pp. 213–17; Margreta de Grazia, 'The essential Shakespeare and the material book' in *Textual Practice*, vol. 2 (1988), pp. 69–86, and *Shakespeare Verbatim: The Reproduction of Authenticity and the 179 Apparatus* (Oxford: Oxford University Press, 1991); Grace Ioppolo, *Revising Shakespeare* (Cambridge, Mass.: Harvard University Press, 1991); Leah Marcus, *Puzzling Shakespeare: Local Reading and its Discontents* (Berkeley: University of California Press, 1988) and 'Levelling Shakespeare: local customs and local texts', in *Shakespeare Quarterly*, 42 (Summer 1991), pp. 168–78; Random Cloud/Clod (Randall McLeod), 'The marriage of good and bad Quartos', in *Shakespeare Quarterly*, 33 (Winter 1982), pp. 421–31; see also de Grazia and Stallybrass's extremely useful short bibliography of McLeod's work, in 'The materiality of the Shakespearean text' (see note 2 above); Stephen Orgel, 'The authentic Shakespeare', in *Representations*, 21 (1988), pp. 1–25; Annabel Patterson,

Shakespeare and the Popular Voice (Oxford: Basil Blackwell, 1989), Chapter 4; Gary Taylor – extensive publications, but see in particular Taylor and Michael Warren (eds), *The Division of the Kingdoms: Shakespeare's Two Versions of* King Lear (Oxford: Clarendon Press, 1983); Taylor's 'Introduction' to Stanley Wells and Gary Taylor with John Jowett and William Montgomery, *William Shakespeare: A Textual Companion* (Oxford: Clarendon Press, 1987); and, more recently, 'The Renaissance and the end of editing', in George Bornstein and Ralph G. Williams (eds), *Palimpsest: Editorial Theory in the Humanities* (Ann Arbor: University of Michigan Press, 1993); Steven Urkowitz, *Shakespeare's Revision of* King Lear (Princeton: Princeton University Press, 1980) and ' "Well-sayd olde Mole": Burying three *Hamlets* in modern editions', in Georgianna Ziegler (ed.), *Shakespeare Study Today: The Howard Furness Memorial Lectures* (New York: AMS, 1986), pp. 37–77); Michael Warren, 'Quarto and Folio *King Lear* and the interpretation of Albany and Edgar', in David Bevington and Jay L. Halio (eds), *Shakespeare: Pattern of Excelling Nature* (Newark: University of Delaware Press, 1978), pp. 95–117, and *The Complete* King Lear *1608–1623* (Berkeley: University of California Press, 1989); and Paul Werstine, 'Narratives about printed Shakespeare texts: "Foul Papers" and "Bad Quartos" ', in *Shakespeare Quarterly*, 41 (Spring 1990), pp. 65–86.

4 W. W. Greg, *The Editorial Problem in Shakespeare: A Survey of the Foundations of the Text* (Oxford: Oxford University Press, 1967), p. 2.

5 Fredson Bowers, 'Textual criticism', in Oscar James Campbell and Edward G. Quinn (eds), *A Shakespeare Encyclopaedia* (London: Methuen, 1966), p. 865. See also R. B. McKerrow, *Prolegomena for the Oxford Shakespeare: A Study in Editorial Method* (Oxford: Clarendon Press, 1939).

6 ibid., p. 869.

7 Hardly surprising, perhaps, given the original provenance of some of the editorial techniques and procedures which the New Bibliographers adopted (derived, as they were, from the field of biblical studies).

8 p. 71 (cited in note 3 above).

9 p. 6 (cited in note 3 above).

10 Harold Pinter, *The Homecoming* (London: Methuen, 1966), p. 31.

11 The one possible exception is the 'Hand D' contribution to the manuscript of *The Book of Sir Thomas More*, but even this is questionable – see Scott McMillin, *The Elizabethan Theatre and* The Book of Sir Thomas More (Ithaca: Cornell University Press, 1987), esp. pp. 135–59.

12 p. 257 (cited in note 2 above).

13 pp. 278–9.

14 See Alan Sinfield and Jonathan Dollimore's opening comments in *Political Shakespeare: New Essays in Cultural Materialism* (Manchester: Manchester University Press, 1985) and the debates recorded in Ivo Kamps (ed.), *Shakespeare Left and Right* (London: Routledge, 1991).

15 See the introduction to Greenblatt's *Learning to Curse: Essays in Early Modern Culture* (New York: Routledge, 1990), and Graham Holderness, 'Production, reproduction, performance: Marxism, history, theatre', in F. Barker, P. Hulme and M. Iversen (eds), *Uses of History: Marxism, Postmodernism and the Renaissance* (Manchester: Manchester University Press, 1991), esp. pp. 156–9.

16 Robert Freeman (ed.), *Marx on Economics* (Harmondsworth: Penguin Books, 1968), p. 51.

17 ibid.

18 Jonathan Goldberg, 'Textual properties', pp. 213–14 (cited in note 3 above).

19 Stephen Orgel, 'The authentic Shakespeare', p. 14 (cited in note 3 above).

20 Jerome J. McGann, *The Textual Condition* (Princeton: Princeton University Press, 1991), p. 21. D. C. Greetham in his Foreword to the 1992 edition of McGann's *Critique of Modern Textual Criticism* (cited in note 3 above) observes that 'if there is one thing that the *Critique* insists upon, it is that there is no "text itself"...' (p. xv).

21 'The materiality of the Shakespearean text', p. 26.

22 ibid., p. 261.

23 'The essential Shakespeare and the material book', p. 7 (cited in note 3 above).

24 p. 261.

25 For the most elaborated statement of this position, see Grace Ioppolo, *Revising Shakespeare* (cited in note 3 above).

26 Stanley Wells, 'Theatricalizing Shakespeare's text', in *New Theatre Quarterly*, VII (May 1991), p. 186.

27 We use this phrase advisedly. The 'onlie begetter' of the sonnets was not, of course, the author.

28 *Textual Companion*, p. 69.

29 A similar metaphor is used to characterize the role of the editor in relation to the author: 'The authority of scholars derives from their capacity or their claim to recover and interpret the revered texts of ... cultural 'fathers'; like priests, they tell us what the father meant; by doing so, they earn the affection of their 'mother' (the Church; or its secular equivalent, the university' (*Textual Companion*, p. 7).

30 p. 279. See also McGann, *Critique*, p. 1.

31 pp. 282–3.

32 p. 283.

33 Paul Werstine, review of *The Complete* King Lear, in *Shakespeare Quarterly*, 44 (Summer 1993), pp. 236–7.

34 Michel Foucault, 'What is an author?', in Paul Rabinow (ed.), *The Foucault Reader* (New York: Pantheon, 1984), p. 119.

35 In H. Aram Veeser (ed.), *The New Historicism* (London and New York: Routledge, 1989), p. 218.

36 De Grazia and Stallybrass, p. 282.

37 De Grazia and Stallybrass, p. 279.

38 'Bowers of bliss: deconflation in the Shakespeare canon', in *New Theatre Quarterly*, VI (1991), p. 361.

Denis Ekpo

Towards a post-Africanism: contemporary African thought and postmodernism

There is indeed a very strong sense in which postmodernism can be said to be of no concern to Africans. First, the crisis of modernity which postmodernism thematizes and wants to exorcise, can be viewed in apocalyptic terms only by those who had previously wallowed so arrogantly and so complacently in the excesses of a rationality and a world-interpretation that virtually deified the European subject by enthroning it the master of the earth and of other men; the origin of meaning, the locus of absolute transparence. It was this reckless self-deification of a subject-centred European reason that translated into all the titanic projects of European modernism whose nightmarish and unforeseeable effects have generated the present postmodern pathologies and tears. The crisis of the subject and its radical and violent deflation – the focal point of postmodern critique – are the logical consequences of the absurd self-inflation that the European subjectivity had undergone in its modernist ambition to be the salt of the earth, the measure and master of all things.

For cultures (such as ours) that neither absolutized, i.e. deified, human reason in the past nor saw the necessity for it in the present, the postmodern project of de-deification, de-absolutization of reason, of man, of history, etc., on the one hand, and of a return to, or a rehabilitation of, obscurity, the unknown, the non-transparent, the paralogical on the other hand, cannot at all be felt like the cultural and epistemological earthquake that it appears to be for the European man. In fact it cannot even be seen as a problem at all. Hence from the African standpoint, postmodernism runs the risk of being seen as no more than an inconsequential coquetery of a still arrogant rationality whose latest hypocrisy and refinement consist in 'the absolute knowledge it has of its very irrationality'.[1]

However, the crucial question to non-westerners and especially third-world intellectuals is whether those proto-western ratiocinations

Textual Practice **9:1**, 1995, 121–135

and paradox-mongering that constitute postmodernism are not merely the symptoms of terminal exhaustion of the European culture demiurge? If so, then the recourse to postmodernist cultural and rhetorical indeterminacies and anarchy, the systematic raids into the founding codes of western culture, the exploding of its instituting dualisms, can all be viewed merely as masks of or compensation for a world-historic culture fatigue of the West. In this regard, it is instructive to note that the postmodern jeremiads are being intoned precisely at a time when the man of the post-industrial West has come to resemble less and less a self-conscious subject full of himself and more and more a simplified, equal and finished product of western industries and democracies. Thus when such a being settles for the indeterminate, the paradoxical, the strange and absurd, it is probably because he bears no more resemblance to the man as we know him, especially here in Africa; he is a post-man whose society, having overfed him and spoilt him, has delivered him over to irremediable boredom. Nothing therefore, stops the African from viewing the celebrated postmodern condition a little sarcastically as nothing but the hypocritical self-flattering cry of overfed and spoilt children of hypercapitalism. So what has hungry Africa got to do with the post-material disgust and ratiocination of the bored and the overfed?

It did happen nevertheless that Africa, at a certain period in its history, came into contact with, and suffered defeat at the hands of, modern European rationality. The modernist culture blanket that Europe cast over Africa in the wake of this conquest meant above all the superimposition of a logocentric rationality on native minds. The fact that such minds have remained incarcerated in this rationality ever since proves the degree of success of the European cultural conquest. But this fact above all serves as the horizon of what constitutes modern Africa. In other words, today, by modern African thought, we usually refer to discourse formations, in European languages created by African intellectuals and elaborated and structured in accordance with the procedures of modern European rationality, and articulating mainly, but not exclusively, African problems. Included in this rubric are philosophical, sociocultural, political and economic thought. (In this essay, emphasis will be placed on foundational formations such as philosophy and cultural thought.)[2] On the strength of the above operational definition, the structural and rhetorical pre-history of modern African thought can easily be traced. Contrary to common sense, such a pre-history is not in Africa, but in Europe, most specifically, in the European Logos. (By Logos we mean here the metaphysics, the logic and the rhetoric of modern western rationality.) For modern African thought came into being when African intellectuals, using the European Logos, conceptualized, problematized and thematized Africa for the first time by postulating the existence of a specific African rationality – an Afro-ratio – different from logocentric European reason. Now the implication of staying within the metaphysical and logical closure of the Western Logos to conceptualize an African rationality was that modern African thought – as the discourse of an African rationality – became embedded in, structured and delivered in accordance with the grammar of western reason. On account of this logocentric preconditioning, i.e. pre-structuring, modern African thought, right from inception, acquired an a priori isomorphic relationship to the logic, metaphysic and rhetoric of modern European thought.

The purpose of this essay is to use the resources of postmodernism to show how the isomorphisms between European cultural modernity and modern African thought can be exploited to elucidate the functional mechanisms as well as the performative impasse of the modern African thought systems whose founding metaphors as well as operational procedures are all drawn from European cultural modernity. Our ultimate aim also is to show how the cracks and wounds that postmodernism has inflicted on western rationality and power can be fully exploited to cause a radical rethinking of the ideology of Africanism especially, as it affects our conception of and relationship with the West. In this sense, our rapprochement between postmodernism and modern African thought (Africanism) should enable us to tackle the present crisis in modern African thought. I understand by 'crisis in modern African thought' the problems that crystalize around the following question: In the context of an irreversibly logocentric modernity, can the pursuit of a specific African rationality, originality and legitimacy embodied in the Afrocentric ideal of contemporary African cultural and strategic thoughts, still be justified? Or is it misleading, warped and counterproductive?

The logocentric trap of modern African thought

Let us first see how postmodern critical strategies can help us uncover the implications of the logocentric overdetermination of modern African thought. We have already noted how African thought came to acquire its structural isomorphism with western thought systems. Now the reason for this congenital isomorphism was that it was not the African mind which on its own terms set out to problematize its Africanness. It was the European Logos which, through the agency of colonial culture, provided the context in whose pre-comprehension and pre-structuring suppositions, i.e. in whose logic and metaphysic, Africa became thematized as a problem. This means that the European Logos being the metaphysical and structural horizon through African 'reality' shows itself to the modern African mind, the meaning which the modern African thinker gives to African 'reality', African originality, rationality and legitimacy, is logocentrically predetermined or over-determined and has nothing original and African in the sense in which most thinkers understand and use these terms. However, the pragmatics of modern African thought, i.e. the very existence of this thought as a separate and distinct discourse formation, imposed the rhetorical and ideological necessity to dissimulate, mask, misrecognize or distort the logocentric structure, conditioning and orientation of modern African thought. But this very process of concealment or misrecognition of the logocentric condition of our modern thinking harboured at the same time a basic and enduring conceptual as well as pragmatic snare and disability which we referred to as the 'logocentric trap'.[3] This we defined as the masking of the logos plus the lack of full awareness of the deeper implications of the logocentric conditioning of modern African thought and of the practices woven into it. But then where does postmodernism come in here?

My answer to that question derives from our very definition of modern African thought as a logocentrically over-determined reflexion of African intellectuals on Africa and on the West. Such a definition establishes, at both the structural and the performative levels, an isomorphism between modern African thought and the logic and rhetoric of modern European reason. Postmodernism, being the most radical critique and disruptive of the manifold logocentric games which modern European rationality plays, appears to provide an almost unexpected opportunity for the modern African mind, largely conditioned by the Western Logos, not only to sort itself out of the logocentric trap, but also to get into real power games of European modernity. Postmodernism furnishes the most uncanny access and insight into the production mechanisms of the basic texts of western rationality/power. And since it was largely in the logocentric intertextuality of this rationality that the modern African mind formed itself, an insight into the structures of the Western Logos will certainly help to uncover some of the conceptual snares which the modern African mind got into while trying to stay in the Logos to assert its own rationality and difference vis-à-vis the Logos. Now the critical weapons and strategies of postmodern thought provide the shortest and, so far, the most effective route to the arcanes, i.e. the power ruses and games of modern European reason. Accordingly, it is our opinion that only these postmodern critical tactics and games can perhaps help us fully to understand and elucidate the workings of the mind, i.e. the modern African mind – entrapped in, and bewitched by, the modern European rationality and culture. Let us now look more closely at some of the ways in which the strategic resources of postmodernism can be tactfully diverted to serve, first, the elimination of conceptual snares and performative handicaps from modern African thought, and, second, to legitimate the formulation and formation of a new African thinking.

Postmodernism and the de-obstruction of the African mind

The modern African mind set is framed mostly by two historical events, namely, European colonialism and the African reaction to it in the form of African nationalism and cultural awakening. It was the perception of these two events that generated the foundational structures, the paradigmatic conceptualities as well as the general orientation of modern African thinking. It was indeed through the strong desire to impart a wholly 'Afrocentric' interpretation to these two events that the modern African mind got entangled in a conceptual as well as rhetorical trap – the logocentric trap. For instance, while the first event, European colonialism, was interpreted through the 'Afrocentric' prism of the elite into a collective racial cum cultural trauma, the second, anti-colonialism cum cultural awakening, involved the metaphysical hypostatization of an essential Africa as the basis for a specific African rationality, cultural authenticity and political legitimacy. Subjected to the prism of this hypostatized Africanity, the two events were extracted from the complex of causes to which they belong.

This of course, made the grasp and mastery of their specific dynamics and logics difficult if not impossible. Consequently, European imperialism and its aftermaths came to acquire in the modern African mind, the eternity of absolute evil, while all the categories and paradigms of the African cultural and political self-awareness become inviolate positivities. In other words, the emergence of the modern African mind involved on the one hand the occultation or distortion of the specific cultural and historical logic and dynamics of European cultural cum political imperialism and, on the other hand, the invention of a voluntarist and hybrid doctrine called Africanism. Under this umbrella doctrine, totalities, labels and paradigms such as African identity, African nation, African rationality, African personality, African authenticity, etc. were created and turned into metacodes of modern African self-awareness. In this discourse of Africanity, the modern African subjectivity was formed. That is, Africanism became for the modern African mind, the discursive as well as mythic horizon in which the a priori principles of action, knowledge of Africa, and perceptions of the West were formulated and articulated. The implications and consequences of this were many and far-reaching. The first was the emergence of the 'Afrocentric ideal' as a structuring motif or the categorical imperative of modern African cultural, political and strategic thinking. This ideal which can be defined as a voluntarist drive to re-make our own world in our own, i.e. African, image, serves as a picture held before the modern African mind to inspire and direct it. But then, in the hypostatized metacodes of the Afrocentric ideal, the lived, everyday realities of Africa, including its irreconcilable cultural and natural differences, incompatibilities and obscurities were magically frozen or simply palmed. The doctine of Africanism out of which the modern African mind emerged, legitimated itself by imposing a psychic and emotional cellophane on the diversities and opacities of Africa. Under the shibboleth of African identity, Africanism 'erased' the 'scandal' of ineradicable differences between one tribes-people and the other and went on to anaesthetize all other 'embarrassing' cultural and natural incongruities of the continent. Formed out of the seductive yarn of these Afrocentric master narratives, the modern African mind appears to have emerged into the modern world enveloped in the fog of warped idealism and misleading voluntarism; and coupled with a high propensity to self-affection, it appears right from the onset to have misconstrued itself, Africa and the West. In the Afrocentric frame of mind was foreclosed not only newer, more useful and flexible re-interpretations of Africa, but also and above all, newer, more advantageous and efficacious perceptions and re-interpretations of the West. For the modern African mind appears to have definitively conceptualized its identity, its destiny, its past and present, in the horizon of a conspiracy theory, that is, in perpetual accusation of, opposition to and fight against, the West. From this perspective, the West seems to have acquired the static eternity of an imperialist demon whose every move may conceal a conspiracy to underdevelop Africa. Thus this frame of mind along with other Afrocentric idealities has imparted an activist moralism to modern African thinking and has placed our minds in a perpetually resentful posture towards the West on the one hand, and in a permanent complacency towards Africa on the other hand. Modern African thinking in many respects has come to be synonymous with perpetual accusation of the West; denunciation of western duplicity, hypocrisy, double standards; the search for historical guilt, responsibility and reparations have become the only form of radical thinking.[4]

Meanwhile, this Afrocentric form and perspective of mind has so far imparted to modern African thought a record non-performativity if not outright negative performativity. That is, when translated into practical applications in politics, development, social engineering, etc., Afrocentric thoughts have so far engendered mostly confusions, instability, aberrations, failures and woes. Is modern African thought largely a piece of logical and ideological incongruity? Are the meta-codes that legitimate and structure its enterprises rather mental blockages and misleading totalities? How do we explain the self-subversive dynamics of a heroic search for an Afrocentric knowledge, i.e. Afrocentric rationality and legitimacy, which merely leads us into a dead-end in politics and development? The change of knowledge/critical paradigms occasioned by postmodern reflexivity offers perhaps the shortest route to the structural and conceptual snares, blockages and deadweights that appear to have so far undermined the efficacy and creativity of the modern African mind. How then do we ride on the back of postmodernism to de-obstruct the modern African mind set?

Our study above of the foundational processes of modern African thought involved taking its founding notions such as African rationality, African originality, etc. back to their forgotten source in the European Logos from which they derived their logical and rhetorical pre-history. What this process of deconstruction was able to show were: (1) In its foundational structures and orientation, modern African thought is logocentrically over-determined; (2) Consequently, it is possible to reformulate the paradigmatic notion of an African rationality (or African originality) to show that it is not so much a different, indigenous, non-logocentric reason, but merely the same western rationality misunderstood, masked, distorted or misrecognized. However, this very process of occultation, distortion or misrecognition of the Western Logos is borne by, entrenched and actualized in the idioms of our African self-awareness, i.e. the metanarratives such as African identity, African originality, African presence, negritude, African nation, etc., through which we conceptualized and which have since governed our modern African self-consciousness. Now a deconstructionist or postmodernist re-reading of these foundational categories of modern African thought show them to be merely metaphorical amalgams whose signifiers and structure of argument both belong to the logocentric tradition. Being logocentrically mediated notions, their purported origin from, their coincidence with, or even their real concern with, an original pre-logocentric Africa, are a priori excluded or deferred and at best express a mere desire. In reality, these notions function as decoys, created partly by desire and partly by the logocentric trap in which the modern African mind is held captive even in its most strident posture of African authenticity. This means then that the foundational concepts of our modern consciousness are mostly incongruous totalities, false positivities or misleading labels. Above all, they appear to be metaphors through which the Western Logos play tricks on and bewitch the modern African mind. Consequently, if these concepts cannot really bear their explicit Afrocentric argument, i.e. their African origin and structure, then Africanism, the metaphysics of the affirmation of an African rationality, originality and legitimacy, becomes a problematic philosophy. The proto-Africanist ambitions of certain strands of modern African thought can then be shown to be an exercise in self-delusion. Such thinking can subsist merely as a utopian ideology or poetry.

The first stage towards the de-obstruction of our modern consciousness is to disentangle it from the obscure and incongruous textuality of this impossibile Africanism. By returning the founding metaphors of Afrocentric ideology to their rightful place in the western thought system, and by showing them to be no more than romantic scaffoldings erected by a logocentrically bewitched mind, a postmodernist critique of Africanism will simply render its arguments aporetic, its goals impossible and its motivations confused and misleading. The shibboleth of an African identity and the necessity to posit it, become an imposture, since the conceptualities that validate and support such an idea are shown to be metaphors that contradict their explicit Afrocentric argumentation. Now the metaphysical ideal that the African must necessarily postulate its difference from Europe in order for him to be himself, can now be shown to derive not from any 'Afrocentric' reality, but from the idealism of a warped desire and voluntarism of misplaced hubris. Though one understands and perhaps sympathizes with the historical imperatives that necessitated this heroic desire and search for a special Afrocentric place in the modern world, one cannot but criticize the self-deluding, warped, and misleading form and content of the thinking that governed it. Now that it has become clear that such thinking has engendered mostly disastrous voluntarism in politics and in development, it is time to retrieve the modern African mind from the Afrocentric trap. One way of doing this is the shedding of all the deconstructed metacodes, totalities and scaffolds that formed the material out of which the modern African mind emerged – African rationality, African identity, African originality, African nations, African legitimacy, etc. The aim of this psychic and mental load-shedding is to liberate the mind and discourse for newer, de-totalized, polycentric, and more useful interpretations of the African world. Another step in this project of de-obstruction of African thinking is the total deconstruction and re-interpretations of the Afrocentric perception of and relationship with the West.

Even though the chimerical proto-Africanism of the earlier Afrocentric thinkers and of their new-conservative successors[5] has often been officially criticized and in some cases even denounced for its uncritical fundamentalism, the Afrocentric paradigms and metacodes they created had already wholly permeated our perception of imperial Europe and continues till today, to govern our perception of and relationship with 'post-imperial' Europe. However, since the basic concepts and codes of Afrocentricity appear to have already severely prejudiced our ability critically to distantiate ourselves from Africa, our capacity to position ourselves advantageously within the Europe-controlled world power complex seems to have suffered adversely from any fundamental Africanism or Afrocentricism. The question now is: in this postmodern era in which the humanist, moralist self-understanding of the European man has come to an end and new technocentric or system paradigms have taken its place, can the modern African mind, nurtured and bewitched in the forgotten grand imperialist tales of Europe and equally in the heroic but empty dream of an African rationality and originality, still hope to profit from an Afrocentric commerce with the West? Do we still stand to gain from a conspiratorial interpretation of our encounter with western culture and power? Perhaps the most interesting thing that the postmodern turning-point has brought about through its radical and uncanny unmasking of the principles and ruses of western culture, power and history, is opening the way for non-westerners in general and Africans in particular to radically re-think the fundamental categories through which they have hitherto perceived, received or rejected the West. Through such thinking as Foucault's power theory, Luhmann's systems theory, Lyotard's de-legitimations and Derrida's deconstructions of western logocentric rationality, what we now know about the dominant discourse, form of life and mode of historical action of modern Europe is that these are masks for power. Hence European modernity is distinguished by the paradigmatic alliance of reason and power in the legitimation and prosecution of Europe's major historical actions such as imperialism, neo-colonialism, etc. Now the African thinker is accustomed to judging European imperialism and neo-colonialism from the perspective of a moral-humanist interpretation of history because he thinks that such was the horizon against which the West accomplished such actions. What the postmodern unmasking of western historical forms of power reveals is that the West, by the time of imperial capitalist expansion, had already abandoned the moral-humanist mode of legitimation (Legitimation by Grand Tales) and adopted the logic of systematic rationality – i.e. the logic of legitimation by the success, efficacy and maintenance of systems. If such were the logic and dynamic of European imperialism, then a critique of it (imperialism) that starts from a perspective other than that of power rationality or system logic, simply misses its mark and is condemned to shooting at the no-man's land of the modern European mind. Now our Afrocentric critique of the West is deeply embedded in the old Hamanist tradition of Europe with its moral world order, truth, justice, etc. It is from this perspective that we have never stopped pointing accusing fingers at Europe; we sentence her guilty and consider her responsible for exploiting and under-developing the African. However, had these acts been committed against Africa in the name of a moral world order, truth and justice, then of course our African thinkers would have had a point. But this was not the case it seems. Europe acted not in order to conform to truth or justice but simply to increase its power. The question was not whether it was right or wrong to colonize Africa, but whether it could be done. In other ways, it was purely a technocratic problem. Accordingly, any indictment of the West couched in terms other than those of the power signs or systems logic of the West is bound to produce little or no real effect on its target. It is not for nothing that one talks of 'postmodern cynicism'[6] as the distinctive character of the technocrative logic of modern European reason/power. For post-modernist re-interpretations of modern European history do not try to place the European man above the charges of immorality, injustice and arbitrariness; it only renders such charges without object and pointless. Thus when we dangle our conspiracy theory before the postmodern West, sentence it guilty and ask for reparations, accuse it of hypocrisy, double-standards, etc., the postmodern West may not necessarily dismiss such charges out of hand; they might probably even concede that we are 'right' – i.e. from our old 'moral' perspective. However, they will be quick to add that since all these acts and attitudes of which they have been accused were necessary for the maintenance and strengthening of their power system, they had really no choice in the matter. In any case, (they will add) what we Africans call conspiracy, double standards, hypocrisy, are for the West merely strategies for the optimal performativity and efficiency of their systems. After all, as Nietzsche, the proto-postmodernist, pointed out, 'a thousand fold craftiness belongs to the essence of the enhancement of man.'[7] Now there can be no question of approving or not approving of this postmodern cynicism of western systems or power rationality, for the simple reason that (1) It does not need our approval; (2) It is not based on any metaphysical principle but, as Luhmann tells us, is grounded in meta-biology.[8]

In contact with this type of thinking, the modern African mind, burdened as it is with deadweights and shibboleths inherited from the Afrocentric tradition, may probably find material for further hysterical declamations against the West or may even sink into depressive impotence. However, if the strategic insights of postmodern unmaskings are fully grasped, such a mind should rather undergo a profound undeceiving and look up to European postmodernism as a tremendous restorative. The de-obstruction and self-liberation of the Afrocentric mind can then be seen to be synonymous with a full awareness of the real nature of the western 'trap'. As revealed by postmodernism, it is not just a culture trap; it is a bio-power trap. Meanwhile, the stock-in-trade of angry Afrocentrics has been to denounce any attempt to 'satellize' African nations to western economic power systems. What postmodern power or systems theory has shown, and what the post-communist era has confirmed, is that this state of affairs – the satellization of Africa to the western economic power complex – has already been reached. Not only are we caught up in the implacable systemic rationality of the western economic power complex but our very capacity to develop and modernize depends solely on our ability to come to terms with the postmodern systemic imperatives of this power complex. Now since the western power systems have so far proved to be so impervious and so hostile to the moralistic idealism of the Afrocentric perspective, and given the implacability of the systemic imperatives that govern them, how should the modern African mind come to terms with the West?

One possible way will be to abandon the old ineffectual Afrocentric route since all the strategic possibilities inherent in the Afrocentric traditions of thought have merely led us into either a futile confrontation with the West or a depressive prostration before it. Indeed, it appears that in contact with the systemic cynicism of modern European power, Afrocentric moralism and idealism merely bring about frustration and decline. So now is the time to search for new routes, new interpretations since the old ones have proved powerless and groundless in the modern era. Our thinking is that in this era, only the strategic weapons and insights of postmodern thought could point to a way through which the modern African mind can finally come to terms with the West. The starting-point of this new route is the complete re-conceptualization, reconstruction or re-interpretation of our perception of the West, not with a view to knowing it more deeply, but with a view to enhancing our power by gaining cognitive control over the West. We have already seen how a systemic re-interpretation of western action in the past and in the present day renders the notions of guilt and reparations irrelevant. Now the same power or systems perspective could be re-deployed to enable the modern African mind cognitively to transform or overcome the depressive idea of the West as an awesome enemy, a predatory beast, a hostile force, etc. into a representation of the West as a useful tool for power enhancement and growth. In such an extramoral reconceptualization of the West, the ideas of enmity and hostility are no longer needed or useful.

However, such a radical shift in perspective necessitates first of all a change in our old, Afrocentric perception of western reason as a static uniform entity whose nature can be fully grasped once and for all. One must place oneself in a postmodern perspective in which European reason is apprehended through its variable and multifarious power games. It is only from this games approach to European reason/power that one can find the conceptual and strategic energy needed to overcome frozen rigidities of our Afrocentric ideal and to return our minds to newer, more useful conceptualizations of the West. Hence to come to terms with the West, via postmodernist thought, we need not to know the nature and essence of its reasons, but to understand the various power games it plays so as to see if one can play it to our advantage.

One possible way of getting into the various knowledge/power games of the West is the strategy of 'guile' furnished by Derrida's deconstruction and which revolves around the notion of a 'double-game' or 'double-science'.[9] The idea behind this strategy is that given, first, the western culture trap (that is, the fact that for us modern Africans, 'the order of Western rationality is absolute, since it is only to itself that an appeal against it can be brought')[10] and given also the formidable weight of the western power complex, what should the modern African do first in order not to be crushed by the West and, second, so as to transform these two constraints into advantageous, power-enhancing resources? The double-game/double-science) strategy has it that since one is playing against such a formidable Master 'who is certain to win at a game with rules which he himself has fixed', there is no point denouncing or criticizing; to win, one can only play double-game by 'feigning obedience to the Master's rules' while at the same time taking advantage of little openings to outwit him. Now the double player is one who has 'bad intentions but whose moves are impeccable'.[11] His intention is to beat the Master at his own game or at least to play as well as he. So the first thing he does is to learn to play the games strictly according to the Master's rules. But while doing this he is guided by the ulterior motive that he is only doing this in order to gain power and undo the Master of the game.

In less allegorical terms, what one is saying is that for the modern African mind to come to terms with the irrepressible West, he must first strategically immerse himself in the West, not in order to know it, but through guile, to master its various knowledge/power games strictly in accordance with the Master's knowledge rules. The ulterior motive of course is to gain cognitive control over the West by transforming an erstwhile adversary, complex-ridden perception of it into a means of gaining advantage and increasing our power. This can be achieved by rethinking, re-interpreting the whole gamut of western power configurations in a manner most favourable to our power enhancement. Indeed, such a rethinking is itself power, for as postmodern theory has shown, 'the cognitive process is not a means of acquiring "knowledge" but is quite simply a means of gaining power.'[12]

From postmodernism to post-Africanism

At first glance the novelty in this double-game strategy of coming to terms with the West might appear a minor one – especially if one still sees this from the viewpont of traditional knowledge paradigms. But if the postmodern perspective which sees the world as nothing other than a complex maze of power or systems relationships is understood, then such a strategic re-interpretation of the West; such a repositioning of ourselves in the western power complex, is not just a paradigm shift but amounts to a change in the character of what the modern world as such is for us. In this sense, one can talk of cultural revolution. As a commentator on Nietzsche put it,

> From the perspective of any given power-centre, when its system of power relationships changes, the world in which it exists undergoes a corresponding alteration of character.[13]

For, from this power game perspective, what is happening is that the whole cognitive tradition, i.e. the Afrocentric tradition, from which the modern African mind construed itself and its perceptions of the West, is shown to be neither true nor false, merely another power game but one which is no longer useful because it is powerless. If all knowledge is power game, then the only knowledge that matters is precisely one that enables me to gain power and to ensure the maintenance of my system. To grasp fully this power perspective is to open oneself to an alternative, non-Afrocentric strategy of thought and action as well as a different order to meaning. By accepting and adopting this alternative strategy, we will already have overthrown Afrocentricism; we will be standing already in a post-Africanity. For, from the perspective of this new thinking, we will have already suspended or jettisoned all the grandiose totalities and pseudo-codes that formed our modern African consciousness. The major advantage of this leap out of Afrocentricity is of course the freeing and the unburdening of the modern African mind from the pseudo-meta-physical deadweights and shibboleths that imprisoned it in an arti-ficial Afrocentric trap. The second advantage is the embracing of the postmodern free and gameful spirit in the search for knowledge. Since such a post-Africanist mind now knows that western knowledge tools are not 'truths' or facts about any ultimate reality, but merely power signs, metaphors and fictions which happen to work or have succeeded, he will now be ready to vary his knowledge games freely in his search for more effective means to master western power. With such advantages, the post-Africanist mind can retrieve all its power and creative potentials by repossessing himself of the Western Logos and using it as a power tool rather than being possessed and bewitched by it and forced into either a romantic search for an impossible Afrocentricity or the depressive rhetoric of perpetual accusation of the West.[14]

University of Port Harcourt, Nigeria

Notes

1 Jacques Poulain, 'Cynisme ou Pragmatisme? Le temps du jugement', *Critique*, no. 464–5, Jan./Feb. 1986, p. 63.
2 This foundational work can be found in the texts of these commonly referred to as the pioneer African Philosophers, e.g. Alexis Kagames, Lufuluabo, Senghor, etc.
3 Cf. 'The African mind in the Logocentric Trap', paper presented at the Faculty of Humanities Seminar Series, University of Port Harcourt, Nigeria, April 1991.
4 For instance, Chinweizu's *The West and the Rest of Us* (Lagos, NOK, 1978).
5 Cheikh Anta Diop, *Nations Africaines et Culture* (Paris: Présence Afri-caine, 1955, 3rd edn, 1979), and Chinweizu, op. cit.

6 Jacques Poulain, op. cit., p. 72.
7 Neitzsche, *The Will to Power*, trans. Walter Kaufmann (New York: Random House, 1968), p. 293.
8 'We can use the term metabiological for a thinking that starts from the "For itself" of organic life and goes behind it – the cybernetically described, basic phenomenon of the self maintenance of self-relating systems in the face of hypercomplex environments.' Habermas, *The Philosophical Discourse of Modernity*, trans. Frederick G. Lawrence (Cambridge: Polity Press, 1987) p. 372.
9 Jacques Derrida, in Vincent Descombe, *Modern French Philosophy* (Cambridge: Cambridge University Press, 1980), pp. 138–41.
10 Jacques Derrida, *Ecritures et Difference* (Paris: Seuil, 1967), p. 59.
11 Vincent Descombes, op. cit., pp. 139–41.
12 R. H. Grimm, *New Nietzsche's Theory of Knowledge* (Berlin: de Gruyter, 1975), p. 182.
13 ibid., p. 183.
14 Chinweizu, *The West and the Rest of Us*; Cheik Anta Diop: 'Civilisation ou barbarie?', *Présence Africaine*, 1981.

Reviews

Catherine Belsey

Jonathan Goldberg, *Sodometries: Renaissance Texts, Modern Sexualities* (Stanford, CA: Stanford University Press, 1992), 288 pp., $12.95 (paperback)

James Grantham Turner (ed.), *Sexuality and Gender in Early Modern Europe: Institutions, Texts, Images* (Cambridge: Cambridge University Press, 1993), 224 pp., £10.95 (paperback)

Richard Wilson, *Will Power: Essays on Shakespearean Authority* (Hemel Hempstead: Harvester Wheatsheaf, 1993), 320 pp., £12.95 (paperback)

What troubles Jonathan Goldberg about the Gulf War is an American T-shirt showing Saddam Hussein's face superimposed on the rear end of a camel, and the problem he identifies in *Sodometries*, the aspect of the T-shirt that disturbs him most, is not so much the gross imperialism of the image, but its homophobia. The point, made at the beginning of a scholarly work on the undecidabilities detectable in the texts of Renaissance sexuality, is as arresting as it is scandalous, and that, of course, is part of the point. Only a dull, lumbering mind, we are to suppose, would fail to recognize that Goldberg's analysis *takes for granted* the outrage of the systematic Allied demolition of a third-world infrastructure (and numbers of their own side into the bargain). But can we, should we, I am compelled in my pedestrian way to ask, ever assume a shared revulsion against instant militarism, in a world where the West increasingly undertakes to police every dispute and to 'resolve' political problems by violence?

Within pages of this surprise opening, *Sodometries* gets down to its real topic, which is the homophobia of current Renaissance studies. Goldberg's primary addressees are his colleagues, and the book has at least as much to say about prevailing readings of the texts as it has about the different disposition of sexual meanings and values in the early modern period. The main protagonists of *Sodometries* are not Renaissance figures at all, but the New Historicists on the one hand, and the feminist critics on the other, the only identified radical groupings. It is almost certainly the case that both these schools have paid insufficient attention to homoeroticism. Goldberg is right, in my view, to draw attention to the fact that the New Historicists largely ignore sexuality, collapsing it into power, and that feminist critics have given most of their attention, not surprisingly, to the ways in which male sexual power works to oppress women. But, quite unlike Foucault, who addresses a general intellectual public, unlike Alan Bray and Bruce Smith, Goldberg has very little to say to a reader who is not already fairly steeped in current debates about Elizabethan and Jacobean literary texts.

The debates he considers are largely American. One or two of the Allies get an honourable mention: Alan Bray, of course, and Simon Shepherd and Philippa Berry, deservedly. Foucault is uneasily appropriated from the beginning; deconstruction features, but Derrida gets only a single footnote; Lacanian psychoanalysis appears momentarily, but to account for personalities rather than meanings. In so far as it is concerned with the present, however, *Sodometries* is specifically about America, where the law seems to be a good deal more homophobic than it is in Britain, and where 'sodomy' seems to have no very specific meaning, including, as it does, sexual practices that do not involve the anus, and confining itself to relations which are not either within or a prelude to marriage. A Supreme Court decision of 1986 denied the right to perform homosexual sodomy in private, but in the process effectively restricted the meaning of sodomy to homosexuality, while paradoxically extending it to cover whatever homosexuals choose to do. 'Sodomy' in American English, and this is Goldberg's point, is more or less any sexual practice which white, male, heterosexist judges disapprove of, and that in turn means virtually any erotic activity that challenges Family Values.

Goldberg's political analysis therefore has a specific local reference, but his thesis also has wider implications. The discursive policing of sexual desire is an important issue in any country where right-wing governments are busy co-opting the Family against homosexuals, single parents and other versions of 'the enemy within'. *Sodometries* supports the view that what Adrienne Rich has called 'compulsory heterosexuality' is a relatively recent invention, and is intimately related to state power. Inscribed in the allocations of academic praise and blame is an important hypothesis, which is that the institution of English is currently reinforcing, whether wittingly or not, the homophobia of the state.

Goldberg's main thesis is that in the Renaissance, too, sodomy names everything that is transgressive, including political transgression, but that the precise character of the extra-textual erotic relations between men at that moment is beyond recovery. In a chapter on Spenser he puts the case that what is at stake in the relations betwen Colin and Hobbinol, between Spenser and Sidney, and between Sidney and his sister, is so elusive, and so effectively textually veiled, that criticism can probably hope to find no more than a mirror image of its own sexual values. But in the course of the argument he also makes clear the historical relativity of our own longing to see men and women as *opposite* sexes, and the union of those opposites as the only imaginable object of the only thinkable form of desire. The account of Marlowe brilliantly argues that the homoeroticism Marlowe's work so positively affirms is not to be understood as un-masculine, effeminating, or in any sense a travesty of heterosexuality. The object of homosexual desire in *Edward II* is neither a substitute for nor an improvement on a woman. Women, in fact, hardly come into it. And as the chapter on Prince Hal demonstrates, in a world of war and power, of imperialism as the explicit continuation of politics by violent means, women count only as objects of exchange between men, which is to say as instruments of masculine self-advancement.

This is a genuinely engaged, highly intelligent, very inventive and sophisticated book, and it's one I shall return to. It is difficult, but not wilfully so, and the analyses never become predictable. On the contrary, in fact: at moments the unexpected deconstructive turn of the argument renders the writing itself an object of desire, in its elusiveness, for the reader. But at the same time, and paradoxically, it is also a book I find quite difficult to like. The explicit argument makes a case that I support wholeheartedly, namely, that we misread the Renaissance, and indeed the possibilities of human sexuality, if we interpret them in the light of nineteenth-century notions of sexual difference, taking heterosexuality both as a personal identity and as a norm which all other modes of desire either simulate or parody. The sexual options are altogether more various and more discontinuous than the Victorian binary model would lead us to suppose. But what I seem to detect, perhaps unfairly, in the book as a whole, is a distaste not just for heterosexism, but for heterosexual relations, a reversal of the common prejudice which does not entirely escape its terms.

Moreover, when Goldberg cites Foucault as placing the pre-modern world 'before the advent of sexuality' (p. 6), does he not risk collapsing sexuality in its entirety into precisely the segregation of sexual identities that Foucault locates in the Victorian *scientia sexualis*? This scientific sexology is the main topic of *The History of Sexuality, Volume I*, and 'sexuality' is named as the correlative of the knowledge sexology represents, but as the volumes go on it becomes clear that Foucault is tracing sexuality as the object of a succession of power-knowledges back at least to the Greeks, and treating it as a means of recruiting and disciplining subjects, whether in the classical *ars erotica*, or in the modern science which names and fixes sexual identity. There is in Foucault no innocent world of bodies and pleasures outside sexuality, or indeed regimes of sexuality. We can, however, begin to delineate in textual terms, it seems to me and, I think, to Goldberg, at least the ambiguities and evasions of an epoch before sex was officially required to express a unified and consistent interiority, when sexual pleasure was potentially dispersed and differential, and divisions might exist within desire, as well as between desires.

Sexuality and Gender in Early Modern Europe, meanwhile, is certainly dispersed, and the differences within the book make me wonder who in the world can be the addressee of the collection. A good deal of the material here is outstanding, most notably the art history, which attends more closely than some of the literary criticism to the work of the signifier, but what is this random assemblage of material doing in a single volume? Sexuality *and* gender? In Italy, France and England, all of them quite separate cultures at this time? Accounts of sexual difference, prostitution, childbirth, pornography? In art, furniture, letters, fiction, poetry? And all these very disparate essays on this immense range of topics named as 'chapters'? The authors are all working in American institutions, but the collection is published by Cambridge University Press, presumably because the American market is much larger than any other. The book is beautifully produced, but issued in paperback. Why? Am I alone in feeling increasing irritation that I am obliged to buy expensive anthologies for the sake of the two or three essays that I want to read closely?

These certainly include Mary Pardo's dazzling account of 'Artifice as seduction' in Titian, Cristelle L Baskins on *cassoni* images of Esther, Janel Mueller on lesbianism in Donne, and David Kuchta's reading of the semiotics of Elizabethan masculinity. But what is disturbing in the collection as a whole is its curiously wayward appropriation of European theory. Poor Foucault is invoked as an influence here too, but this time he is also explicitly reprimanded for being boring and unscholarly. The editor quotes with approval another American comment by David Halperin on *The History of Sexuality, Volume One*: this, they both assure us, is 'dogmatic, tediously repetitious, full of hollow assertions, disdainful of historical documentation, and careless in its generalizations', for all the world as if Foucault were being denied tenure, and for good reason. After this it is no real surprise to learn that Halperin's own collection of essays, called *Before Sexuality*, 'sets the standard to which historians of early modern sexuality should aspire' (p. xvi), though this time the culture before sexuality was apparently located in Ancient Greece.

If *Sexuality and Gender* is offered as an example of the alternative to Foucault, give me repetitious dogmatism any time, especially when it brings with it a wholly new framework for understanding the history of modern sexuality as the story of a culture which produces coercive norms and thereby perversities. Meanwhile, oddly enough, a number of the essays invoke poststructuralist vocabulary, though the purpose of this is not always clear to me. It seems as if it's good to employ the terms, but it's evidently not necessary to do so with any fidelity to the European texts. A 'discourse', for example, is variously, and in the same paragraph, the inscription of a specific knowledge, an exchange of utterances, and a way of talking (p. 311). In other words, 'discourse' has become a handy, all-purpose term which effaces distinctions and thus saves a lot of intellectual effort. Elsewhere, there's evidence of a very shaky purchase on the difference between a signifier and a sign (p. 237), even though it might be argued that that particular distinction is one of the most radical in twentieth-century linguistic theory. But the most dispiriting moment of all must be the bland dismissal, in a discussion of *Othello*, of all the intellectual labour that has been dedicated, during the course of the twentieth century, to the introduction and differentiation of the notion of the subject:

> Iago's speech, and, indeed, his actions, indicate how complicatedly intertwined the relationship between body, reputation or name, and gender becomes in defining what seems (both to him and to us) to be somehow opposed to it, the 'private' character, what an earlier age with a theological discourse called the soul, what used to be the 'self', and what is now termed the 'individual subject'.
>
> (p. 208)

I'm not sure who now terms it the 'individual subject'. Althusser discusses 'concrete individuals' and the process that makes them into subjects. But I am sure that the subject (that which speaks) is not the same as the self (the unified origin of meaning), the soul (the immortal element, distinct from the mortal body), or the private character (those aspects of personality which are not on public display). The sentence sweeps away carefully argued historical distinctions between the postmodern subject as effect and in process, the modern *cogito*, and the medieval animating principle, replacing them all with the old universal, transcultural, liberal individual.

Is this casual appropriation of poststructuralist vocabulary to be read as carelessness, or is it, on the contrary, a deliberate recuperation of all that is radical in recent theory? Or worse still, is it another kind of imperialism? In the sixteenth century, Europeans could pick up a Persian rug, initially made for use, and hang it on a shelf for display; in the twentieth, Amerians pick up a French theory, made to challenge oppression, and put it on show, but domesticate it in the process so that it can do no possible damage.

Will Power, to my relief, returns me to familiar territory, which is to say to a Renaissance characterized above all by conflict, both social and discursive. Richard Wilson is fluent, witty and committed to an account of the early modern period as the site of economic and sexual contests for power. His introduction explains the project of the book in the light of recent developments in Renaissance cultural history; the first four essays interpret Shakespeare's texts in the context of contemporary class struggle; and the final essays invoke Foucault to discuss James I's sinister use of 'mercy', the womb as a blind spot in the move to a medicine based on 'observation', and the will to paternal power grounded in the desire to acquire and transmit property 'freely', which is to say without conventional or legal constraints. The strength of the book is the picture it presents of an economy in turmoil, and the corresponding turbulence of the population in the half-century before the English Revolution of the 1640s. The textual repercussions of the London clothing-workers' struggle against deregulation, the grain riots and the resistance to the enclosures all combine to dispel any last traces of the imagined harmony and hierarchy of the Elizabethan World Picture. This is a thoughtful, scholarly and highly intelligent book on Shakespeare, which draws on what is best in American New Historicism as well as European theory. I have found it altogether instructive.

Even-handedness, however, seems to require that I should have a reservation here too, and it is this. The book seems to share a (peculiarly British, mostly male?) dedication to the process of unmasking and dethroning Shakespeare, which in the end leaves me oddly indifferent. Wilson shows Shakespeare 'himself' to be complicit with the worst and most oppressive elements in his society, and the dramatist's collusion with power is apparently unrelieved by any indications of conflict or anxiety. It is true that we could well afford to dispense with the image of Shakespeare as a wise, benevolent, transcendent spectator of human heroism and folly. But to replace it with a picture of an exploitative, conniving snob is surely to stop at what Foucault calls a 'reverse discourse', which stays within the original frame.

Why are we still concerning ourselves with the Author at all? Predictably, Foucault, or a version of Foucault, comes in here too. It is in my view a misreading of his essay 'What is an author?' to see it as legitimating a retreat from Barthes's prior polemic, 'The death of the author'. When Foucault describes the imperative of individualist cultures to fill the space vacated by the author, he is not, I think, inviting us to obey that imperative. His 'author-function' is not, as I read it, a substitute version of the Author, but a way of naming the figure who defines the inscription of a knowledge. We cannot, and this is his argument, claim to understand Marxism, for instance, or psychoanalysis, without reference to the works of Marx or Freud. Similarly, and this is not his argument, but it might well be where it leads, we cannot discuss recent theory without distinguishing between Lacan, say, and Derrida, not to mention Foucault himself. In each case the name of the author *functions* as the marker of a specific knowledge, and a specific position, inscribed in a specific vocabulary.

The case of Shakespeare is not analogous to any of these. We should in my view do well to begin the process of dispensing with the Author of Shakespeare's plays, whether as sage or shark, so that we can allow the texts themselves a degree of internal dissonance, which would locate them *in* the conflicts which characterized Renaissance culture, rather than *in relation* to them.

If there is an irony which runs through all three books, however, in their invocation of Foucault's influence on our understanding of the Renaissance, it is precisely the destiny of that silent (implied?) bid for authorship, Foucault's attempt, if that is what it was, to lay claim to the meanings of his own work. In that respect, he was no more successful than Lacan and Derrida have been, nor more successful, indeed, than Freud and Marx, whose works have been invoked in causes that would give their authors grounds for some surprise. 'Foucault's account of the Renaissance has clearly shifted the paradigm for a generation of scholars.' What is less clear is the degree to which that account is recognizable as Foucault's.

University of Wales, Cardiff

Paul Hamilton

Anthony J. Cascardi, *The Subject of Modernity* (Cambridge: Cambridge University Press, 1992), x + 316 pp., £11.95 (paperback)

Andrew Bowie, *Aesthetics and Subjectivity from Kant to Nietzsche* (Manchester: Manchester University Press, 1990), vii + 284 pp., £35.00 (hardback)

Modernity is a strangely lithe concept in the hands of contemporary theorists. They use it both to describe the up-to-date and also to reach back to a mental set in western culture dating from Descartes. Modernity is ostensibly superseded by postmodernism, yet the latter has been influentially presented as simply the historical uprooting or mobilizing of its parent, modernity. Postmodernity then either carries to a logical conclusion modernism's insistence on its own epistemo-logical break and novelty, or else reveals it to be an evolving project in need of completion, in search of a future. In the former case, centuries of cultural history are erased and the modernist pulse beats audibly from the early moderns to the postmoderns. History offers itself up with a contradictory immediacy, but the negotiation of contradiction characterizes modernity, and immediacy typifies mod-ernity's consumption of its own past, daring us to overlook this covering of its tracks in our enjoyment of the pleasures of contempor-aneity. In the paradigmatically modernist history of *Gerontion*, for example, 'the giving famishes the craving', and the reader pivots exquisitely on the dilemma of a past etiolated by being made avail-able, by being made modern. Nevertheless, Eliot's poem offers this through a senile consciousness which expresses itself in images of cultural confusion, 'Hakagawa, bowing among the Titians', converg-ing on a vulgar, irredeemable anti-semitism used crassly to figure the levelling of value by capital. Great art has, after all, to be beaten down in order to leave the modernist lament for it unrivalled.

In the awful daring of a moment's surrender, the subject momen-tarily recovers history in present pleasure but seems compelled to figure this climax as a debasement. 'History is now and England' involves the same degeneracy, religious and agrarian immediacy this time inadequately masking manifest destiny. But such Nietzschean seizures are arguably another stage in a project of self-understanding in which, eventually, the selfish immediacy belonging to the satisfac-tions of consumption will be replaced by a more fulfilling reconstruc-tion of understanding as mutual and intersubjective – a kind of action presupposing society rather than a myth of solitary eating. The world is not to be represented – as though we could, impossibly, compare it with our experience of it; rather it is to be reproduced as a lifeworld, to be identified and criticized to the extent to which it is constituted through our communicative actions. Heideggerian nostalgia for the world of pre-understanding, an ontological world somehow prior to ontical, instrumental science and the unverifiable distortions of representation, is out. In are post-metaphysical aspirations towards an ideal speech-situation composing the consensual, comparably unexploited solidarity of the rationalized lifeworld. For those, however, who argue for modernism's absolute, epochal definitiveness, no such genealogy can get round the postmodern heritage of spontaneity, the demonizing of rational precedent and the loss of philosophically credible historical narrative.

Current theorists of modernity tend still to emerge from these opposite camps. When Richard Rorty tries to 'split the difference' between Lyotard and Habermas, he tries to make postmodern, unruled spontaneity a form of socially specific communication – 'one of the prettier unforced blue flowers of bourgeois culture'. He curiously undermines his case, though, by reinforcing the romantic fit of his proposed dovetail by an Eliotic allusion when he further characterizes the postmodern sublime as making one 'want to cut free of the words of the tribe'.[1] Eliot's Mallarmean echo, itself entombing Poe, is, of course, far from progressive; if it signals the end of philosophy desired by Rorty, it does so in a sense very different from Habermas's post-metaphysical thinking. It comes during a passage in *Little Gidding* full of that modernist, Yeatsian self-disgust with which Eliot so disingenuously laments and overcomes episodes from Dante's *Inferno*. But a reader looking here for the modern shape of a sometime philosophical project, now ongoing in another form, would be disappointed. The difference between that and Eliot's vexed presentation of the unpresentable, in which again the giving famishes the craving, is irreconcilable.

Anthony Cascardi, in *The Subject of Modernity*, tries like Rorty to maintain a stance of 'equal dissatisfaction with Habermas and with poststructuralist thought.' Cascardi thinks that the contradictions of modernity go deeper than Habermas would admit; since Descartes they have been forcibly solved by bestowing on science the power of attorney to settle discursive disputes. In fact Habermas may, argues Cascardi, be perpetuating this Hobbesian sovereignty of reason through his emphasis on good communication's power to establish an ethical body of speakers. The startling notion that Habermas might be rewriting *Leviathan* only hovers for a moment, but it is symptomatic of Cascardi's real sympathies which lean distinctly towards Lyotard. Modernity, he thinks, typically splits its subject across different discursive spheres of value. Unitary and progressive theories of the modern subject are insufficiently aware of the extent to which only novelistic or narrative modes can encompass the disintegration involved. This predictably leads Cascardi to revisit Lukács's *Theory of the Novel* in which, Cascardi writes, the novel has become an epic which 'thinks in terms of totality even in a disenchanted world' (p. 73). *Don Quixote* and *Robinson Crusoe* expose respectively the lack of a master code for the variety of discourses explaining this world and the lack of a natural grounding for a human essence or standard of significance. Hegel is no novelist and neither, of course, is Habermas. Cascardi shares Rorty's fondness for an excursus into a novelistic sphere which unlike philosophy is unanxious about superior systematizations of the events it narrates because it is not in competition with such bids for totality (p. 93). The increase in theoretical generosity or charity enjoyed by the novel becomes exemplary, according to Cascardi, for his own attempt to encompass 'the antinomic configuration' represented by our two strains of modernity, Habermasian and Lyotardian, taken together. And the Hegelian whiff of *Aufhebung* here is to be erased by Cascardi's irreducibly narrative philosophical mode.

The tactic for avoiding Hegelianism, though, does appear to take Cascardi back into the opposition he was above all trying to avoid. In three long and packed chapters he considers different responses to the Weberian 'disenchantment' of the world on which he thinks the moderns have been engaged since the narrative efforts of Descartes and Cervantes. The 'stunning vacuity' of Habermas's contribution comes from his habit of defining communicative action 'so as to confirm the very process of secularization required for its justification' (p. 141). Lyotard, unsurprisingly, is more mildy rebuked when his aesthetic suspension of discursive conflict in *Just Gaming* is argued to be insufficiently appreciative of the self-critical potential in classical novels which enact the freedom aesthetics theorizes. The arrival of aesthetic theory, for Cascardi, is another stage in 'disenchantment', as fictions outlive their power to command belief and so require a new form of justification. Modernity, in other words, is typified by its need for an aesthetic function to mediate 'the antinomy of history and theory', or past determinations and present interpretative pleasures (p. 300). It is as if Cascardi retells *Gerontion*'s story so as to discount the significantly decaying narrator. In order to recognize ourselves in history, we have to preserve a positive idea not disabled by the historically limited and contradictory discourses available. Out of them we must construct an idea expressive of the divided state in which they leave us. While Eliot's poem is full of a pessimism about the worth of this kind of success, Cascardi brims with optimism about the role of the aesthetic, referring it confidently to 'the ongoing project of self-imagination in the postmodern age'. In its Lyotardian form, however, the aesthetic seems in its turn to have outgrown its original function.

Accordingly, Cascardi finishes with a recasting of the plot of the *Critique of Judgement* to serve his postmodern critique of modernity. In this he appears to do the opposite of Kant. Instead of taking aesthetic experience as our mode of imagining the coherence of noumenal and phenomenal worlds, Cascardi's aesthetic becomes the means of reasserting their heterogeneity. His aesthetic introduces 'a principle of mobility' between antinomies, leaving them intact by providing us with the vehicle for occupying them successively. This aesthetic rationalizes incoherence rather than coherence. Resigned to that function, generous to a fault, it foregoes all future reconciliations which are typified as crude in comparison with the slick 'mobility' between different identities which Cascardi valorizes and which, he thinks, differentiate his Kantianism from Lyotard's exclusive emphasis on heterogeneity.

This does sound at times like a hankering after a pre-Kantian, straightforwardly sympathetic imagination, prized for its ability to project us into another identity without loss of our own, enriching moral behaviour and supplementing justice. The thought that the Kantian system might revert in this way, though, comes from a highly abstract and partial consideration of the *Critique of Judgement* within Kant's overall system, and a complete lack of interest in post-Kantian philosophy before those writings of Nietzsche which favour the postmodern reinterpretation. Andrew Bowie's *Aesthetics and Subjectivity* is an effective supplement here, and a dangerous one too for Lyotardian postmodernists, because its wider understanding of the aesthetic threatens to displace their own.

Bowie suggests that the value or not of taking Romantic philosophies at their own estimation of themselves should convince in proportion to our knowledge of them. His book begins the task, which he wants to continue, of remedying a deficiency in this knowledge going back to Coleridge. The fact, though, that Bowie's book also uncovers a Romantic problematic in recent philosophy from Adorno to Lyotard is not an inadvertent, collateral effect of the history he relates. Idealist philosophies of the subject are obvious targets of those who by contrast see the project of modernity as ungrounded and its subject (replacing God, the State, Nature and any other source of legitimation) as dispersed. Bowie maintains, first, that the categories of subjectivity are displaced rather than eliminated in the postmodern reductio, endowing with pathetic efficacy localities such as language, discourse or power. Second, Romantic philosophies of the subject confronted in their time many of the complexities for which contemporary theorists like Cascardi appear to have found self-defeating accommodations. In particular, in aesthetics they found ways of reformulating ideas of self-consciousness which, commonsensically, we are incapable of abandoning however sophisticated our philosophical understanding.

Bowie claims that Romantic theories of the subject articulate 'what is repressed by our cognitive and economic domination of nature' (p. 34). At a single bound, then, a path seems cleared for the philosopher from Kant to Heidegger, and at the same time, the commonsensical subject puzzled by increasingly technological and abstract know-how of herself as a cognitive or economic object is given a new recourse for self-consciousness. Of course this is too simple, as Bowie explains, but the common cause made here by ordinary and philosophical intuition arguably originates in the space cleared by aesthetics. Aesthetic experience, therefore, is not simply about grasping myself; it is about grasping myself in the process of apprehending nature in an alternative manner to science. Divorce aesthetics from this metaphysics, and you end up with its postmodern skeleton, shuttling from one ungrounded identity to the next, underwritten instead by Schopenhauerian or Nietzschean will. Yet mistake the ordinary consciousness empowered to disclose its own ontological authenticity for a specific *Volk*, and you have Heidegger's notorious conjuncture with national socialism. Bowie favours a third option, and concludes with an Adorno-like vigilance for the historical mutations of the aesthetic, perpetually saving art for society by, in a typical paradox, refusing to allow it to become contaminated by instrumental social ends. For Bowie as for Adorno, it is music which sets the standards for this autonomy, and also exposes its perennial difficulties: its liberated self-expression grows too conventional, or, in the attempt to avoid cliché and commercialism, music becomes solipsistic, losing the ordinary resonance with which it had awoken our collectively more authentic self.

Fundamentally, Bowie's book argues that the story of modernity as an immediate apprehension of the subject at the expense of objective or historical grounding changes if you read carefully the German critics of Kant's Copernican turn. Kant's *Critique of Judgement* has to be taken as a whole, as a critique of teleological as well as aesthetic judgement, if his aesthetic theory is to be understood. The third *Critique* certainly answers to the impossibility of grasping the subject within the circle of science; but the plot of Kant's recovery of this subject for aesthetic reflection is the same as his plan to recover an idea of nature as it too exists beyond scientific rationalization. The subject's intuition of itself in aesthetic experience must be linked to an intuition of itself as part of this intelligible nature. Only if we surmise such a purposiveness in nature can we explain how science comes by its contents and how the subject's experience of itself outside scientific understanding is still, as it were, a natural one. Modernity, therefore, ceases to invoke a relatively straightforward tale of the increasingly subjective reading of a correspondingly secularized or disenchanted world. Rather it records the subject's accompanying aesthetic search for its lost grounding in nature as precisely that dimension omitted by advances in technological discovery but making them possible. Kant's critics, however, argued that to concede this much was to incur the philosophical obligation of describing a natural activity which must, by definition, be unconscious or pre-scientific, although somehow disclosed. Heidegger and Gadamer, Bowie argues, were precipitate in accusing Kant of 'subjectivizing' the object through his aesthetics, and this is proved by the prompt which Kantian aesthetics gave to post-Kantians to develop his ideas further. Kant had shown, as Bowie puts it, 'that nature is not just an object and is part of ourselves as subjects in ways we do not understand, and could not ever fully understand' (p. 45).

Art apparently gives us a model for how we might apprehend ourselves in ways we do not understand; and a concept of nature as Spinozan productivity, *natura naturans* rather than *natura naturata*, gives us a metaphor for how our sciences might be the products of their natural objects. By now we are deep in Schelling's development of Fichte's notion that the 'I' is an activity, and deep also in his disagreement with Fichte's picture of nature as nothing more than a field for moral action. Along the way, Bowie examines ideas of Friedrich Schlegel, Hölderlin and Novalis; but Schelling most conspicuously takes up the definitive challenge to articulate a philosophy of nature which will not be fancifully animistic and which will provide a philosophical vocabulary for disclosing the natural grounding of the subject. For Schelling, whatever self-expression I achieve in art cannot be reduced to the rules for its subsequent understanding: that initial embodiment of self is of an unconscious activity, my natural self prior to scientific rationalization. Kant's explanation of genius is here transformed into a licence for a *Naturphilosophie* in which the purposive organicism of the work of art now models the production of thought out of nature within the subject. This post-Kantian deployment of the *Critique of Judgement* is obviously very different from Lyotardian aesthetic liberalism, but it answers the demands of otherwise opposed modern philosophers such as Heidegger and Adorno for a philosophical attention to the possibility which Kant's philosophy had seemed to rule out – nature free of our technological regulation of it within and outside ourselves.

Schelling's philosophy of nature has further fascinating ramifications which Bowie explores at more length in his new book on Schelling. There, the Cro-Magnon lookalike stares out at us from an 1850 photograph so balefully that his neglect seems almost understandable. But the East Anglian revival of Schelling studies is persuasive, and Bowie draws on work by Peter Dews and others to show the relevance of Schelling's view of natural productivity to other differential systems of significance we tend to think of as originating with Saussure. Schelling's philosophy here is one of identity, though, not of difference, concerned to find a language for the constant play of forces out of which difference is generated rather than imagining that, philosophically, we can just go with the flow. Another of Bowie's aims is to make English readers aware of contemporary German philosophical debates which are often focused by Schelling. (So many continental philosophers have written on Schelling – Jaspers, Heidegger, Marcel, Tillich, even Habermas's 1954 Bonn Ph.D. thesis.) Manfred Frank, Dieter Heinrich and others live as usefully on the page, especially by throwing a different, German perspective on Habermas, as some of the nineteenth-century revivals.

From all this emerges an entire tradition which is anti-Hegelian from the start; it resists Hegel's philosophical subordination of art, however symphonic his logic, and, insisting on the ultimate recalcitrance of the natural individual to conceptualization, it already launches into the task of finding an alternative philosophical language. Especially neglected in this precocious critique of the twentieth-century critique of modernity, claims Bowie, is Schleiermacher. Bowie works out his dialectical position from untranslated writings. Believing in the free productivity we have seen idealists identify at the root of self-consciousness, Schleiermacher concludes that the 'aim of publicly accountable knowledge is to diminish destructive social conflicts generated by our irreducible otherness to each other.' At the same time, his traditionally *aesthetic* grasp of this original difference supplies him with an occasional reason (which Habermas's theory of communicative action perhaps lacks) for necessarily valuing it above social reconciliation (p. 152). This reflective grasp of individual identity and difference, though, is always dependent on a prior natural productivity, and 'only gradually develops in human beings after their physical life has already begun' (p. 156). Bowie here finds a theory explaining why Lacanian mirror imagery and Derridean differance presuppose an identity which 'could only see *itself* if it *already* were in some way familiar with itself' (pp. 156–7). Familiarity cannot be retrospective, and to suggest it comes from aesthetic experience is not in neo-Kantian fashion simply to suspend a symbolic order already in place, but to describe the unconscious and natural production of ourselves as possible subjects of the symbolic order. Art's dialectic of spontaneous production and technical reception again provides the model.

These hinted correctives to poststructuralism remain as hints in Bowie's commentary. We still want to know how much of post-Kantianism's metaphysics we have to take on board in order to maintain its proleptic critique. Bowie's book is very much part of work-in-progress, and he clearly intends to provide answers to the questions raised by *Aesthetics and Subjectivity*, perhaps across the axis of Adorno's and Heidegger's critiques of instrumentalism. In his single-minded exposition of neglected German philosophers, Bowie has little time for cultural or political context. The result is a history of ideas partly redeemed from pure ideality by its perpetual ferreting out of the forgotten materialisms of the philosophies he studies. Marx's materialism famously necessitated a complete inversion of his Hegelian inheritance, and the evident circumscription of Marxism by post-Kantianism highlighted by Bowie cries out for more explanation. To be able to ask such questions, though, is the result of reading a book which makes so newly visible this tradition and the revision of ideas of modernity it entails. This is a dialect our tribe ought to be able to speak.

University of Southampton

Notes

1 See Richard Rorty, 'Habermas and Lyotard on postmodernity', in *Habermas and Modernity*, ed. R. J. Bernstein (Cambridge: Polity Press, 1985), pp. 161–76.

Steven Connor

Patricia Waugh, *Practising Postmodernism, Reading Modernism* (London: Edward Arnold, 1992), vi + 176 pp., £10.99 (paperback)

Francis Barker, Peter Hulme and Margaret Iversen (eds), *Postmodernism and the Re-reading of Modernity* (Manchester: Manchester University Press, 1992), vi + 322 pp., £35.00 (hardback)

Stephen Pfohl, *Death at the Parasite Café: Social Science (Fictions) and the Postmodern* (Basingstoke and London: Macmillan, 1992), 319 pp., £12.99 (paperback)

Lawrence Grossberg, *We Gotta Get Out of This Place: Popular Conservatism and Postmodern Culture* (New York and London: Routledge, 1992), viii + 436 pp., £11.99 (paperback)

More postmodernism. If, like me, you have been trying to keep tabs on the appearances and uses of the term in academic writing, you will have noticed that titles and subtitles of books tend now to include the phrase 'and postmodernism' as though it were a kind of nutritional supplement. Politics, truth . . . and postmodernism. Media, society . . . and postmodernism. The range of postmodernisms investigated in the four books I have a chance to say something about here is wide, but I am pleased to say that in none of them is postmodernism just this kind of decorative attachment. Each, in fact, offers a substantial and distinctive account of what it takes the postmodern to be.

Patricia Waugh's study is divided into two sections, which correspond roughly to the division proposed in her title, between the practice of postmodern theory and criticism and the exercise of reading modernism (though it is necessarily a reading in the light cast backwards from the glare of postmodern preoccupation). The first section offers a characterization of the postmodern through a discussion of five of its aspects or recurring topoi: Romantic aestheticism; the sublime; the question of period; questions of aesthetic form; and the relationship between postmodernity and Enlightenment. The second section offers readings of a number of modernist texts through the lessons established in the first section: *Heart of Darkness*, *To the Lighthouse*, Eliot's criticism and *Ulysses*. In this second section there is also a chapter which, without the aid of a particular literary case study, astutely considers the relations between feminism, Enlightenment and the postmodern. (But why is it here, and not in the first section?)

Patricia Waugh's purpose is, by disclosing the conveniently narrow characterizations of modernism which postmodernism has used to define itself, to suggest some of the more fundamental ways in which modernism anticipates and persists in postmodernism. As if this were not enough, Waugh pledges herself to uncover a further continuity, in showing that the family resemblance of modernism and postmodernism derives from their shared origin in Romantic styles of thought. The thread that connects Romantic, modernist and post-modernist for Waugh is the primacy of the aesthetic. Where Kant and contemporary Romantic thinkers established the nature and force of the aesthetic by carefully distinguishing it from other areas of life and thought, the dominance of the aesthetic in postmodernism comes from its incontinent flooding into the areas from which it had pre-viously been sealed off – philosophy, politics, sexuality, economics and social life generally. The aestheticism whose prestige had been assured by an act of sacralization in Romantic thought thus achieves postmodern hegemony by being thoroughly secularized.

Waugh is shrewdly alert to the different qualities and meanings attaching to the aesthetic ideal. It manifests itself first of all in the principle of subjective self-making or self-narration, in a tradition that Waugh traces from Coleridge through Nietzsche to contempor-ary fans of self-fashioning like Richard Rorty. 'If the "I am" is cut loose from the divine "I AM" ', as Waugh so niftily puts it, 'then divinity has to be relocated in a self which must aesthetically con-struct its own ground in a transformation of the body through the body' (p. 21). This last detail here links this particular habit of thought with the sense of radical 'situatedness' which is also identified with the aesthetic, the acknowledgement of the always-already embeddedness of the self in temporal and spatial contexts. Waugh tracks this idea through – with a hop, skip and a jump, here and there, let it be said – from Wordsworth to T. S. Eliot, Heidegger and Gadamer. Such situatedness is postmodern in its refusal of the non-perspectival vantage point or 'view from nowhere' of disem-bodied reason. As Waugh carefully points out, it also imparts a complicating kink to the standard argument that sees aesthetic disin-terestedness leading to modernist 'autonomy' in a straight line from Kant to Clement Greenberg, and most stations in between.

Central to the re-readings of modernist texts which make up the second half of the book, in fact, is the attempt to excavate a different and expanded sense of the meaning of 'aesthetic autonomy', that modernist extrusion of the Romantic tradition in which 'the notion of autonomy as the separation *from* life paradoxically also implies a form of aestheticism, the existence of art *in* life' (p. 17). Waugh argues that the work of writers such as Virginia Woolf has been read too narrowly as concerned with textual or formal autonomy, for in it the autonomy of the work of art is constituted on the analogy of the autonomously self-creating human person. The source for this kind of aesthetic autonomy is not so much Kant as Nietzsche. Waugh comes close to offering her reader a Nietzschean reading of *To the Lighthouse*: 'Why not', she enquires,

> maximise the liberatory potential of art by aestheticising the totality of one's experience so that instead of preserving art by withdrawing into an autonomously self-referential aesthetic realm one bursts out of the enclosed circle and treats the world as a work of art giving birth to itself and the self as an infinitely plastic entity which is free to 'author' its own life.
>
> (p.112)

(Nietzsche gets a pretty smooth ride through most of this book, by the way. If the early rejections of Nietzsche as proto-fascist ignored much that was important and premonitory in his work, the widespread contemporary approval of that work, especially among feminists, seems to me to smile too easily on the stupidity and malignity that lurk in it.)

I think that Waugh's is a powerful argument and one that contributes much to the recent rethinkings of the status of the aesthetic in postmodernism, and its relation to ethical thinking. It is a pity then that, despite the keenness of her own historical account of the aesthetic and its meanings, Waugh sometimes tends to fall back into simplistic or incurious assumptions about the nature of the aesthetic, for example in the sentimental primitivism of her claim for the priority of art as experience over the abstraction of theory:

> Whereas theory inevitably uses a conceptual mode in attempting to vindicate the authenticity of the non-conceptual, works of art can inhabit the position in their irreducible particularity. Postmodern art is less at the mercy of its own performative contradictions than postmodern theory (p. 81).

One among many obvious objections here is that the alleged immediacy and particularity of art are cultural values and ascriptions rather than given or natural conditions, and as such always in some sense the result of precisely the kind of theoretical abstraction which is said to be foreign to the aesthetic.

Waugh has a rather complex and nuanced argument to stage, with a large cast and proliferating sub-plots. She does not make things any easier for herself by trying to keep the attention of many different kinds of reader at once. At one moment she is developing a no-holds-barred discussion of Heideggerian ontology; at another, she is giving the novice reader ground-level introductions to Foucault and Deleuze. Waugh is in fact an extremely reliable guide and skilful expositor even in this back-of-the-envelope vein, and in its own way, the first section of this book is as good an overview of postmodern thinking as a newcomer could look for; the problem may be that the argument of the book does not really need or benefit from this width of preoccupation and splintering of address. At times, reading the book is like watching a hard-pressed cook trying to deal with a collapsing soufflé just as the Hollandaise sauce is bubbling over and the baby has started to climb into the oven. This is, in fact, a hugely authoritative account of postmodernism, in which every page flares with intelligence and insight and which has an important and provocative argument to offer. But it takes a cool head and a good sense of direction to keep oneself orientated in what turns out to be the very complex terrain that it charts. (I normally get irritated by reviewers who suck their teeth elaborately at matters of presentation, but I am also sure that, when she is asked to do another edition of this book, Patricia Waugh will be keen to clean up the dozens of typographical errors contained here; between pages 112 and 114 alone, for example, I found 'iself', 'absurbly','aesthertic' and 'anithetical', along with some mispunctuation.)

The retroactive transformation of modernity by our current concern with the postmodern is also the subject of the most recent volume in the series of publications emanating from the Literature/Politics/ Theory symposia at the University of Essex. There are twelve very substantial essays here, which, though they may at first appear heterogeneous in terms of their topic or occasion – Kristin Ross writes about postmodernism, spatiality and detective stories, Jonathan Benison considers the status of science fiction, Nancy Fraser criticizes the constitution of the public sphere in Habermas, Jane Flax argues for the affiliation of feminism and postmodernism, Michael Newman discusses the work of Anselm Kiefer and Christian Lenhardt – in fact worry collectively and intriguingly at a set of closely related problems regarding modernity, memory, temporality and politics, and set up an unusually high degree of implicit dialogue and cross-talk, of affiliation and divergence.

The essays are also connected by two factors relating to the moment of their emergence at a symposium at the University of Essex in 1990. First, there is the mingling of euphoria and unease occasioned by the chain reaction of revolution in eastern Europe, which gives urgency and substance to even the most stratospheric of the theoretical reflections contained in it. And second, there is the (then) imminence of the centenary of the birth of Walter Benjamin. The figure of Benjamin broods over the whole collection, and it is to the melancholy lucubrations on time and history in his late 'Theses on the philosophy of history' that many of the essays consciously or unconsciously seem to return. For those contributors who argue for the continuing responsibility of critical theory to the ideals and progressive temporality of modernity, Benjamin seems to provide a model for the complex proleptic remembering which is entailed by continuing the project of modernity – a remembering of the progressive possibility once confidently projected in modernity, in a version of the backwards advance into the future of Benjamin's famous Angel of History. For those, like Jane Flax, in her essay 'Is enlightenment emancipatory?' and, more qualifiedly perhaps, Kenneth Lea, whose essay 'Traducing history' attempts to assimilate Benjamin to Lyotard's postmodernity, the question seems rather to be how the process of mourning the modern may be brought to completion – though none of the essays in the collection forget Freud's lesson that the recovery from and forgetting of loss always involves its preparatory repetition. For others again, it is a question neither of how the modern is to be kept in mind, nor of how it is to be left behind, but of how we are to live with the newly paradoxical time of postmodernity which lies both beyond and within the temporality of the modern. Here, Benjamin's work, with its obstinate suspicion of totalized or continuous historical narratives, which he regarded as the mesmerizing fraud of the political oppressor, and his interest in the redemptive discontinuity of collage-time, the time of historical break and reconfiguration, provides a model for some of the strange loops in postmodern time and time-consciousness – in which, for example, postmodernism finds itself prefigured in modernism and the modern finds itself subject to uncanny recapitulation in the postmodern.

The collection divides broadly into two kinds of essay, the reflective or theoretical, and the analytic or concrete. Among the most absorbing of the former is Peter Osborne's careful analysis of the qualitative transformation in the nature and experience of temporality in modernism in his stolidly titled essay 'Modernity is a qualitative, not a chronological, category'. Nancy Fraser's careful revision of Habermas in her 'Rethinking the public sphere: a contribution to the critique of actually existing democracy' is a fine example of the kind of judicious and particularized critique that a social theory pluralized by postmodernism can originate. Jay Bernstein's 'Whistling in the

dark: affirmation and despair in postmodernism' is a precise, pris-
matic attack on the value of affirmation in postmodern thinking,
which, he says, voluntaristically refuses the difficulties and aporias
demanded by an authentic working-through of modernity. In 'Writing in the lifeworld: deconstruction as paradigm of a transition to
postmodernity', Peter Dews is similarly unpersuaded by the claims
of postmodernism, though his fine, nuanced account of the significance of metaphor in Derrida reaches a different conclusion from
Bernstein about Derrida's relation to postmodernism. (For Bernstein,
Derrida is the diagnostician of postmodernism, for Dews he is the
carrier of it.) I read Peter Dews's essay with the usual admiration for
the tireless tenacity of his analysis; right up to the conclusion, that
is, which suddenly became extremely spindly in argument. Perhaps
it is a little unfair to home in on this one portion of the essay, but,
as the final words of the final essay in the collection, it is rather
caught in the spotlight, so here goes. The essay ends up convicting
Derrida of an 'ultimate erasure of the proper and the proximate'
which is said to be typical of the 'reflexive self-deracination' of
postmodernistic thinking. But it defines this charge by first of all
deploying the later work of Derrida which, as Dews acknowledges,
is far from denying the constraining power of human contexts of
meaning, against the more overheated Nietzschean moments in his
early work, and then applying the charge mounted implicitly by that
later work against the earlier indifferently to the *whole* body of
Derrida's work, early or late. This coercive approximation is then
reduplicated in the forced association of Derrida and postmodernism
as a whole, such that what is true of Derrida is held necessarily to
be true of postmodernism, and vice versa. I realize that it is always
necessary to cut a few corners to come to a firm judgement, but I
found the giddy skid of synecdoche here just a little too breathtaking.

I have just distinguished the theoretical essays in this collection
from the studies of particular cases or examples, but this is perhaps
itself too nonchalant an approximation, since there is much that they
share in method and subject. Indeed, the very problem of the status
of the case or example for modernity and postmodernity is one of
the subliminal sub-topics which connect the two kinds of essay. For
might it not be, as Kenneth Lea suggests in his discussion of Lyotard's
aesthetics of the sublime in his 'Traducing history', that the newly
(or recurrently?) problematic sense of the relation between the 'case',
and that of which it is a case, is a defining feature of the postmodern
itself? For Lyotard, the postmodern becomes modern precisely at the
moment that it is deformed into demonstrability, when it becomes
possible to index and display its instances. In his 'The long run of

modernity' Adrian Rifkin has a similar apprehension of the narrowing effect of approved or canonical exemplifications of the modern,
but, rather than proclaiming the postmodern to be hostile to every
kind of instancing, draws the rather different conclusion that a postmodernist sense of plurality might allow for a closer and minuter
investigation of the differences within the modern itself. The agility
with which Rifkin's essay itself moves between different examples of
the modern, from theoretical works like those of Benjamin, to the
inter-war Parisian music-hall, the kiosk and the taxi meter, is itself
evidence of the value of just such an expanded attentiveness. (The
bounce in Rifkin's own style is also a relief from the jaw-jutting
earnestness that affects some of the essays here.)

The particular kind of case that is in question in many of the
essays is of course cultural or artistic. Some of these essays take
the modernism/postmodernism break for granted in ways that the
essays I have been discussing so far do not. Margaret Iversen's
'Spectators of postmodern art' is an effective survey of some of the
reactions against hard-line artistic modernism, in minimalism and in
the feminist appropriationist art of Cindy Sherman and Mary Kelly,
though it might have entered a little more into the conversations
going on in the essays around it. Elaine Jordan's account of the
feminist postmodernist fiction of Christa Wolf and Angela Carter is
intelligent and has its heart in the right place, though the conventional
preferences of postmodernism, for categorial disruption, fictionalized
history, and so forth, are here asserted rather than inspected. I hope
Elaine Jordan will forgive me two little sniggers about this essay. I
think that the person called 'Linda McHale', whose optimistic reading
of postmodernism Jordan says she shares on page 178, is a com-
mingling of two separate writers, Linda Hutcheon and Brian McHale,
though, admittedly, they are both pretty cheerful about postmodernism. And, in a reminder of the revenges that time is always wont to
bring in: in the light of the allegations (possibly mischievous) about
Christa Wolf's sideline as a STASI informer before 1989, Jordan's
ringing declaration that 'Wolf's imperative has been to bear witness'
(p. 69) might now sound a little hollow. Kristin Ross's 'Watching the
detectives' is a skilful attempt to read the important question of space
in postmodernism via a reading of the modernist and postmodernist
depiction of the city in the detective fiction of Raymond Chandler
and the contemporary French writer Didier Daeninckx; and Jonathan
Benison's 'Science fiction and postmodernity' is an authoritative and
discerning discussion of the triangular relations between the modern,
the postmodern and science fiction. 'Suffering from reminiscences',
Michael Newman's study of Anselm Kiefer, Christian Lenhardt and

Gerhard Richter makes high demands on the reader, but delivers correspondingly rich rewards. Its conjoining of the question of memory with the question of the possibility of art in the contemporary world, makes for an essay of enormous compass and gravity, and one which draws together many of the preoccupations of this excellent volume. Such collections often achieve coherence only through the muting of difference; here, difference and disagreement are actually structuring principles. What they enable the book to construct is not so much a unity of perspective on the relations between postmodernism and modernism, as a kind of parallax – which gives dynamism and dimension to questions that are too often flattened into formulae.

And there is no shortage of dynamism in Stephen Pfohl's *Death at the Parasite Café* either. The book is part of the CultureTexts series which has been publishing titles at intervals for the last decade or so under the joint editorship of the magi of Canadian postmodernism, Arthur and Marilouise Kroker. The series produces works of social theory which are as crass and extravagant as they are ambitious and exploratory. This one is an extended Baudrillardian meditation on the apparently lethal conditions of contemporary global cyberculture. The mood of the book is one of a curiously exhilarated gloom. There was once a time – call it modernity, maybe – when the political authority of the white male middle class was secured, in the order of fact and of representation alike, by iron binarisms, which defined, expelled and excluded 'others' of all kinds. If this was once the case, then political power has undergone a bizarre contortion in the epoch of what Pfohl calls 'ultramodernity'. For the contemporary explosion of information and means of reproduction, along with the growth of the society of the spectacle and the arrival of a libidinal economy of ephemeral intensities as the dominant mode of capitalism, has made excess not the abjected other of contemporary society, but its organizing principle.

> Excess is being reduced to the self-same realm of access.... Those experiences which had previously exceeded or fractured the social constructed 'commonsense' of the modern order, are today being manufactured in a simulated form and then fed back for our consumption without their once disturbing potential for creating a critical difference.
>
> (p. 15)

The problem which the book poses to itself is the traditional one of incorporation: with what principles of dissent or difference should a critical social theory line up, in a situation in which dissent and difference are not only disarmed, but are the very engine that drives an oppressive system? The 'parasite café' of Pfohl's title is his metonymy for the 'commanding communicative circuitries . . . of ultramodernity itself' (p. 20). It is 'a terrifying place where a simulated return of the repressed does little but fuel desires for continuous consumption and where the ideal purity of fascist mastery might be terminally realized in the telecommunicative aestheticization of everyday life' (p. 35).

Phew. Things are obviously not looking too good. Nevertheless, the book does identify itself with the possibility of subversion, of a resistance to a system that appears to become more total and more monolithic the more it decentres and differentiates itself in the varieties of critical postmodernism which Pfohl pits against the protean adaptability of ultramodernism: ethnographic postmodernism, drawing on early twentieth-century criticisms of anthropological reason; sex/gender postmodernism, mounting challenges to heterosexist patriarchy; multicultural postmodernism, involving resistance to white hegemony in colonial and postcolonial contexts. So convinced is Pfohl of the corruption or superannuation of any kind of political critique, whether in a liberal or Marxist tradition, which would derive its validity from the reasoned and unconstrained negotiation of interests, rights and values, that he is forced towards a Dionysian or ecstatic politics whose legitimacy would be grounded not in reason but in the intensity of transgression. The middle chapters of his book, which are really the most sustained and substantial parts of it, develop a fascinating, though often also rather obscure ethnographic reading of the 'elementary forms of ultramodern life', in terms borrowed from Durkheim, Freud and Bataille. Durkheim's analyses of the operations of ritual and the sacred in archaic cultures are here read back suggestively into ultramodern culture, though only to yield the grim conviction that 'WHITE MAGICAL MEDIA TECHNOLOGIES extend the violence of sacrificial hierarchies into the realm of omnipresent environmental effects' (p. 190). But at the same time, and sometimes almost in the same breath, Pfohl looks to the experience of certain kinds of somatic intensity, to the carnal knowledge of submerged cultural traditions (witchcraft, voodoo, magic) and other 'pagan epistemological practices' (p. 175) to provide principles of political resistance and renewal.

Of course, given the defeatist totalization of Pfohl's initial account of the ultramodern culture of accessible excess, there is absolutely nothing, apart, perhaps, from a faith in the principle of extremity itself, to guarantee such corporeal counter-discourses against incorporation. If the book manages to convey accurately something of the power of modern capitalism to include everything which it once seemed imperative for it to exclude, it deliberately cuts itself off from the kinds of intellectual resource needed to analyse such a situation and recognize any kind of auspicious flaw in it. For all its passionate hostility to political violence and exclusion of all kinds, the book is too mesmerized by the principles of extremity, violence and excess to develop plausible or human-shaped political values and alternatives. Given its principled (though unargued) certainty that the traditions of reasoned critique are the tools of the oppressor, this is condemned to be an argument governed not by the movement of dialectic, but by arbitrary mood swings.

This is appropriate, perhaps, in a book, where the argument is conducted as much through the form as through the subject of its discourse. Throughout, exposition and argument are interrupted by images seemingly derived from a video-text by the author on the same theme and with the same title, passages of autobiography, real and fictionalized, dream-sequence, fantasy, self-dramatization, and enlivened throughout with prankish typography. I would not be at all surprised if a hypermedia version of the same text were soon to disseminate through academic hyperspace. At odd moments, Stephen Pfohl hands over authorship of his book to imagined characters, notably the crackpot alter-ego Professor Jack O. Lantern and a figure who acts as the carefully correct good conscience of the book, the mythic female figure of Black Madonna Durkheim, who breaks in at intervals to deliver reproofs to its author, slapping his wrist for indulging in male fantasy and nagging him (though wholly in his own idiom and cadence) about his narcissism.

When it comes to its own form, this is a book that emphatically, even oppressively, knows its own mind. At regular intervals, it breaks off the fun and games to deliver strict little lectures about their form and purpose: 'Methodologically this text may be read as an effort to deconstruct the dominance of a positivist aesthetics in the (w)riting of contemporary social science' (p. 75), we are instructed at one point. The kind of social theory which this book aims to exemplify will have got beyond the vicious and guilty reduction of the world to a mere theme for knowledge, along with theory's fond dream of being able to subtract itself from the scene which it surveys. Social theory of this kind must not repress awareness of its own forms of historical positioning, and its practitioners must 'open ourselves to questions and methods falling between the forced fields of philosophy, literature, linguistics, HIStory, economics, women's studies, psychoanalysis, the iconic or performing arts, and even theoretical

physics' (p. 78). Following the hint of James Clifford and some
other postmodern ethnographers, Pfohl looks to the 'ethnographic
surrealism' of Georges Bataille for a model. The purpose of all this
is to allow social theory to unpick itself from the political oppression
with which it has for so long been wickedly complicit. The book
wants to describe and exemplify 'a language that dissolves itself fes-
tively. A language that opens out to and materializes itself in a
dialogue with others' (p. 14). And if it knows what it wants, it knows
how to get it, too:

> The text you are reading stupidly mixes *social-psychoanalysis* with
> *collage-(w)riting, deconstructive ethnography,* and a *genealogical
> approach to HIStory....* I am trying to construct a reading
> environment that disinFORMs as much as it shares knowledge.
> Hopefully this will offer an experience closer to the uncertainties
> of *dialogical research* than the more masterful pleasures of dialecti-
> cal analysis.
>
> (p. 95)

Why is it that such modest and come-on-in declarations in academic
texts always sound so cocksure and hectoring? The problem seems to
be partly in the assumption that a text can be dialogic or monologic as
a matter of simple authorial or stylistic choice. But if the condition
of all texts is to be only partly aware and in charge of the conditions of possibility that make them readable in different contexts,
then to include that condition of partial mastery as part of a conscious
programme is always going to be futile – since the text will continue
to be readable and be read in terms of constraints and contingencies
that are not entirely in its ken. Consciously embracing or bracing
itself against such contingencies will make them neither more nor
less operative, since they are by definition a matter of what exceeds
the text's intentions with respect to itself. Indeed, it might be said
that the will to self-unmaking that this book so voluptuously indulges
is anyway no depletion of the masterful intentionalism that it finds
so revolting, but a stock item in its repertoire. Oddly, for all the
animus it displays against the abstractness of traditional social theory,
and for all its desire for performative immediacy (in a curious postmodernist recall of the modernist ideal that texts should not mean
but merely be), this text itself remains curiously prospective, like a
kind of model or simulation of the text it would like to have been:
it reads like a trailer that has turned out to be as long as the movie
it is promoting.

There are at least three books stitched together inside the covers of

Lawrence Grossberg's *We Gotta Get Out of This Place*, all of them well worth the cover-price on its own. Its first section, 'Cultural Studies: Theory, Power and the Popular', is a rich and detailed consideration of the theoretical resources necessary for cultural studies in its reading of popular culture. The next section, 'Another Boring Day in . . . Paradise' (Grossberg's ellipses, not mine), is a fascinating and abundantly contextualized study of what Grossberg calls the 'rock formation', by which he means the patterns of meaning, identification and affect configured by and around popular music since the late 1950s in the US. Finally, in the last two sections, 'Where the Streets Have No Name: Hegemony and Territorialization' and 'Real Power Doesn't Make Any Noise: Capitalism and the Left', we encounter a set of arguments, which manage to be boldly speculative and authoritative at the same time, about the transforming conditions of capital in the US and beyond, along with an impressive plea for corresponding renewals in left social critique. But, though each of these separate enquiries has its own defining tow and momentum, it would be unfair to suggest that their association is purely arbitrary or opportunist. For the book is powerfully organized, not in linear fashion, nor around a set of invariant propositions, but in a pattern of radiating concentric circles, each widening the field of application and implication of its predecessor. There is so much local excellence in the book that the reader might be forgiven for not registering the positively heroic sweep of its total design; though, as may soon appear, I think the question of how to draw such an enquiry into a total design has more than accidental application to the enquiry itself.

For indeed, the question of how to do cultural studies is a question posed with particular urgency by the conditions of cultural life that this book analyses. For Grossberg, cultural studies must find a way of maintaining that hold on particularity and plurality which has been its great contribution, must develop a critical practice 'appropriate to the terrain of daily life itself, to its rhythms and forces, its shapes and dimensions' (p. 106), without falling into the pulverized, paralysed condition of postmodern disconnectedness. I think the title of the book is one of the few things about it that badly misfires, but there is this to be said for it, that it neatly hinges together the two idioms or perspectives on offer in cultural studies: in the demotic matiness of its preliminary title, and the somewhat clipped propriety of the subtitle that interprets and completes it. The titles of the individual sections in the book which I quoted a moment ago enact a similar balancing of the mimetic-participative and the abstract-analytic modes of cultural study.

The first section of Grossberg's book attempts to develop a

theoretical vocabulary of sufficient suppleness and bite to remain true to the complexity and mobility of the 'lines of flight' in contemporary cultural life while also maintaining the possibility of bringing to light the forms of its organization. Central to Grossberg's analysis is the notion of what he calls a 'structured mobility' in contemporary social life, a framing or constraining, with specific effects and purposes, of the very patterns of change and movement that seem to deny the possibility of any such constraint. Also central to the book's argument is a focus upon feeling and affect, which Grossberg believes have played too little part in a cultural studies restricted by its definition of culture as made up of signifying practices, or the communication of ideological meanings and beliefs. An account of the present must learn to attend to what Grossberg calls the 'maps of mattering' of which every individual's life is made up. Like 'structured mobility', this phrase attempts to hold together the force and the form of social life, without either subordinating one to the other, or losing the sense of their dynamic opposition. Sometimes, the attempt in this section to maintain the tension of this relationship between force and form, and to take account of the sheer multiplicity of their articulations results in a kind of overload of specificity, usually involving geomorphic metaphors of boundaries, territories, points, lines, planes, sites and locations. When this happens, the writing can slip into a sort of reverie of quasi-exactitude:

> A map of territorialization ... is a map of the circulation of practices and sensibilities through space and time, and of the effects of and constraints on this circulation. It locates them in a dispersed field in order to ask how they occupy different places in relation to the ongoing structuring of the field itself. Hence it measures not only places and spaces, but also distances and accesses, intensities and densities.
>
> (p. 107)

When I read this passage for the first time (and the second, and the third), I felt rather like Alice confronted with the poem 'Jabberwocky', in *Through the Looking-Glass*: 'Somehow it seems to fill my head with ideas – only I don't exactly know what they are.' But I must acknowledge that the succeeding sections of the book manage to fill out very effectively the terms that may seem abstract or content-less on first encounter. There, Grossberg elaborates his case about the relationship between rock music, postmodernity and cultural conservatism. Unlike other critics who content themselves with enquiring whether rock music is, or is not, authentically postmodern, Grossberg sees rock music as in a sense articulated both against and within postmodernism. This is because rock music and its associated forms, styles and practices come into being as a way of simultaneously exceeding and anchoring identity. I found the analysis of this effect subtle and percipient:

> Rock was always about the transitions between investments and differences. It was not only a territorializing, but a differentiating machine as well. . . . Rock was about the control one gained by taking the risk of losing control, the identity one had by refusing identities. Its only stability was the investment one made into the formation itself. It reified its own transitional status, locating itself as the permanent 'between'.
>
> (p. 180)

If rock music, defined in these terms as a form of 'structured mobility', is in one sense itself a symptom of postmodernism, in another sense it is vulnerable to a postmodernity which, Grossberg tells us, threatens 'the historical collapse of specific relations within everyday life . . . the "fact" that certain differences no longer matter' (p. 221). Rock music continues to offer intensity, transcendence and transgression, but in a form that is now exactly coincident with the multiple and manufactured intensities of postmodern consumptionism. At this point, Grossberg's argument begins to resemble Stephen Pfohl's argument in *Death at the Parasite Café* about the incorporation of previously transgressive energies by ultramodernism (indeed Pfohl has a short, rather rickety account of Grossberg's analysis of the place of popular music). But where Pfohl's analysis can only crackle around the intricate circuitry of defeat, Grossberg's sensitivity the unevenness and mobility of cultural meanings and affects leads him to recognize in the rock formation a continuing principle of resistance or at least indigestibility.

Here, however, another irony prowls. Grossberg argues that, precisely because of the possibility of transgression it represents, and the reservoirs of intensity to which it gives access, the rock formation has been the subject of a concerted attempt at appropriation for the purposes of the political right. Grossberg notes that it is important for the new conservatism to appropriate rather than to attack rock music and its energies precisely because the former 'has been built on an affective politics, on sentimentality and passion, in which meaning and political positions have become secondary' (p. 269). The appropriation involved here is not a crude matter of translation or impersonation, as though the presidential press office were to sign up its own rock bands and insist on its own political agenda in the lyrics of their songs (though something of this kind is not completely unimaginable either). Rather, if I understand Grossberg's argument aright, it is an appropriation of something like the logic of intensity itself, since the new conservatism in the USA 'does not need to deploy specific commitments or beliefs, but it has to foreground the need to believe in belief, to make a commitment to commitment' (p. 271). Achieving control over the meaning and experience of intensity and desire makes it possible to depoliticize them, to disconnect affect from political interests or motivations. Far from being contained, channelled or regulated in the older, cruder forms of social discipline, affective intensity is now controlled precisely by being unfixed, by means of a heightened mobility which prevents affect from settling into any stable form of effectivity. Where earlier regimes of power worked by keeping us in our places, postmodern neoconservatism – and the advanced global capitalism which works its purposes through it – achieves the same effect by keeping us on the move. If all goes well for the new conservatism, the carceral society will become the evicted society, meaning will dissolve into feeling, the semantic will slide into the somatic and politics will be banalized into spectacle. The 'disciplined mobilization' of rock music is essential to this process:

> By rearticulating rock's structured mobility to a specific hege-monic struggle, it has constructed a different territorialization of everyday life. In this new apparatus of power, the homelessness of the rock formation is normalized. And more importantly, the rock formation's lines of flight are disciplined so that they can no longer point to another space. They must always return into everyday life, reterritorializing themselves without becoming lines of articulation. It is simply that their flight now has to be enclosed within the space of everyday life.
>
> (p. 296)

The picture that Grossberg projects here is only a whisker away from the wish-fulfilling defeatism of Stephen Pfohl and the Baudril-lard from whom he (Pfohl) draws so much. What distinguishes Grossberg's analysis from theirs is his continuing conviction that if analysis can explain social process, it can also evaluate it, and inter-vene to change it. The final section of Grossberg's study is a friendly but unflinching criticism of the failures of the cultural left either to acknowledge the successes of the right, or to engage with them. Central to this failure is a willingness to allow left critique to be disaggregated into the politics of identity, in which any actual or posited horizon of common interest risks being howled down as incipient fascism. Just as disabling, Grossberg believes, is the failure to acknowledge the importance of the affective in forming and sustaining political identification and purpose. Grossberg's fine, commanding study ends with a call for a left politics that would accept the challenge of imagining and forming an open or non-dominative totality, that would neither dissolve differences nor dissolve its own responsible authority in the idolatry of absolute difference. The achievement of Grossberg's book lies not just in the force of its analysis of contemporary conditions, nor even in the power of its political imagination, but in its exemplification of the very mode of attention to cultural life that would be necessary to such an open totality.

Birkbeck College, London

Lynne Pearce

Kathy E. Ferguson, *The Man Question: Visions of Subjectivity in Feminist Theory* (Berkeley: University of California Press, 1993), 236 pp., $40.00 (hardback), $13.00 (paperback)

Gerardine Meaney, *(Un)Like Subjects: Women, Theory, Fiction* (London and New York: Routledge, 1993), 255 pp., £35.00 (hardback), £11.99 (paperback)

Pam Morris, *Literature and Feminism* (Oxford: Basil Blackwell, 1993), 217 pp., £10.99 (paperback)

As we move into the 1990s it is perhaps unsurprising to discover that feminist theory, in particular literary and cultural theory, is still struggling to process the critical debates that emerged during the late 1980s. These debates, centring on the question of how to develop a feminist project which can combine attention to the historical and cultural specificity of different interest groups with a rigorous anti-essentialism, have become so intense that the majority of feminist authors now feel obliged to 'declare their position' each time they set pen to paper.

It is significant, for example, that all three of these volumes – although dealing with different textual referents and addressed to widely different audiences – are united by a theoretical anxiety which may be paraphrased as follows: how do we lay claim to a female subjectivity without falling prey to some species of essentialist thinking? And yet it is clear, too, why the same question keeps being asked: de-centring woman has, as the commentators in the late 1980s predicted, radically decentred feminism, and it is hardly surprising that, as a consequence, all those working in the field should find themselves in a metaphorical courtroom desperately searching for a line of argument persuasive enough to defend their particular theoretical position.

I will begin my review with an account of Kathy Ferguson's *The Man Question: Visions of Subjectivity in Feminist Theory* since it deals with the issues I have just introduced at a metatheoretical level. Despite its title, this book has really very little to do with masculinity except for the fact that the different feminisms Ferguson considers (identified here by the terms 'praxis', 'cosmic', 'linguistic') have each, in their different ways, displaced masculine (Hegelian) theorizations of subjectivity. Ferguson's own theoretical mission centres on a brave attempt to philosophize the polarization of 'genealogy' and 'interpretation' in current feminist epistemology, and then to suggest ways in which we might strategically utilize (but *not resolve*) the differences between the two.

Before evaluating her success in this project, some definition of terms is necessary: following Judith Butler, Ferguson employs 'genealogy' to refer to these theories focused on the 'deconstruction' of the category 'woman', and 'interpretation' to refer to those focused on articulations of women's experience. While most contemporary feminist critical practices (e.g. 'praxis', 'cosmic' and 'linguistic' feminism) are informed by *both* genealogical and interpretative tendencies, one or the other is usually dominant. Thus 'praxis feminism' (incorporating the various expressions of 'standpoint theory') is predominantly interpretative, and 'linguistic feminism' (incorporating French Feminism and American 'deconstructionists' such as Judith Butler and Gayatri Spivak) is predominantly genealogical.

Central to Ferguson's own philosophical negotiations is an attempt to reveal the falsity of the opposition between the genealogical and interpretative traditions within feminist theorizing. She illustrates repeatedly the way in which 'the deconstructive project is itself parasitical upon the claims it seems to unfound' (p. 27), and similarly how many feminist projects centred on women's experience are self-deconstructing. Beyond this evident hybridity at the level of praxis, moreover, Ferguson argues strongly – and here we return, once again, to her central thesis – that neither genealogy nor interpretation is, in itself, a sufficient basis for an effective 'feminist political theory' (p. 29). Deconstructive practices, while theoretically radical ('which strike[s] at the categories which allows sexism to exist', p. 29) leave the 'enormous [material] inequalities between men and women intact'

(p. 29), while interpretative practices are often blind to their own foundationalism. This statement of the current impasse within feminist theory is, in itself, hardly original, but Ferguson does offer some useful suggestions for how we might deal with the dilemma.

First, and most importantly, she is strongly resistant to attempts to 'resolve' the differences between the genealogical and interpretative projects: the political future of feminism depends rather on a frank acknowledgement of their competing and contradictory investments, and on the continued legitimacy and necessity of each. The only rhetorical/philosophical vehicle she believes capable of sustaining such contradiction is *irony* and this, combined with a commitment to coalition politics, becomes the touchstone of her political and theoretical agenda.

Ferguson's biggest obstacle in selling irony as a legitimate theoretical strategy is that it is perceived to be intrinsically opposed to political activism. Irony usually signals a lack of commitment 'one way or the other'. For Ferguson, however, a sense of irony is just what today's feminists need to *enable* them to act:

> Irony is a way to keep oneself within a situation that resists resolution in order to act politically without pretending that resolution has come.... Irony can be a public virtue for feminism when it enables political action that is both committed to its values and attentive to its incompleteness.
>
> (pp. 30–2)

The competing demands of genealogy and interpretation have become so acute and are so evidently irresolvable that irony is the only way in which we can cope with our shifting loyalties and investments:

> The tensions between longing for and being wary of a secure ontological and epistemological home, if handled ironically, need not be a source of despair; it can instead produce an appropriate humility concerning theory and an ability to sustain the contrary pull of continuing to want what cannot fully be had.
>
> (p. 35)

One of the strengths of Ferguson's book is that she offers plenty of concrete examples of how such irony can be used to mediate (but not resolve) the tensions between the different groups of theorists. This can be illustrated by reference to her chapter on 'Linguistic Feminism'. As I noted earlier, what Ferguson identifies as 'linguistic feminism' centres on the work of the French Feminists and the American genealogists. It 'emphasizes the power of discourse as an economy, that is, the power to produce and distribute opportunities and resources that make available or deny entry into various subject positions' (p. 121). This emphasis on the wholly discursive construction of the subject means 'Linguistic feminism has no patience at all with identity politics in either its praxis or cosmic forms' (pp. 126–7). Yet while Ferguson frankly admits her own alliegance to this genealogical camp, she is acutely aware, too, of the problems: if linguistic feminism 'counsels a vacation from subjectivity ... who is it, then, who is going on vacation?' (p. 130). In other words, how do we account for the 'identities' which, however fictitious, contradictory and provisional, remain a material/political experience for all of us? It is at this sort of philosophical impasse that Ferguson calls upon irony as a strategy which will enable us to sustain the logic of the genealogical project (which, following Foucault, urges us to interrogate the *construction* of subjectivity rather than the forms it takes) while at the same time acknowledging the solipsism and intellectual elitism of such an enterprise. Indeed, there are moments, she counsels, at which it is appropriate to regard the endlessly self-perpetuating discourses of deconstruction as a kind of kitsch: in the hands of the most skilful theorists the arguments are followed through with such tenacity as to resemble a sort of intellectual macramé; until, that is, you recognize the irony of this hermetic claim to 'truth'.

Ferguson's book ends with a chapter entitled 'Mobile Subjectivities' which, following in the footsteps of Judith Butler, Donna Haraway, Teresa de Lauretis, Gayatri Spivak, Denise Riley and Trinh Minh-Ha, makes a bid for the reconceptualization of subjectivity based on the principle that it is a chameleon skin to be inhabited differently at different times. As such, it is a model which brings together the principles of both the interpretative and genealogical traditions, inasmuch as identities are allowed to exist but not to become fixed. In lifestyle terms, this theory can be translated into what Ferguson describes as 'hyphenated identities': 'Hyphenated identities that range along particular axes of definition, such as used-to-be-working-class-now-professional, or divorced-mother-now-lesbian, mark the ordering trajectories across which mobile subjects roam as also in motion' (p. 161). Undoubtedly this is a formulation of subjective experience that demands the perspective of irony and good humour; both on behalf of those theorizing it *and* those living it! To be so provisionally situated is not necessarily an easy option. Indeed, an ironic awareness of this might cause us, on some occasions, to reject the theory of 'mobile subjectivity' altogether. It might be theoretically persuasive without being psychically or politically desirable. To lay claim to a single/stable identity might be more pragmatic. For Ferguson, however, irony allows this to be an option *within* a theory of mobile subjectivity: we can drop anchor at any point we choose.

In conclusion, I would recommend Ferguson's book as a lucid and thought-provoking intervention into the current debates on subjectivity, identity politics, and anti-essentialism. Her invocation of 'irony', while clearly part of the 'deconstructive' tradition of negotiating problematic philosophical issues through rhetorical devices (cf. 'parody', 'mimicry', 'masquerade'), is persuasive as a strategy that will enable us to 'act politically' without the promise of resolution or completion.

Gerardine Meaney's (Un)Like Subjects: Women, Theory, Fiction explores the question of subjectivity at a textual rather than an abstract, philosophical level and is unusual (and, I feel, successful) in using three contemporary feminist novelists (Doris Lessing, Muriel Spark and Angela Carter) to engage with and interrogate the 'Big Three' of French Feminism: Hélène Cixous, Luce Irigaray, and Julia Kristeva. Not surprisingly, Meaney's own engagement of the 'female subject' is via the mother–daughter relationship and, although it is nowhere explicitly stated, I think we might see her project as an attempt to reclaim the French theorists from the cruder accusations of matriarchal essentializing/myth-making that have been levelled against them.

This re-evaluation of 'the maternal' is achieved principally by textual readings (both fictional and theoretical) which challenge the more utopian accounts of oedipal and pre-oedipal relations. In Chapter 1 ('Between the mother and the Medusa'), for example, Meaney uses Cixous and Lessing to explore the role of the 'monstrous mother'. Her argument here is that while Cixous attempts to engage with, and hence *transform*, 'the territory of the Medusa, the mother, the monstrous enemy', Lessing rejects her and 'identifies with the hero' (i.e. the masculine principle) in order to 'write as something more' (p. 45). To this extent, Cixous's project may be seen to be more radical than Lessing's, although Meaney's section on 'The dark stranger' offers an interesting twist to the issue of gender identification in subject formation by proposing that many male literary heroes (e.g. Heathcliff in *Wuthering Heights*) may be *symbolically* female: the 'dark continent' of repressed sexuality and desire. Hence the possibility that authors, like Lessing, whose texts repeatedly offer their heroines salvation through the arrival of a 'dark stranger' (e.g. Thomas in *Landlocked*) might be confronting the Medusa in disguise.

In the chapter '(Un)like subjects', Meaney continues her 'degradation' of the mother-figure by reading Julia Kristeva's *Stabat Mater* (and Jane Gallop's reading of *Stabat Mater*) against Angela Carter's

novels. (I use the term 'degradation' here in the more positive, Bakht-
inian sense of 'bringing back to earth with the purpose of
regeneration'.) What she reveals is that both Kristeva and Carter
replace mythic/archaic constructions of motherhood with an alternative celebration of its fraudulence and trickery. In Carter's novel *Wise
Children* this 'fraudulence' is written into the plot via the disputed
maternity of Dora and Nora Chance, while the audacious trickery
and artifice of Fevvers in *Nights at the Circus* (and the obvious
question marks over her own parenting) may be seen as another
ironic comment on female 'authenticity': 'The Fraudian mother constructs herself through language, and the place where language fails'
(p. 158). Kristeva, meanwhile, signals deception through her textual
strategies. The fraudulence and duplicity of the 'mater' is reproduced
in the way she elects to write about her: to signal, indeed, the
impossibility of writing about her: 'Kristeva's use of the double columns is a sublime fraud. No reader will read both columns exactly
simultaneously. . . . The double columns signify the doubleness of
every text, the inextricable strands of poetry and analysis' (p. 153).

Alongside this 'degradation' of the maternal role through an
attack on its archetypal status, Meaney also connects Kristeva and
Carter in their refusal to see mother–daughter relations in terms of
an oppressively self-reproducing chain. Through their focus on the
'nothing natural' aspect of the connection, both writers promote a
vision of *discontinuity* which enables mother and daughter to relate
to one another as 'unlike subjects': 'It therefore dispenses with the
necessity of a mediation through the distant son and substitutes
the possibility of a relationship between (un)like subjects for that
between like objects' (p. 156). This is, I think, an interesting re-
reading of Kristeva via Carter which might offer subsequent readers
and critics a means of formulating less claustrophobic models of
mother–daughter relations.

Another aspect of Kristeva's theory that Meaney is interested in
is *the abject*. Defining abjection as 'the first separation of the subject
from that [i.e. the maternal body]' (p. 192), it is, for Kristeva, the
phase which re-figures and 'precipitates the process by which subject
and object take (their) place(s)' (p. 192), and recurs in adult life as
the (distressing) apprehension of an object who is 'opposed to I'.
Meaney's particular interest in the role of the abject in the construction of female subjectivity is its relationship to *the sublime*. Noting
the association of the two in Kristeva's *Powers of Horror* (1982),
Meaney goes on to argue for the way in which the subject's 'loss of
self' in another (a reflex typical of the sublime) is clearly a defence
against abjection: 'The ideal of the sublime in art testifies to its

residual desire not to separate' (p. 209). Where Meaney challenges Kristeva's configuration of the abject, however, is on the question of death: the conjunction of the abject and death 'is not really admitted into Kristeva's account' (p. 213). And once again it is a feminist novelist, Muriel Spark, who is called upon to expose this limit in Kristeva's own writing. For Spark's characters, instead of saving themselves from abjection through processes of sublimation disarmingly *embrace* it. Her novel, *The Hothouse by the East River*, for example, eschews all consolation: 'The abject–ideal is the substance of the novel: the absence of the ideal is its end' (p. 215). In this respect, Spark takes Kristeva's theory through to a conclusion that she herself evades.

In Chapter 3, 'History and woman's time', Meaney moves from the particulars of Kristeva's theories of subjectivity to a consideration of the relationship of *the maternal and history*. She writes:

> Two strands of thought have emerged in feminism with regard to maternity. One concentrates on maternity as exile from history, the other on the maternal as a powerful disruption of linear history from which women have been excluded. In general, Carter is more concerned with the perils and snares in which maternity confines femininity and Kristeva with maternity's challenging and subversive aspects.
>
> (p. 78)

Acknowledging this difference between these two writers, Meaney once again employs Carter's fiction to problematize French feminist ideals of an (alternative) 'monumental' and 'cyclical' time as inherently subversive. Carter's novels are as profoundly resistant to the notion of the 'eternal feminine' (as a time/space 'outside of history') as they are to the archaic status of 'the mother' *per se* ('If a woman takes time off from thinking, it seems, she is in danger of becoming a mother goddess' (p. 91)). This is not to say that the alternative conceptualizations of subjectivity associated with the maternal cannot be usefully employed to help us rethink history, but that we should not necessarily expect this to be a *utopian* alternative. While Kristeva, in 'Woman's time', speaks of the maternal as a 'space which can disrupt, traverse and transgress history' (Meaney, p. 99), Carter warns: 'The theory of maternal superiority is one of the most damaging of all consolatory fictions and women themselves cannot leave it alone, although it springs from the timeless, placeless, fantasy land of archetypes where all the embodiments of biological supremacy live' (p. 98).

In conclusion, then, it can be seen that Meaney's 'method' in

(Un)Like Subjects has been to use Carter, Spark and Lessing to challenge and displace the more utopian readings of mother-centred psychoanalysis that have come out of French Feminism. This is not to say that Kristeva, Cixous and Irigaray are guilty of matrophilia themselves (a good deal of Meaney's text demonstrates quite the reverse), but to acknowledge that this has been a tendency in followers (understandably) desperate for an alternative to phallocentric psychoanalytic theory. It should be acknowledged, however, that knocking the mother off her pedestal in this way does very little to lessen her significance. While Meaney's re-readings of Kristeva and Cixous may have the immediate effect of turning the 'good mother' into the 'bad', she remains 'Mother' nevertheless. Although Meaney never spells out her theoretical objective very explicitly (and this is my one real reservation with the book as a whole) it is clear that she is one of a large number of feminists for whom the future status of 'women's writing' (as a legitimate canonical category) will depend on a successful defence (or rewriting) of the principles of *écriture féminine*.

Another text which accounts for the difference and specificity of women's writing largely through its focus on French feminist theory is Pam Morris's *Literature and Feminism*. As one of the few books of literary theory *genuinely* targeted at an undergraduate audience, its inclusion of illustrative textual readings (to demonstrate 'theory in practice'), end-of-chapter summaries and student exercises, means that it has clearly been conceived (rather like Raman Selden's *Practising Theory and Reading Literature*) as a course-reader.

While such introductory volumes are vitally needed for teaching purposes, however, problems are emerging in the way students are making use of them. Although Morris's own text is, I feel, generally very successful in the way in which it explicates complex theory in a non-reductive way, the students themselves have an alarming capacity for 'simplifying' the concepts of Lacan *et al.* to such an extent that they become ludicrous. (It should be said that I write here from bitter experience since a volume of which I am myself a co-author (*Feminist Readings/Feminists Reading*, 1989) is now widely 'rehashed' – sometimes to the point of plagiarism – in essays and examination scripts around the country!). This obviously raises a difficult pedagogical point over to what extent we can or should 'spoon feed' our students such material, but I am equally aware of the absurdity of presenting them with unannotated 'original' material (Lacan or Kristeva in the raw, for example) or, indeed, of expecting the majority to cope with a more complex commentary like Meaney's. Despite the obvious pitfalls, I therefore believe we must be grateful for texts like Morris's (although I fear her 'summary points' might prove even more liable to travesty than our chapter conclusions in *Feminist Readings*!).

Morris's book is divided into two parts organized around the twin concepts of 'Literature' and 'Feminism' that she interrogates in the Introduction. While I am still not totally convinced by the rationale behind this structure (since both sections are inevitably concerned with both 'literature' *and* 'feminism', and a more obvious division – like Toril Moi's in *Sexual/Textual Politics* – would seem to be between Anglo-American and French feminism), the book does open by addressing the questions that the students must inevitably ask 'at the beginning' ('What is feminism? What does it mean to be a feminist? What is the purpose of feminist literary criticism? How can it affect the way we read?' (p. 1)), and steers its readers through some possible answers with appropriate skill and patience.

Part I, which I feel is the least successful in that it attempts to cover such a broad historical/theoretical sweep, is a basic introduction to 'feminist critique', Anglo-Americn 'gynocriticism', and the way in which feminism has challenged the literary canon. In these chapters Morris comments on some of the key proponents of feminist critique and gynocriticism (Kate Millett, Elaine Showalter, Sandra Gilbert and Susan Gubar, etc.), and incorporates some useful textual analysis to illustrate what each 'approach' involves. The third chapter ends with a judicious problematization of the limitations of these approaches, although this inevitably sets up the French Feminism focused upon in Part II as the more sophisticated reading practice, and one of the dangers of the book might well be to polarize the Anglo-American and French traditions and to overlook the fact that a great many of today's critics 'belong' to neither.

These concerns aside, however, the chapters on Lacan, Cixous, Irigaray and Kristeva offer an excellent introduction to key concepts and terminologies without being too overtly didactic. They also demonstrate how central a radical reconceptualization of subjectivity is to the feminist critic's attempt to specify the 'difference' of women's writing. In her readings of Cixous, Morris is especially good at demonstrating how the stylistic features of her writings are concomitant with her polemic. On this point she writes: 'For this reason, summarizing her arguments . . . not only simplifies what she is saying, it actually erases the main site of her provocation: her linguistic playfulness and, at times, her lyricism' (p. 128). My main concern with these commentaries, admirably lucid and detailed as they are (Morris is extremely careful in defining terms like the 'semiotic', leaving less room for student 'misreading' than many earlier commentators), is that they are nevertheless rather uncritical. Although each theorist *is* problematized, the discussion is nowhere near as hard-hitting, politically, as Toril Moi's account in *Sexual/ Texual Politics*.

Literature and Feminism ends with a chapter on 'Lesbian, black and class criticism'. Despite the obvious dangers of tokenism induced by grouping these three types of writing/criticism together, Morris moves sharply and sensitively through a number of the key debates and issues which problematize the relationship of 'minority' groups to the critical mainstream. What all three groupings of course share is a challenge to the essentializing/hierarchizing practices of mainstream feminist criticism. Equally, however, lesbian and black critics have had to face their own problems of essentializing identity-politics, and Morris brings the debates reasonably well up to date with discussions of the 'strategic identities' recommended by Bonnie Zimmerman, Gayatri Spivak and the theorists invoked by Kathy Ferguson (see above) in her chapter on 'Mobile subjectivities'. The section of the chapter dealing with class includes a brief but useful overview of the main tenets of poststructuralist literary marxism, and a suggestive exemplification of how an awareness of class specifics challenges some of the more utopian/idealistic representations of the maternal espoused by both French and Radical feminists.

The different audiences at which the three books I have reviewed together here are directed makes any comparative evaluation of them very difficult. For example, one would not expect an introductory text like Morris's to further debate about the theories with which she deals in the same way that Meaney's and Ferguson's do. As I indicated at the beginning of the article, however, the fact that all three authors are united – subtextually at least – in an attempt to define and defend an 'alternative' female subjectivity (that then supports an alternative 'feminine' writing practice) is an indication of the globalization of theoretical discourse that appears to have taken place. Despite the fact that we are often coming from very different disciplinary and political backgrounds, and despite the fact that we are working with very different textual referents, feminists the world over seem to be overwhelmed with the same problem of how to argue for the uniqueness of women's experiences/artistic practices when 'woman' herself has been so radically (and, indeed, so successfully) decentred. Since the future of feminism itself sometimes seems to depend upon our successfully coming up with an answer to this question, it is hardly surprising that, both at the level of metatheory (Ferguson) and pedagogy (Morris) it is never far away. Whether the rhetorical manoeuvres Ferguson *et al.* effect will, in the end, be an *adequate* answer remains to be seen. For while we may, as theorists, be able to convince ourselves that the 'de-centring of the category woman' is supportable if viewed 'ironically', many of us are already facing the more material institutional consequences of 'women's studies' being subsumed into 'gender studies' and 'feminist appointments' becoming 'gender appointments'. Much as I was per-suaded, therefore by the coolness of Ferguson's demand that we learn to live with ambiguity, another part of me wonders just how long we can really keep smiling.

Lancaster University

David Seed

Raymond Federman, *To Whom It May Concern: A Novel* (Boulder: Fiction Collective 2, 1991), 186 pp., $8.95 (paperback)

Raymond Federman, *Critifiction: The Way of Literature* (Albany: State University of New York Press, 1993), vii + 133 pp., $14.95 (paperback)

As a leading member of the Fiction Collective group and as coiner and proponent of the term 'surfiction', Raymond Federman has been associated for years with experimental fiction originating mainly from the USA. Federman, however, has had the advantage of being equally at home in French and Anglophone cultures. Reversing the direction of one of his mentors, Samuel Beckett, Federman left France, the country of his birth, at the end of the war after narrowly escaping deportation to the Nazi gas-chambers, and subsequently adopted American citizenship. His progress as a writer has doubled with an academic career mainly at SUNY–Buffalo, and Federman has been a consistent advocate for writers and critics to jettison the lingering traces of the expectations associated with fictional realism such as verisimilitude or a well-shaped story-line.

Federman has written in an autobiographical sketch: 'my life began in incoherence and discontinuity', and his novels can be read as a series of attempts to give authentic expression to that incoherence and discontinuity. Most of his works to date are thus autobiographi-cal in so far as they focus on different phases of a life which resemble his own. *Double Or Nothing* (1971) describes the experiences of a 19–year-old immigrant to America, and *Smiles on Washington Square* (1985) takes the serial story a step further with the young protagonist falling in love with a student from Boston. To label these works 'autobiographical' runs the risk of totally underplaying their playful formal complexities. Federman has repeatedly returned to a pun in his own name – 'featherman' or 'penman' – whereby it designates the very function of writing. When he names himself in his own texts Federman is therefore not simply trying to transfer life into art, but is creating different provisional selves which will be scrutinized as the narratives progress. Federman's fiction becomes introspective because it constantly demonstrates a postmodernist awareness of its own narrating procedures. Like the work of his friend and colleague Ronald Sukenick, it alternates between composing and dismantling fictions in ways which never allow the reader to forget that s/he is participating in a literary construct.

At the heart of Federman's work until quite recently has lain an absence related to the events of 16 July 1942 (subsequently described by him as his date of birth) when the young Federman hid in a closet while the rest of his family was carried off to the death-camps. This event was referred to by the symbols x-x-x because, as Federman has explained, 'these signs represent the necessity and the impossibility of expressing the erasure of my family.' In 1979 Federman broke that silence by publishing *The Voice in the Closet*, a monologue delivered by the composite voice of Federman's earlier creations which is contained in most editions by rectangular spatial designs. *To Whom It May Concern* follows on from *The Voice in the Closet* by moving closer to that primal scene. The narrative centres on the meeting between two cousins, an unnamed man who has gone to America and Sarah who has gone east to Palestine after the war. The claustrophobia of *The Voice in the Closet* now gives way to more positive and open possibilities as the boy emerges from confinement; and his search for refuge is replayed this time without isolation when the two cousins console each other in a cellar. Federman handles the potentially overwhelming pathos of these situations with great care by dramatizing points where verbal utterance breaks down. Sarah tries to tell her story to the boy but collapses in tears; at a later point in Palestine she breaks down again after shooting an assailant. Again and again Federman demonstrates the sheer fragility or inadequacy of words reaching into a silence which gradually becomes charged with potential meaning, whether it is the silence of those being herded on to trucks in 1942 or the void of the irrecoverable past. The male cousin later returns to his apartment but to no point. He is cut off from his own past which too has been erased metonymically by the erection of new buildings. And so the problem for the two cousins ultimately turns out to be absence not pain because 'their bodies bear no inscriptions of suffering since they escaped physical pain, hunger, and torture'. Lacking the tangible signs of scars or camp numbers, their bodies symbolically represent the blank page of their memories which they try to fill with circumstantial detail. It should already have become clear that this novel does not progress in any kind of linear order, but instead circles around this key event in the past, trying to articulate its significance.

Federman has recorded elsewhere that he learnt from Proust the following lesson: 'to write a novel is not only to tell a story, it is to confront the very process of writing a novel. Since the writer is always interrogating the creative process, he must be present some-how in the text.' Like Federman's other fiction, *To Whom It May Concern* is thus to an important extent a novel about writing a novel. It risks appearing provisional by dating its sections like entries in an author's diary and in that respect, unlike most modernist novels, records the labour of its own composition. The result is almost as if Steinbeck's *East of Eden* and *Journal of a Novel* had been conflated in one work, except that Federman's narrative stays in a preliminary phase. As a result the reader is drawn into a series of speculations about how the story might be told. Story, or more precisely plot, remains a matter of hypothesis, a possible way the book might develop. As in the fiction of Federman's postmodern contemporaries (Pynchon, Coover, Sukenick and others) means of creating continuity in the novel are introduced only to be questioned. Federman's alert-ness to genre as often as not shows itself in an anxiety to avoid clichéd patterns and he moves in and out of temporary story-lines, discarding one as melodrama or another as gratuitously sensational. His sense of being caught between narrative possibilities is written into the novel as a nervous expectancy in the two cousins who are both in transit. Without the awareness necessarily taking him any nearer to satisfactory narrative articulation, Federman expresses within the novel his determination to avoid 'neatly packaged stories'. Instead 'we must dig in to see where raw words and fundamental sounds are buried so that the great silence within can finally be decoded.' One analogue for this struggle is given in the main cousin's profession as sculptor, trying to bring form into being out of raw materials.

The proponents of postmodern fiction have sometimes assumed rather too easily that the metafictional dimension had no place within realism, but what, for example, could be more challenging to readers' habits than Thackeray's impish comments on narrating throughout *Vanity Fair*? What is different in a work like Federman's is the sheer extent to which composing replaces plot as the true focus of the narrative. It is the story of how to begin, which little by little shifts its concern to the problem of an ending. In between the two, narrative segments are projected as hypotheses, predictions or unsatisfactory excursions into other modes. One model for this procedure whom Federman acknowledges in the text is supplied by *Jacques le Fataliste* where Diderot side-steps many initial questions of information by framing his narrative as a dialogue located in textual space between Jacques who gives the *récit* of his adventures and his Maître, an older and wiser audience. Around these two speakers plays a third voice, that of the author.

Dialogue indeed is absolutely central to Federman's method. His title punningly combines formality with emotional engagement in a mode of address and throughout the novel he plays with different aspects of utterance as a reach outwards towards a respondent. *To Whom It May Concern* firmly puts behind it the solipsism of *The Voice in the Closet*. Federman drains off the potential privilege of narrating by subjecting his own drafts to scrutiny by members of his family. This constitutes an act of bonding in contrast with the separations referred to within the narrative. If erasure implies death the inscription of other voices in the text becomes a life-giving act and the text in turn becomes the spatial site for different voices to engage with each other, the projected reader's included. These dialogues operate simultaneously on different levels from author-to-reader, through father-to-children to a fictional correspondence between the two cousins. Partly they repeat the questioning of her young cousin by Sarah in the cellar who tries without result to understand the deportations. Partly the dialogue engages the reader in the emotionally draining process of composition. Federman can even learn from his own creations. Lying awake one night he 'sees' the cousins in a kind of mental cinema and imagines the man telling Sarah: 'One cannot give shape to sentiments, one cannot mold emotions into neat forms. They simply flow in the world.' Here the very impossibility of Federman's own novel is voiced; but, as usual in this work, there is always a countervoice which here rejects failure. The reader has to manoeuvre through these different possibilities which are never resolved. At the end of the novel the narrator has joined an imagined audience and nods off to sleep as the two cousins address each other. In its speculative energy *To Whom It May Concern* is the latest and most moving exemplification of a mode Federman has acknowledged in his own works: 'the governing tense of my fiction is indeed the conditional tense.'

Federman's new collection of essays, *Critifiction*, makes an ideal companion work to his latest novel since it establishes a theoretical and historical context for *To Whom It May Concern*. When he began the title essay for *Surfiction* (1975), an earlier version of which appears here, Federman refreshingly rejected the then fashionable clichés of the death of the novel although he has maintained a consistent position throughout his critical and fictional writing that the demise of realism must be acknowledged. It is a position that was shaped importantly by Federman's reading of Beckett, whose austere presence hovers over all the essays in *Critifiction* as a formative influence. One of Federman's earliest works was a study of Beckett, *Journey to Chaos* (1965), where he examined the progression not towards knowledge but towards uncertainty in the latter's fiction. The condition of epistemic doubt going hand in hand with the persistence of utterance (*The Unnameable*: 'Here all is clear. No, all is not clear. But the discourse must go on.') informs Federman's theoretical statements on the novel. On an analogy with 'surrealism' Federman coined the term 'surfiction' as a novelistic mode which 'challenges the tradition that governs it'. Without necessarily moving towards the minimalism of Beckett this fiction is subversive and self-scrutinizing: it will thus 'unmask its own fictionality'. Surfiction and postmodern fiction in general could here be seen as an extreme and explicit form of self-reflexive element which has persisted throughout the history of the novel. To include allusions to Diderot in his latest novel represents a way of signalling its formal pedigree and therefore of questioning its own novelty.

Federman demonstrates a shrewd awareness of literature as a institution maintained by publishers, key review periodicals and universities. When he examines the respective meanings of 'experiment', 'readable', and 'unreadable', he concludes, with due acknowledgement to Barthes, that the middle term denotes the reader's comfort as s/he is reassured within the familiar attitudes assigned by the prevailing culture. The New Fiction, by contrast, sets out to disturb these attitudes and to force the reader to re-examine the nature of literary consumption. The extent of this purpose rather than the purpose itself constitutes its novelty since even the great works of realism regularly incorporated such an element into their narratives. Consider, for example, George Eliot's brief discussion of authentic versus supposedly 'edifying' characterization at the beginning of Book Two of *Adam Bede*; or Dickens's famous comparison between melodramatic and realistic transitions in Chapter 17 of *Oliver Twist*. In both these cases, and many others could be cited, the reader is temporarily estranged from the fictional illusion and invited to examine the nature of textual pleasure in these works. The fiction which Federman is here promoting goes a considerable way further towards destroying illusion. He assimilates Michel Foucault's notion of 'heterotopia' where the work becomes a field of subversive energy, disturbing language itself. The consequences can be radical in the extreme. A text may change shape as it goes along (Sukenick); it may throw up so many plots as to fill the reader with paranoid uncertainty (Pynchon); or, as in Federman's earlier novels, the text may play games with typography and syntax, and so approach the condition of concrete poetry.

Federman rejects the myth of authorial originality. Probably borrowing his reversal from Barthes, he argues that language creates the author instead of vice versa. The question which his own novels repeatedly explore is: 'what does it mean to compose a text?' *To Whom It May Concern* continues this motif by ruminating on the circumstances of its own possibility. The result for the reader can involve a refreshing irreverence towards literary decorum, but it can also demand a new attitude to the reading process. For example, to describe Federman's fiction as 'autobiographical' can be both a truism and a misleadingly reassuring label. When discussing this issue he quickly disposes of the suggestion that we read novels to gain access to the author's life, but 'autobiographical' was used regularly in the nineteenth century to suggest a resemblance between first-person narratives and their supposed factual counterparts. Federman will have none of this. For him the past is an absence so final that paradoxically an author's autobiographical fictions become the most authentic articulations of himself. But then authenticity and origination are notions which Federman repeatedly questions. His ideal text, he states repeatedly, is one which interrogates itself, and so correspondingly his ideal reader must be ready to question the nature of the novel itself. Although Federman never composes works with central enigmas or buried codes à la Eco, he is well aware of the demands he is making on the reader. Hence the appropriate title for his novel. In *The Human Use of Human Beings* Norbert Wiener has described 'to whom it may concern' as an 'undirected message spreading out until it finds a receiver'. The establishment of the Fiction Collective in the USA and the virtual impossibility of obtaining Federman's novels in Britain both bear ironic testimony to the precarious nature of his own reception.

In broad terms Federman's description of postmodernism approaches quite closely that of Fredric Jameson. For both writers the movement was essentially an anti-hierarchical one where genres collapsed together; where plagiarism ('play-giarism' as Federman calls it) refuses to recognize the status of earlier works, particularly the classics (as witness Kathy Acker's *Great Expectations* and *Don*

Quixote); and where works insistently reveal their own inauthenticity. If genres do collapse together there is no reason at all why criticism should not take on some of the properties of novels, and that is why Federman has entitled his key essay 'Critifiction'. In keeping with his perception that no utterance is ever final but situates itself within a continuous public dialogue, he offers a collage of thoughts rather than a continuous essay. 'Critifiction' thus joins the postmodern literature of fragments which would include William Burroughs's *Naked Lunch* (seen by Federman as a key work in the turn towards postmodernism) or J. G. Ballard's *Atrocity Exhibition*.

Although Federman acknowledges the variety of discourses which play within the culture of any historical moment he tends to understate the political power which such discourses could carry. Bakhtin's instance on the novel's special openness to 'heteroglossia' would be at least congenial to Federman's account of how American fiction has developed over the last forty years. His explanation runs as follows. After the emphasis on existential fiction in the 1940s the following decade was characterized by a tacit agreement between writer and state. The surface complicity screened a latent sense of absurdity which found its expression in the early 1960s as public distrust of official statements grew. The catalyst of the credibility gap particularly during the Vietnam War led to a fiction of black humour which for Federman marks the first phase of postmodernism. The late 1960s and 1970s saw a fiction making an even more radical use of language and anti-illusionist techniques. Finally, and the change was signalled symbolically by the death of Beckett in 1989, we have entered a new phase where the disruptive energies of postmodernism have run their course and where the term itself has now become routinely applied to quite diverse fields of contemporary American life. As a survey of main currents in American fiction Federman is undoubtedly right to see the period around 1960 as a turning-point. To take only one example, comedy offered a means of revision. Bruce Jay Friedman and Jerome Charyn as well as the more notorious Philip Roth undermined the usual solemnity of the Jewish-American novel and Terry Southern used an elegant erotic humour to attack the prudishness of the 1950s. But the latter decade may well turn out to be a more complex and varied period than a label like the 'tranquil-lized fifties' might suggest. In particular the astonishing surge of creativity in post-war American Science Fiction must be assimilated into this account. The latter operated as a none too covert means of social criticism throughout the 1950s, attacking the materialism of the new consumer culture and the lunacy of the nuclear arms race. A particularly striking development of recent years, and one not necessarily limited to American fiction, has been the gradual convergence of Science Fiction and other fictional modes; a change so striking that in one of the most startling examples of revisionist hyperbole Fredric Jameson has described Science Fiction as *the* literary medium of postmodernism. It is one which Federman has himself tried out in *The Twofold Vibration* (1982) which describes an old man about to be deported to another planet on New Year's Eve 1999, so it is a pity that he only gives the genre passing mention in these essays. That being said, the essays in *Critifiction* are still to be recommended as conclusive refutation of the prejudiced assumption that novel and arresting theoretical positions have to be expressed in complex inaccessible prose. These lucid formulations make *Critifiction* an important contribution to the public discussion of postmodernism.

Liverpool University

Andrew Edgar

Michael Taussig, *Mimesis and Alterity: A Particular History of the Senses* (London and New York: Routledge, 1993), xix + 299 pp., £35.00 (hardback), £12.99 (paperback)

The Cuna Indians of Columbia use wooden carved figures, called *nuchukana*, in curing rituals. These figures are remarkable, in part, because they are always representations of Europeans, wearing modern western suits and hats. The most distinctive cultural item of the Cuna is the *mola*, an appliquéd shirt front sewn by Cuna women. Yet these traditional artefacts now incorporate such western images as mousetraps, lunar modules and the HMV logo of a dog listening to a phonograph.

In 1832, the crew of *The Beagle*, including Charles Darwin, made its first contact with the people of Tierra del Fuego. Darwin recorded the fact that the Fuegians were 'excellent mimics', specifically in their capacity to reproduce the coughs and yawns, the pallid faces, and the language of the western sailors. Thus, in part, was the savage to be differentiated from the civilized sailor; except that the sailors also commanded impressive powers of mimicry (not merely in the play of dance, but also in the ability to communicate with the Fuegians through pantomimes of sleep, encampment and sun rise). Yet, from the western viewpoint at least, alterity is maintained in so far as the sailors mimed to the savages as adults do to children, so that mimesis becomes a component of civilized control over the savage. Fortunately, as the Cuna examples show, the savages can mimic back, seemingly reasserting their power over that which is other, through copies of it, so that boundaries (between savage and civilized, between male and female, between self and other) are destabilized.

Through an engaging montage of such images, Taussig evokes the mimetic (which is inevitably inculcated with alterity) as that which at once grounds and disrupts culture. The mimetic is 'the nature that culture uses to make second nature' (p. 70). In this key phrase Taussig expresses his central engagement with the paradox of the apparent intractability and yet arbitrariness of social conventions. He seeks, by leading the reader to reflect on the mimetic, to facilitate our perception of, and reaction to, the mischief, and indeed desperation, of our normal dwelling place between the 'real and the really made-up' (p. xvii).

At the core of Taussig's analysis is the imputed subversive potential within otherwise hypostatized images. Diverse and intriguing illustrations are given. While the mimetic faculty may involve embodiment, as with the Cuna carvings, and thus the fixing of the mimic's power over the mimicked person or object, it also involves a disembodying moment, often manifest in the burning of an image in order to release or transfer its power. A Cuna medicine man would burn photographs of western consumer goods, in order to spread the ashes about the patient's house. The souls of the goods, realized in burning, would, like a giant shopping emporium, distract evil spirits.

A parallel is drawn between this practice and Walter Benjamin's account of the shock effect of advertising, in order to suggest that even fetishized commodities are inherently subversive. They have a 'phantasmogorical potential' of which advantage may be taken (p. 29). Yet it is precisely this attempt to theorize the moment of resistance in mimesis that is most problematic. The two key theoretical chapters of the book (the second and third) present, appropriately enough, a montage of images of Benjamin's accounts of the mimetic faculty, photography and Surrealism. The montage technique, which to a greater or lesser extent governs the structure of the whole book, does indeed serve to destabilize the images presented, forcing the reader to reflect upon the certainties that they bring to the reading of both the book and the other cultures that it mimics. Yet there is a deliberate superficiality, or under-theorization, in this technique.

Taussig acknowledges that he is concerned with surfaces, not depths (p. 251). He delights in Balzac's notion of photography as the capturing upon the photographic plate of a membrane from the original object (p. 21). Yet this superficiality is identified with a physiognomy, and thus with the reading of depths from the surface. At this point, crucially, Taussig appeals to what I suspect is a misreading of Adorno. He suggests that Adorno saw the mimetic faculty as providing an immersion in the concrete (p. 254). While Adorno does indeed appeal to the mimetic more fundamentally than most commentators suggest, Taussig oversimplifies the complex constellations within which Adorno always deploys the term. Crucially, the mimetic is not to be divorced from the disciplined intellectual activity of the mind or spirit. For Taussig, the mere shock of the image is enough to disrupt the social convention. For Adorno, such shocks can equally well blind us to our continuing implication in oppressive practices. Taussig's misreading is most notable in the way in which he dismisses Adorno's criticism of Benjamin, to the effect that Benjamin fails to guard against the absorption of his own work into the very commodity structure that he opposes (p. 29).

Taussig wants to maintain that the mimetic faculty gives the mimic power over their object. (Thus might a non-western culture subvert its colonial other.) Yet the nature and efficacy of this power goes unanalysed. Paradoxically, this is both a failure and a success of the book. As Taussig offers me various images of Cuna healing, or a search for 'White Indians', I (a 'westernized' reader) want to know if the healing 'really' worked, or if there 'really' were White Indians, and at once I am made to feel guilt and self-awareness at my presumption, and my inability to cope when my normal space between the 'real and the really made-up' is questioned. But equally, when I am told that mimesis is a source of power, I still inquire into the efficacy of this power. More precisely, I wonder if I should be satisfied at a blanket account of mimesis, as an impossible yet necessary, and everyday, affair (p. 129). Adorno might respond that this naturalistic image of the mimetic inculcates it with repression, precisely because as soon as we can no longer ask about the difference between essence and appearance, reality and image, the real structures of power may be left unquestioned and unchallenged beneath mere images of freedom.

University of Wales, Cardiff

Sabina Sharkey

Brendan Bradshaw, Andrew Hadfield, Willy Maley (eds), *Representing Ireland: Literature and the Origins of Conflict, 1534–1660* (Cambridge: Cambridge University Press, 1993), 235 pp., £35.00 (hardback)

In their introductory chapter, Hadfield and Maley suggest that, in the early modern period, English representations of Ireland were more often than not representations of England, with Ireland providing a locus of identity formation *and* anxiety. Tracing the political aspirations and tensions through the language of Anglo-Irish relations, they stress the importance of humanist skills for all parties there in an era of competing vernaculars, expanding literary markets and emergent colonial culture. The familiar problematic terms, kingdom/colony, old and new English are considered and their political referents are well discussed. They show how a term such as 'native', when explored etymologically by two dialogically opposed groups, can provide rhetorical ammunition for diverse political interests. One advocate, Sir John Davies (1569–1626), Attorney General of Ireland, argues that since the derivation signifies 'belonging to the land' and the land now belongs to the English Crown, then the people too are properly bound to English subjection. By contrast, O'Flaherty, in a text which was of great importance to the emergent Catholic national identity, *Ogygia* (1685), uses the same Latin etymology to confirm the primacy of the indigenous relation to the territory and thereby to confirm a continuity and status, a nationhood, which resisted the attempt to subject a people to the Crown. The question of whether Ireland is represented as an alternative to or an extension of English society is posed by Hadfield and Maley, in relation to issues of text transmission and censorship, patronage, economic activity and government. In the latter case the volatility of Irish political culture is neatly encapsulated in their query as to whether the Vice-Royalty in Ireland was a representation of the English Crown or an alternative to it. Such questions bring to mind the fortunes of a range of government administrators, Essex, Spenser or Strafford. The editors' view that Ireland to England was as much hammer as mirror in the early modern period is certainly supported by the concern among English governors in Ireland up to 1641 that a process of degeneration was causing the English to approximate towards an Irish identity.

Many of the essays in the collection are excitingly revisionist. Gillingham, sceptical of the supposed division between 'medieval' and 'Renaissance' modes of perception, argues instead for their continuity in terms of representations of Ireland where he views the fundamental shift in English representations occurring in the twelfth and not, as is often suggested, in the sixteenth century. Again issues of terminology are pertinent here, and he argues that the mistaken usage of the term 'Norman' to refer to the early invaders of Ireland facilitates an imposed discontinuity between the early invaders and the sixteenth-century colonizers. The reluctance of modern historians to use the term English flies in the face of contemporary narrative sources where the invaders are referred to as Saxain, Sassanaiq or Anglos. Gillingham is not a little irate that editors and commentators who translate these terms as 'English' then continue in their own commentaries to refer to this group as Normans (a practice which may owe something to a very different revisionism which affected Irish historians from the late nineteenth century until recently). Furthermore, he sees the related reluctance to recognize the era of Henry II as a turning-point in Irish history as inevitably distorting our understanding of sixteenth-century colonial activity in Ireland. For readers of sixteenth- and seventeenth-century discourses on Ireland, this is a persuasive argument since the invocation of Henry as an exemplary reforming conqueror, authorized by the terms of the Laudabiliter, is most frequently invoked as the origin point and legitimating precedent for current efforts.

In Bradshaw's excellent essay on Geoffrey Keating's *Foras Feasa ar Eirinn (A History of Ireland)* (1634), Keating's emphasis on Henry and the Laudabiliter is viewed as of central importance. Bradshaw offers an elegant revisionist reading of Keating's work. Not so much an antiquarian exercise, this carefully wrought vindication against a tradition of denigration by English commentators is viewed as a counter-Reformation humanist text. Keating stresses the authority of ancient sources and is philologically exact, rhetorically inventive and above all 'present-centred' in expounding them. The exigencies of that present prompts Keating to construct, from the lore of the early history of Ireland, an origin legend for a Counter Reformation Catholic Ireland. Again terminology is invoked to adumbrate political change, the hostility of the nua Ghaill (new English) for the sean Ghaill (old English) contributes to the emergence of a new congruent identity grouping of old English and 'mere' Irish, who together are referred to as Eireannaigh (Irish). As the latter term suggests, a proto-nationalist consciousness is invoked here and Bradshaw demonstrates how Keating asserts and assists the same. Most persuasive is his demonstration of how, by careful reading of the Laudabiliter, Keating shows that the normal constitutional consequences of conquest were pre-empted, rather than, as sixteenth- and seventeenth-century English writers would have it, endorsed.

Carlin and Maley continue this radical revisionism. Maley, assessing the impact of Spenser's *View* on Milton and his contemporaries, proposes that, contrary to the established view (see Hill, Hughes, etc.), it is precisely the estranged radicals who exhibit the most fervent commitment to a politics of plantation. Carlin clinches this point in her cogent analysis of the role of the English Independents in the Cromwellian re-conquest of Ireland. During the crucial years 1649–51, the Independents negotiated a dilemma, namely, how to reconcile 'an ideology of individual rights and liberty with the degradation of a particular section of humanity'. Their solution moved them away from a religious deliberation of Irish circumstances to a reiteration of the familiar discourse of barbarism. Concurring with Canny and Quinn that this anthropological discourse placed them within a tradition of negative representation active from the Elizabethan period, Carlin also indicates how they further developed it. By stressing the unreformability, the incorrigibility of the Irish, the rationale for their permanent disarming and subjection was established. This ideology, alongside their defence of Rule by Conquest, positions the writings of this radical group of Independent figures within a mainstream of English colonial thought.

For any reader interested in early modern Ireland this is an excellent collection although not without flaws. The volume offers a comprehensive and useful chronology prefacing the essays, and Morgan's scholarly overview of the career of Tom Lee refers to Myer's analysis of the sub-genre of 'The Elizabethan-Jacobean essay on Ireland', often reform treatises, reiterating their four defining characteristics before making the case for more exact readings of specific groups of texts such as position papers. So to find Kavanagh in 'The fatal destiny of that land: Elizabethan views of Ireland' referring to 'the genre of Elizabethan discourses of Ireland', and then drawing heavily on source texts from outside the Elizabethan period (Rich, Moryson and Davies) to display the 'Elizabethan' view, is surprising. In a book dedicated to investigating representation, her relation to rhetoricity is unclear. At the outset she notes that the account of Irish card players sufficiently addicted to the game to gamble not just their possessions but their very sexual organs, apart from being in her view amusing, is one of a number of 'extraordinary tales' narrated for specific affect. The rhetorical affect of this material she sees as promoting a process of 'reformation' of the Irish by the English 'who hoped to bring the Irish finally under the Crown's domination'. At the end of the essay she returns to the anecdote:

> Our modern sensibilities rightly cringe at the eradication of indigenous social and political structures, but to the sixteenth-century Englishman in Ireland, the lack of recognisable categories defied reason and the need for colonialism was unquestioned. Nothing good could come from the disorder associated with most things Irish. The imposition of English structures seemed the only viable answer. Tragically, for many colonial representatives, this

was only possible if much of the Irish population were moved or killed.

The strip poker players introduced at the beginning of this essay would undoubtedly still be gambling at its close if it were possible. Their story suggests that the Irish have lost the ability to discriminate between articles that matter and those that can be discarded when the betting gets out of hand. This blindness to the evaluative difference normally found between nail clippings and privy members indicated to English observers that the Irish needed to be overseen for their own good.

Had the need for colonialism been as unquestioned as she suggests, then the need for a promoting rhetoric becomes less clear. Of this type of representation she previously noted that it resonated with the 'exaggeration of political expediency'. But here she seems to suppress any awareness of colonial rhetoric, in order to reproduce it. Colonial intervention is represented as a form of benevolent protection, and according to this logic, the subjection which prevented Irish males from willingly castrating themselves had as a tragic side effect the outcome of moving or killing them instead. She cites Barnaby Rich frequently, yet has overlooked his presumably rhetorical advocacy of the wholesale castration of the Irish populace as a mode of colonial control. To invoke Spenser as one who 'loved the countryside and hoped for peace' is an established if surprising representation but her belief that in the *View* he merely succumbed to sensationalism is unpersuasive. She illustrates the latter opinion by quoting the episode wherein the foster mother of Murrogh O'Brien, in her grief at his execution, drinks blood from his severed head. What she seems not to consider is that this account is given by Irenaius in the context of an exposition on Irish Scythianism and as a further example of the unpleasant Gaulish customs of the same. Far from random sensationalism, there is a discourse of ethnicity framing the representation of the Irish in Spenser's text which might merit recognition.

Overall this is a collection that admirably fulfils the high ambitions outlined in the editors' introduction. It ably tackles the relations between literature and the origins of the conflict and is essential reading for those interested in early modern Ireland.

University of Warwick

Christa Knellwolf

Joseph Graham, *Onomatopoetics, Theory of Language and Literature*
(Cambridge: Cambridge University Press, 1992), xiii + 311 pp., £35.00
(hardback)

In his book *Onomatopoetics* Joseph Graham draws on studies of the
human brain in order to argue for the viability of a certain literary
theory. He claims that there is an inherent link between the structural
organization of the sign and the thought process informing it. The
title invokes the figure of speech 'onomatopoeia', which describes
the reproduction of a non-linguistic noise by the human voice. But
although the existence of onomatopoetic words might suggest that
the relation between the linguistic and the non-linguistic noise is a
'natural' one, onomatopoetic words are still subjected to the linguistic
sounds realized in the language of some particular cultural community, as the fact that the self-same rooster crows differently in
different languages illustrates. Apart from that each language contains
only a fraction of all the sounds (phonemes) which occur world-
wide.

Graham adopts the thesis of Noam Chomsky that the linguistic
faculty is physiologically preconditioned, which entails that both the
generation of language and its interpretation is a congenital faculty.
The argument that language is innate, whose philosophical implications Chomsky takes over from Descartes, supports the point of
view that language is natural. According to the theory which Chomsky formulated the child is not born with language but with the
ability to acquire any existing human language. It possesses what he
calls a mental programme which ensures that the structures relevant
to the language to be learned are recognized and selected to form a
mental representation of the mother tongue. The existence of this
unconscious linguistic knowledge then makes it possible to decide
whether an utterance is well formed.

The idea of mental programmes belongs to the view that a
universal language inspires the origination of all (human) languages,
hence that a universal language exists as an abstracted version of
every natural language. The only difference between the theory
of mental programmes and that of a kind of collective linguistic
subconscious is that the former relies on structures that are materially
present in the brain, although it is unclear how objectively provable
they are. This probably explains why Graham's usage of the term
'brain' (which embraces the concept of 'mind') is fuzzy and confused.

For example he says that 'Both infants and animals can think, though neither can talk. And humans can think alike, while talking differently. All it takes is a separate and different language of thought' (p. 115). Passages like this one mix up different topics; they blur the conceptual framework and show his carelessness in dealing with claims that cannot be proved. While being hostile to empirical studies, he is happy enough to take on board claims which originate out of a homespun intuition of how meaning works in everyday life. But although he argues his theory both too carelessly and too dogmatically, it contains a challenging potential for the project of establishing a relatively objective literary theory.

In spite of the biologically oriented argumentation, the thought that there is one universal language, of which all existing languages are a mirror image, sounds Platonic. And indeed Graham's argument starts with the language theory propounded in Plato's *Cratylus*. This dialogue concerns the question whether the meaning of words or names is natural or cultural (the Greek term 'onoma' contains both meanings and suggests that words are names for things). Graham focuses on Socrates' solution that 'some names are conventional while others are natural' (p. 9). In the interpretation of Socrates' compromise Graham distinguishes between a semantic and a syntactic meaning. He relates the syntactic component to the possibility of expressing meaning, for which reason it is a priori and natural, while claiming that the semantic component is subjected to the demands of convention and therefore arbitrary. Thus the reading of Plato is a preparation for the contrast between Saussure's semantic and Chomsky's grammatical theories.

Graham chiefly attacks Saussure's understanding of language as a system of differences. Since there is no logical connection between any given sound sequence (the signifier) and the mental representation behind it (the signified), on the level of lexical semantics, the relation between the formal linguistic concretization and the mental image which it represents is arbitrary. As literary theorists took up Saussure for their own purposes, they extended the applicability of arbitrariness to the general field of signification. A result of this is the claim that since an utterance (be it one in philosophy or literature) is language, it is subjected to the law of arbitrariness and therefore cannot have any claim to truth. In order to refute this idea Graham launches an attack on Saussure because he only looked at the relation between the signifier and the signified. Moreover he argues convincingly that Chomsky's grammatical theory, which focuses on the relation between signifiers, is better suited as the basis for a theory of meaning, but the criticism aimed at Saussure is excessive and simplistic.

Graham focuses on Chomsky's claim that deep structures underlie concrete utterances in order to argue that meaning is generated according to a system. He elevates what Chomsky called mental programmes into a language of thought, called Mentalese. Thus he says, 'Unlike English and all the others, Mentalese is not a language that you learn. The language of thought is innate' (p. 107). To call these deep structures a language is however problematical since from the point of view of cognitive linguistics it is still very much a matter of conjecture how the brain works. This means 'Mentalese' is a model for how the physiological organization co-operates in order to produce a language. Chomsky himself has never gone so far as to talk of a congenital universal language. What he calls *universal grammar* relates to the capacity of the human brain to construct any natural human language. For him speaking is not a matter of projecting a pre-existing mental language but it is a case of possessing a mental system which can, by recognizing patterns that are vital for the linguistic system, establish a language-generating mechanism. For him only the ability to select the right patterns is innate. This means Chomsky's model is by far more abstract, although it is still a variant of the Platonic, or Cartesian, notion that the practically spoken language is an imitation of 'another' language. In spite of the fact that it regulates the production of language, it is never accessible because the property of being language intervenes in the analysis of the language-generating principle. Therefore the biologically based argument cannot escape the fact that the understanding of the controlling system of language always has to be mediated by language, which easily leads to the conclusion that everything is language. So instead of supporting his search for objective criteria of categorization, the thesis of a mental language can just as well say that every utterance is a reflection of Mentalese and therefore possesses equal claim to accuracy and objectivity.

Graham's major argument in his search for constraints to the seeming arbitrariness of interpretation draws on Jerry Fodor's model of a modular structure of the mind; although he suppresses Fodor's admission that his theory is in fact 'a thought experiment'.[1] The term module is taken from computer science and denotes a self-contained sub-unit. A modular system, as postulated here, therefore depends on the idea that the brain consists of a range of units with specified tasks, such as, apart from basic abilities like that of balancing the body against gravitational force, the senses and language.

When Fodor, in collaboration with Chomsky, speaks of

modularity, he distinguishes the linguistic function from all other mental functions. Since his study was carried out in a research community interested in artificial intelligence, his model is primarily concerned with the possibility of categorizing language in such a way that it can be reproduced by a machine. This means that the Chomskyan claim of language being innate can lend itself to an understanding of language as a mechanical function. Thus Graham says, 'The mechanism of speech perception is modular; it works fast and it works automatically, like a reflex which gets triggered or immediately activated' (p. 152). To look upon the brain as a computer has become fashionable, but to reduce language, which is still complex beyond comprehension, to the very basic level of a reflex, pushes the comparison to a machine to an extreme degree. Then there is the further problem that Graham wants to subscribe to an extremely mechanistic view of the human being while adhering to the idea that literature teaches us by force of example (cf. p. 189). Since everyday conversation suffices for the acquisition of language, the purpose of literature cannot be to teach language, but behaviour. If we are however simply machines – indeed such simple machines that it is possible for us to comprehend ourselves in the same sense as the comparatively simple computers which we construct – there is no reason why we should behave in any particular way. On the other hand, if he reduces the socio-historical contextual dimensions of language to mechanistic forces, it is doubtful whether the conceptual range of the metaphor permits him to make a statement at all. The problem lies in the very fact of comparing, in the force of the metaphor. Undoubtedly an aura of objectivity clings to the natural sciences, so that the statement that the brain is a machine may be no more than a performative act of celebrating the idea that it is finally possible to gain access to an objective understanding of ourselves.

Graham's major focus is the interpretation of literature. When he talks about the implications for literature he claims that, following the example of the linguistic theorists, it is necessary 'to go mental and modular. That is, to consider literature as a product of the mind and then to compare it with others like language' (p. xiv). The natural sciences have geared us towards accepting the view that the brain (or the mind) directs all 'intelligent' processes of the human being. But how is it possible to distinguish between different products of the mind and specifically to differentiate between literary and non-literary language as an effect of biological specification? It is generally accepted now that different faculties are located in different areas of the brain. Concerning language, several 'linguistic' areas have been detected, and not all of their functions have been explained.

Language is not one self-contained unit but consists of different parts involved in the process of encoding and decoding meaning. Then it is connected to several other areas of the brain necessary for the reception and the production of sounds and written symbols (so among other things acoustic and visual abilities are indispensable). For the co-ordination of thought the different cognitive fields have to be connected and therefore it is problematic to demarcate the individual areas too narrowly. A complicating aspect is that the connections have to be extremely intricate in order to be efficient, and that co-ordination would be unfeasible without transmission of information, which is indeed a further form of language, which moreover embraces the whole mental apparatus.

This excursus into the anatomy of the brain yields the information that the brain is structured according to a hierarchic architecture, and that there are high-level processes which control low-level processes. Fodor distinguishes between modular and central faculties, the central ones being unencapsulated and therefore capable of a kind of analogical reasoning.[2] In that sense it seems to be possible to distinguish between a subject-specific, strictly ordered way of perceiving the world and one which is not limited to any strict mode of categorization. What the distinction into modular and central processes describes is that thoughts are constructed by different kinds of mental work. But the model cannot be used to distinguish between different text types. Nor does it make sense without taking into consideration that language has to be used to categorize language. Furthermore, arguing for the possibility of transferring structures (figuratively) to all areas of linguistic usage undermines the task of finding (objective) categories.

With regard to literary theory Graham starts off with an analysis of aesthetic effects and leads up to Paul de Man's statement concerning the impossibility of theory. Aesthetics is supported via the relationship between seeing and understanding, which means that Graham looks upon metaphor as being central because it transforms an abstract idea into a form that is graspable for sensual perception. This means figures of speech are understood as presenting an alternative way of understanding, of giving the brain the abstract idea alongside its translation into a code that is aimed at the senses. The conclusion drawn from the existence of different forms of representation is that different ways of parsing them must be involved, and that the brain must be capable of recognizing that several channels of informational transmission are involved. In a further move Graham argues that the brain must be able to recognize the presence of different points of view in a theoretical argument. Although Graham's way of relating these differences to the language Mentalese does not explain them, he is still right that we can tell whether an argument jumps from one order of logic to another. Or, in his terms, a faculty of non-categorized analogical thinking can be aware of leaps between categories.

When he concentrates on de Man's notion that theory can only confirm the impossibility of theory, Graham says that 'the basic issue turns on the possibility of one being certain about uncertainty, or at least having sufficient evidence concerning insufficient evidence. For that to be, there has to be a difference in modes of manifestation or representation' (p. 275).[3] The very possibility of reflecting on argumentative weaknesses of our language, hence of our cognitive faculties, demonstrates that there is a mental level at which it is possible to reach absolute certainty. Graham therefore concludes that a viable literary theory should recognize that the brain is capable of different degrees of certainty, and especially that it is capable of reflecting back on itself. Although it may indeed never be able to come up with any final insight as to what meaning is, it can still reject solutions which are manifestly wide of that goal.

The most interesting aspect of Graham's literary theory concerns the attack on relativism from within these imputed linguistic structures. However, he tries to move from absolute relativism to absolute certainty and the attempt is made to set up modularity as a unified, all-encompassing theory. Still, it yields the useful insight that a number of systems have to co-ordinate in order to produce meaning; and the overlapping of different structures may then be a way of eliminating a range of random associations. For the interpretation of literary texts (or of any feature of the 'world') it is not necessary to know which mental mechanism is responsible for which information, but only that there are different kinds of knowledge. The concept of modularity as taken from the observation that the brain works according to the principle of division of labour, confirms the claim that understanding is impossible without categorization. On the other hand the notion that linguistic styles correspond to mental sub-modules is an unfeasible extrapolation from the theory of modularity. It only makes sense if it stays aware that it cannot explain more than that there is a way of ordering language and thought by means of loosely demarcated possible ways of expressing oneself, and that there are no clear-cut borderlines.

Stanley Fish's notion of self-consuming artefacts also receives particular attention in Graham's study. Fish moves away from the text as the place where meaning is located and, as the title of his recent publication of essays, *Doing What Comes Naturally*, indicates, understands the interpretation, or the reception, of a work as its meaning. As Fish formulates it, 'Analysis in terms of doings and happenings is ... truly objective because it recognises the fluidity, "the movingness", of the meaning experience because it directs us to where the action is – the active and activating consciousness of the reader.'[4] Graham takes this up and reformulates it as follows: 'the very sequence of experience in reading forms the substance of meaning. . . . In a word, the act of parsing is part of the meaning' (p. 260). But Graham goes beyond saying that meaning originates at the moment of decoding it, hence that it is exclusively a product of the consciousness of the reader, as Fish does. Apart from that Graham attacks Fish's undifferentiated relativism, which works according to the principle that the reader somehow intuitively knows how to react (what to *do*) when confronted with a text. Graham's argument against Fish is that the range of one's reactions is limited and that they have to correspond to a certain preconditioned pattern.

Unfortunately Graham does not engage in his critique of Fish with a view to actually setting up an alternative literary theory. Otherwise he might have come up with a hermeneutic theory of reading which takes account of both the text and the response of its readers. Graham strongly rejects the extremes of, on the one hand, exclusively focusing on the text, as in W. K. Wimsatt's notion of the 'verbal icon', and, on the other, of concentrating exclusively on reader-response. He foregrounds the idea that text as well as any reaction to it follows rather rigid structures. But how they interconnect in the process of reading is left open.

Graham's point against Fish can be summed up by the formula that you can only do what can be done, which leads on to questions concerning the conditions of possibility for speech. Although the name of Jacques Derrida is not mentioned in Graham's study, his project seems to be the closest point of comparison for what Graham has in mind.[5] The major difference however is that Derrida locates the possibility for the origin of meaning in an abstract potential while Graham relegates it to the material structures of the brain. This is what Derrida refers to by specifically coined terms such as 'differance' and 'trace', which he tries to exempt from being treated as concepts because that would imply that their import is clearly definable and that they belong to readily comprehensible categories. But since categories are made up by that which exceeds them (to avoid talking of something like a category of a higher order), it is impossible to define them exactly. Therefore categories are themselves only elusive and the purpose of Derrida's coinages seems to be to demonstrating the interrelation between the originating principle of categories and the way they manifest themselves in practical examples. Graham's mentalistically oriented approach follows exactly the same lines. But while Derrida moors his argumentation about the transcategorical element to some high-flown talk about 'being' as connected to 'Being' (which he takes over from Heidegger), Graham's approach evades pathos in that it can be reduced to the formula that we know more than we can express, and thus that one part of our knowledge is the co-ordination of knowledge. What goes beyond the limits of language in both theories generates and controls it. Because there are categories, which moreover have to be rigid in order to ensure a certain degree of stability of the language, changes of meaning (including social changes) have to pass through a network of categories. Consequently changes are slow, indirect, and innumerably varied.

Finally it is indispensable to remember that language is above all a social phenomenon. Complete arbitrariness would only be possible if language were practised in an autistic vacuum. As soon as it is shared, there are fixed conventions which stabilize the possible ways of reacting to it. Textual interpretation therefore depends on the categorizations which conventions have shaped, and on the constant unconscious (or semi-conscious) re-definitions of them, as language is adapted in order to render the differences of a changing world. For this reason it is not so much a nuisance as a necessity that linguistic meaning be loose and open-ended. From this point of view it is possible to look upon categorizations as modular, and their constant re-definitions as central processes. But to repeat, Graham himself does not evaluate the meaning and implications of the concept of modularity with a sufficiently critical eye, and only superficially explores the potential contained in this model of how meaning is constructed. This is all the more regrettable since his study could provide a novel and interesting background for an understanding of how meaning is connected to text.

University of Zürich

Notes

1 Jerry Fodor, *The Modularity of Mind, An Essay on Faculty Psychology* (Cambridge, Mass.: MIT Press, 1983), p. 46.
2 Cf. Fodor, *Modularity of Mind*, pp. 106ff.
3 Graham explicitly focuses on Paul de Man's article 'Semiotic and Rhetoric'

in *Allegories of Reading* (New Haven: Yale University Press, 1979), but the claim about the impossibility of theory of course mainly refers to the title essay of *The Resistance to Theory, Theory and History of Literature*, vol. 33 (Minneapolis: University of Minnesota Press, 1986).
4 Stanley Fish, *Self-Consuming Artifacts* (Berkeley: University of California Press, 1972), p. 401.
5 See especially *Margins of Philosophy*, trans. Alan Bass (Brighton: Harvester Press, 1982). The essay in this collection entitled 'The supplement of copula: philosophy before linguistics' is a particular example of Derrida's investigation into the structure of categories on the one hand, and the relation between them on the other.

Robert Mighall

Ed Cohen, *Talk on the Wilde Side: Toward a Genealogy of a Discourse on Male Sexualities* (London and New York: Routledge, 1993), 244pp., £10.99 (paperback)

Wilde is hot property again. April 1993 witnessed the first international Oscar Wilde conference in Birmingham. Contributions by, amongst others, Reginia Gagnier and Richard Dellamora suggested that theory could provide the way forward for Wilde studies. *Talk on the Wilde Side* is a further step in this direction. Cohen's book represents an important attempt to substantiate the thesis put forward by Michel Foucault in the first volume of *The History of Sexuality*, that the dominant movement of nineteenth-century medico-legal discourse on aberrant sexuality is characterized by a shift in focus from acts to identities. This shift is most effectively illustrated in the discursive formation of the new legal and cultural species: the 'homosexual'. Cohen's study traces this formation. His book historicizes the strategies employed by the bourgeoisie to construct for itself a 'class body',[1] and to oppose itself to various forms of counter-hegemonic otherness. The latter category is for Cohen 'sensationally embodied'[2] in the figure of Wilde, who, as the result of his trials, became 'the figure around which new representations of male sexual behaviour in England coalesced' (p. 99). These two positions – the hegemonic and the counter-hegemonic – are reproduced in the two parts of Cohen's study. The first part, 'Against the Norm', explores a variety of discourses, ranging from Malthus to Max Nordau and from bankruptcy to 'self-abuse', which served to define and enforce the ideology of maleness in the nineteenth century. The second part, 'Pressing Issues', reconstructs Wilde's trails in 1895 as they were mediated through contemporary jounalistic comment. Its micropolitical analysis effectively balances the broader historical sweep of the first section. For Cohen these newspaper accounts are significant as they provided a public articulation of the 'homosexual', a concept that was, until then, largely the preserve of medico-legal discourse. The press, according to Cohen, gave this creature life. One of the most important considerations which *Talk on the Wilde Side* foregrounds is that what is usually treated as the 'official version' of the 1895 trials – the accounts provided by H. Montgomery Hyde – relies almost solely upon these journalistic mediations of events. Cohen's highly detailed analysis of Hyde's sources offers an insight into the way the concept of the 'homosexual' was made meaningful by the newspapers' concentration upon Wilde's embodiment of non-normative cultural practices, thereby 'crystalliz[ing] a new constellation of sexual meanings predicated upon "personality" and not practices' (p. 131). According to Cohen these meanings are still very much operational today. Wilde thus plays, or is made to play, a crucial role in this epistemological process. I say 'made to play', as Cohen's representation of events unfortunately allows Wilde little autonomy. Indeed, Wilde's status in this book is somewhat problematic. For a start, *Talk on the Wilde Side* 'talks' about Wilde only in the second half. When he is discussed, Wilde, the famous talker, is scarcely, if ever, presented in direct discourse, but is represented largely through the mediated accounts offered by the press, the accounts which Cohen had previously problematized. Wilde is thus effectively silenced in Cohen's text. This has the unfortunate effect of casting Wilde, to an extent, in the familiar role of victim, as the 'tragic' subject of forces beyond his control. Throughout Wilde is 'constructed', 'figured', 'typed', 'designated', 'constituted' and 'placed' by hostile forces, and allowed little autonomy or resistance to this process. Indeed, for Cohen 'the emergence of "homosexuality" under the mark of pathology and *powerlessness* is clearly governed by the violent assertion of "heterosexual" superiority' (p. 13; emphasis added). In other words Cohen's study suggests a decidedly un-Foucaultian model of power. As such it might be contrasted with Jonathan Dollimore's use of Wilde in *Sexual Dissidence*. Dollimore also employs the Derridian concept of the 'violent hierarchy' to show how the dominant 'forcefully governs' the subordinate/deviant, and how Wilde played an important oppositional role in this process.[3] However, this role is for Dollimore an active one, with Wilde seeking to subvert the fixing of meaning by means of his 'transgressive aesthetic'. According to Dollimore, Wilde's use of paradox enacted a 'perverse dynamic' which exposed and subverted those meanings which sought a transcendent fixity by their repudiation of difference/

deviance. In the final chapter of *Talk on the Wilde Side*, in which he discusses current gay strategy, Cohen similarly calls for a deconstructive erotic politics, for an attempt to

> historically problematize the ways the 'oppositional' terms of dominance come to be embedded within the categories of resistance. My own current attempt to theorize such an analysis invokes the notion of 'ec-centricity' as a way of moving beyond the binary structure of either/or.
>
> (p. 213)

In other words he calls for a strategy in many ways similar to the one Dollimore ascribes to Wilde, whose own 'perverse' aesthetic moved towards a displacement of the binary, and thus of the 'moral and political norms which cluster dependently around its dominant pole and in part constitute it' (Dollimore, p. 66). In Cohen's final chapter, however, Wilde has once more been abandoned, left in 1895 or in decline after his release from Reading Gaol. Wilde's contribution to current debate is, therefore, the largely negative one of providing, against his will, the most consummate representation of the very opposition Cohen seeks to dismantle. By silencing and disempowering Wilde, Cohen rejects the possibility of Wilde's own 'transgressive' or 'perverse' models contributing to future strategy. In short, *Talk on the Wilde Side* would perhaps have benefited with more talk from Wilde's side. This is the one criticism of what constitutes an informative and skilfully handled piece of historical exposition.

Merton College, Oxford

Notes

1 M. Foucault, *The History of Sexuality. An Introduction* (Harmondsworth: Penguin Books, 1984), p. 124.
2 E. Cohen, p. 93.
3 J. Dollimore, *Sexual Dissidence. Augustine to Wilde, Freud to Foucault* (Oxford: Clarendon Press, 1991), p. 65.

Edward Neill

Paul Bové, *Mastering Discourse: The Politics of Intellectual Culture* (Durham, N.C. and London: Duke University Press, 1992), 252 pp., £14.50 (paperback)

Transatlantic critical practitioners who write against the grain of 'The idealism of American criticism', as a famous (if summary) article by Terry Eagleton has it, may indeed be comparatively few. Most of us know something of Said's explorations of culture and, or as, imperialism, of Jameson's plumbing of the political unconscious, of Lentricchia offering life after the new criticism, and have heard Gayatri Chakravorti Spivak speaking for, if not entirely as, the 'subaltern'. Less 'exportable' perhaps only because less 'commodified', to use one of Paul Bové's own favourite terms of abuse, are the constellation of critics in the *Boundary 2* group, all of whom have published interesting, and sometimes brilliant, work – Jonathan Arac, Joseph Buttigieg, Daniel O'Hara, Donald Pease, W. V. Spanos, and Paul Bové himself. Indeed, in a startling article, Donald Pease claimed that the *Boundary 2* school, as a genuine 'site' of 'oppositional' critique, was specifically superseded and suppressed, in effect, by the apparently iconoclastic but actually quite malleable or recuperable new-fangledness of Yale-School-style deconstruction.

One might retort that at least the Yale School members, or 'boa-deconstructors', to use Geoffrey Hartman's coinage, while they occasionally spoke well of each other, felt no compulsion to do so, while the (perhaps rather notionally) 'suppressed' *Boundary* people are prone to emit 'team-calls', cite each other fulsomely, and review each other's books with strident encomia. But it was ever thus with repressed minorities. One takes the point, though, and it is rather a large part of what Paul Bové is saying here, that opposition practice in America tends to be rather swiftly 'co-opted', plushly accommodated, and the prospect of a *'Prison Notebooks* of J. Hillis Miller' was never seriously on the cards. *'Amerika, du hast es besser'*, wrote Goethe, and for Bové this is obviously part of the problem. Even those critics for whom 'critical negation' is a congenial posture, become unwitting conscripts for that 'affirmative culture' (remembering Marcuse's great essay) which subtly convoys *hegemony* (or is cashed as 'hege(l)mon(e)y' – to adopt momentarily the verbal privileges of a Derrida. In this respect Bové's work compares interestingly with Steven Connor's *Theory and Cultural Value*, with its sustained and subtle interest in whatever resists recuperation as a cultural 'positive', even (or especially) by 'theory' itself. Indeed, for both writers a key text is Derrida's recapitulation of Bataille on Hegel to the effect that 'in discourse ... negativity is always the underside and accomplice of positivity'.

It's the 'accomplice' idea here which bothers Paul Bové, the feeling that institutionally as well as discursively even the most resolutely 'oppositional' practice is 'always already co-opted' as a consequence of its own hubristic procedures, which generate master discourses whose very victories end as collaborations no matter how they begin as resistance, partly because 'power affects the forms which our resistance to power can take' (although this reflection seems to me to derive from what has happened rather than from what has to happen). As a result, the book's progress begins to remind one of the 'sad pageantry' of Shelley's *Triumph of Life*: Kierkegaard, for example, although he 'experiences and describes the socio-cultural forces reducing intellectual activity to a mere commodity', is finally in his strategic withdrawal scarcely distinguishable from Candide cultivating his garden; Paul de Man, traducing the Nietzsche of the *Use and Abuse of History* by reducing him to a play of textuality, and himself traduced by his doodling, disfiguring followers; Jeffrey Mehlman traducing the Marx of *Dix-Huit Brumaire* with his more repetitious than revolutionary *Revolution and Repetition* (the Mehlman always rings twice?), Derrida perhaps finally more sirenic than Socratic; Tate, Ransom, Penn Warren and other Professional Southerners (as he calls them) attempting to be organic intellectuals to the despoiled South and to reverse the fortunes of war by capturing the imagination, but ending as miserably 'co-opted' figures, at best right-wing populists; Stephen Toulmin legitimating scientific 'rationality', J. Hillis Miller a little too canny by half in his hosting of the uncanny. . . . So it (mostly) goes.

These 'reflections' give a muted, almost elegiac tone to the book rather at odds with its polemics, while its slightly old-fashioned postmodernism surely secretes a poignant nostalgia for its official *bête noire*, the 'discourse of modernity'. Consider, for example, Bové's elected genealogy, an idiosyncratic and perhaps contradictory amalgam of Marx and Nietzsche, Gramsci and Foucault, Said and Jameson. (About the great masters of textuality, de Man and Derrida, he is intelligently ambivalent). In fact the very orthodoxy of this 'oppositional' lineage or ancestry serves to make its salient aboriginal bend sinister (to the right?) in the form of that Heidegger, once the presiding genius of *Boundary 2*, whose 'rhetoric of temporality' enabled Bové's highly effective excoriations, not only of the 'scientistic mysticism' (to borrow a phrase from Joseph N. Riddel) of the

New Critics, but of the strong tendency even among subsequent and subtle critics to 'mate with their own self-created phantasmagoria in the voids of past texts', as his fellow-editor Daniel O'Hara demonstrates in his *Romance of Interpretation*.

O'Hara writes professedly as a 'comrade in theory', and the phrase happily suggests that even theory has, ineluctably, an 'occasional' ingredient (I agree with Jonathan Loesberg in his important assessment of the responses to Paul de Man's wartime journalism, that the attempt to separate august, mothballing 'theory' from the 'occasional practice' of journalism in order to dismiss the latter out of hand, is despicable as well as inappropriate – see his *Aestheticism and Deconstruction*.)

Bové's own strengths have always been connected with an ability to bring theory and occasion together in a potentially explosive way, and in this mode his timeliest and greatest 'performance' (in the best sense) was 'Closing up the ranks: Xerxes' hordes are at the Pass' (*Contemporary Literature* (1985)), when he contested (or, in American idiom, 'protested') Walter Jackson Bate's Harvardian exclusiveness.

Nothing in the book under consideration here has, I think, quite the force of that essay, while the fact that the chapters are, for the most part, reprinted articles or extended reviews makes the whole thing a bit of a *collage*, in which the (formally despised) notion of a presiding authorial presence is required to guarantee a vague sense of congruence. Even the Introduction, which might be expected to pull things together, however provisionally, is a virtual reprint of the entry on 'Discourse' for *Critical Terms for Literary Study* (ed. Lentricchia and McLaughlin) – itself, surely, a rather 'commodified' work.

Curiously, although Paul Bové and the *Boundary 2* team were very early on the scene of the 'postmodern', or 'postmodernism', as it quickly became, subsequent developments gave the term what must have seemed a fairly dismaying inflection. As a result, they have much more in common with such cisatlantic masters of critique as Professors Eagleton and Norris, who tend to offer pretty severe reflections on postmodernists and all their works than would originally have seemed at all likely. However, as Bové's work here illustrates, especially in his deployment of the sociologist Stanley Aronowitz and that 'master of nuance and scruple', R. P. Blackmur, he continues to offer resistance, not only to 'affirmative culture', thus casting a cold eye on the various modes of 'political and cultural legitimation', but also to facile and fashionable versions of 'critical negation' offered to the 'sceptical mind placed eccentrically within an inhospitable society'.

Middlesex University

John Moore

Zhang Longxi, *The Tao and the Logos: Literary Hermeneutics, East and West* (Durham and London: Duke University Press, 1992), xix + 198 pp., £15.95 (paperback)

Readers anticipating a comparative study of oriental and occidental critical theory, an exciting disclosure for westerners of previously unknown eastern theorists whose work exposes the ethnocentric relativism of Euro-American criticism, will be disappointed by this text. In this respect at least, the subtitle to Zhang's book remains something of a misnomer and a source of frustration. Hermeneutics here refers not to the general theory and practice of interpretation, but more narrowly to the theoretical project of Heidegger, Gadamer, Hirsch *et al.* In fact, *The Tao and the Logos* constitutes a transcultural application of (largely Gadamerian) hermeneutics to a selection of poetry from both East and West, and as such belongs, one would have thought, squarely within the western critical tradition. Challenging this notion remains one of the key themes in this text.

Zhang usefully reiterates the point that much contemporary western theory, by fetishizing the concept of difference, actually produces a totalizing discourse of consensus, where the only consensus remains the tenet that consensus is no longer possible. He then attempts to resist this totalizing tendency by the strategy of appropriating Heidegger's distinction between the identical (an absence of difference through reduction to a common denominator) and the same (the belonging together of what differs). This allows an investigation, not of the difference or radical unknowability of the East (as in Barthes's *Empire of Signs*) for the West, but of their underlying sameness. And nowhere is this sameness more apparent than in the matching hermeneutic concerns that Zhang discerns in the literature and criticism of these supposedly polarized cultural topographies. As the author comments in his Epilogue:

This book has argued for the recognition of the shared, the common, and the same in the literary and critical traditions of the East and West beyond their cultural and historical differences, and yet what is recognized as the same is the presence of difference in all understanding and interpretation, the hermeneutic difference in aesthetic experience and literary criticism.

(p. 192)

In a rebirth of universalism, problems of hermeneutics are seen not as the province of post-Schleiermacherian western philosophy, but as the world-wide concern of poets and critics, writers and readers, occidentals and orientals.

As the book's title suggests, the trope used to overcome the alleged incommensurability of East (*vide* China) and West remains that of the tao and the logos. And it is at this fundamental juncture that the fallacy in Zhang's thesis becomes evident: in the attempt to trim concepts so that they may be fitted into a narrow interpretative schema. The author perceives a 'striking similarity' (p. 32) between the tao and the logos, even going so far as to equate them: 'there is no reason why Plato should not be considered as in harmonious company with Laozi in the contemplation of logos or the *tao*' (p. 29). This astonishing manoeuvre is achieved through the prestidigitation of characterizing *both* concepts as embodying ideal fusions of thinking and speaking, a self-sufficiency of presence which produces a hierarchical privileging of inward thought over outward expression due to the inadequacy of language in conveying meaning in utterance contexts. In other words, in contrast to Derrida's emphasis on logocentrism as a characteristically western trait, Zhang attempts to establish it as a universal condition of human intellection:

> It is obvious not only that the dichotomy of meaning and word, content and form, intention and expression, is deeply rooted in both the Chinese and Western traditions, but that the two terms always stand in a hierarchical relation. Therefore, the metaphysical hierarchy of thinking, speech, and writing, exists not only in the West but in the East as well, and logocentrism does not just inhabit the Western way of thinking but constitutes the very way of thinking itself.
>
> (p. 30)

To engage in this act of recuperation of decentredness in Eastern thought, the author has to undertake some acrobatic contortions.

In the Western tradition, the logos is originary: in the beginning was the Word, and Adam imitates God's creativity through naming. Art constitutes a mimesis of an unattainable Platonic Ideal. Furthermore the universe remains structured in a series of binary oppositions configured as violent hierarchies. In Taoism, however – and it is to

Taoism that Zhang most frequently refers in his discussion of the tao – these elements are absent. In a recent translation and commentary on the *Tao Te Ching*, Michael LaFargue examines in detail what he terms 'origin sayings'[1] in the Laoist tendency of Taoism. These sayings all ascribe an originary function to the tao, but none refer to the logos as a creative principle. In fact, not only is the tao (as Zhang is forced to admit) 'beyond the power of language' and 'ineffable' (p. 27), but, as LaFargue points out, one of the major themes of Laoist thought remains a hostility to 'naming' – a tendency in other philosophical schools to use language to establish fixed meanings as a basis for determining normative forms of social behaviour.

As A. C. Graham suggests,[2] Taoists practise a radical agnosticism with regard to language: meaning is arbitrary, shifting, delusory, and as a result the textual strategies utilized by Taoists like Zhuangzi contain a pronounced levelling function. Zhang concedes that 'In the Chinese tradition ... the power of writing as such avenged itself the very moment it was debased; the metaphysical hierarchy was thus already undermined when it was established,' and comments 'perhaps this is precisely where the *tao* differs from the logos' (p. 33). But to press the point to its logical conclusion and suggest that the tao and the logos, far from being 'remarkably comparable' (p. 27) or even merely differing, are actually completely divergent, would be to explode the author's thesis. Yet such a conclusion remains inevitable. Taoist (if not all Chinese) thought is structured around the yin–yang polarity – not the hierarchically-ordered binary oppositions of the West – and as Alan Watts remarks: 'The key to the relationship between *yang* and *yin* is called *hsian sheng*, mutual arising or inseparability.'[3] Yin and yang are dynamically interdependent, constantly shifting, perpetually alternating – not crystallized in the mutually exclusive categories of a violent hierarchy. Art is not mimetic, but regarded either as a loss of plenitude due to the closure of other possibilities or, as Zhang indicates, as a mere trace of the tao. 'In such a view, words can never fully convey meaning because "of all things, words can discuss the coarser ones, and the mind can grasp the finer ones. But what words cannot discuss and mind cannot grasp is neither coarse nor fine" (Zhuangzi)' (p. 53). Zhang interprets this phrase as evidence of a rupture in the tao between inward thought and outward expression similar to that perceptible in the logos. But in fact it demonstrates the contrary: the tao remains beyond the binary oppositions characteristic of the logos.

En passant, The Tao and the Logos makes some interesting points about poetic language, but as a whole its conceptual framework remains decidedly flawed. The same may be said of the book's closing advocacy of interpretative pluralism. Lacking any awareness of the political dimension of the project he advances, the ideological connotations of his text appear to escape Zhang. Studies promoting 'intercultural dialogue' (p. xiii) are to be welcomed, but texts which do so on the basis of a perceived sameness must be regarded with suspicion. 'Oh, East is East, and West is West, and never the twain shall meet' was Kipling's rubric for nation-state imperialism. But in a context where Western corporate multinationalism aims for global domination, and where China's communist totalitarianism gradually reforms itself into a capitalist political economy, the refrain is likely to change. Assertions of liberal pluralism might just help to prise ajar a new Open Door policy which would lead not to cultural difference, but mind-numbing regimentation and uniformity – the false plurality of commodification and the market economy.

University of Luton

Notes

1 Michael LaFargue, *The Tao of the Tao Te Ching: A Translation and Commentary* (Albany: State University of New York Press, 1992), pp. 207–13.
2 A. C. Graham (trans.), *Chuang-Tzu: The Inner Chapters* (London: Mandala, 1986), pp. 25–6.
3 Alan Watts, *Tao: The Watercourse Way* (Harmondsworth: Penguin Books, 1979), p. 22.

Robert Eaglestone

Roger Sabin, *Adult Comics: An Introduction* (London and New York: Routledge, 1993), 321 pp., £10.99 (paperback)

Recently a number of books have come out about comics – if 'comics' is what the subject-matter is called. The terms vary: graphic novel, sequential art, bandes dessinées. *Adult Comics* is the choice of Roger Sabin, reflecting the choice of the industry itself and its pigeon-holing of what appears to be a new boom in the sales and social acceptance of comics. Writing on comics is not new, of course. Umberto Eco's article on Superman[1] dates to the 1960s, and enthusiasts, or more derisory 'fanboys' (the relationship between comics and gender is a particularly interesting issue) have been bringing out histories and criticism for ages. However, perhaps because of the growth of

cultural and media studies, or even because of a sea-change in the
perception of the art form, new sorts of writing are emerging. Martin
Barker has produced some of the best analyses of comics from a
cultural history perspective.[2] Richard Reynolds followed Eco in producing a structuralist reading of the superhero comic.[3] M. Thomas
Inge claims that as an art form

> comics also deal with the larger aesthetic and philosophical issues
> mainstream culture has always defined in its arts and humanities.
> The comics are another form of legitimate culture quite capable
> of confronting the major questions of mankind ... they should
> ... be respected for what they have contributed to the visual and
> narrative arts of the world.[4]

Peter Middleton uses the American superhero comics he read as a
child to help draw up representations of male subjectivity.[5] Sabin's
book, which has an excellent bibliography of publications on comics
in the US, Britain and elsewhere,[6] is one of the latest, best researched
and most comprehensive to deal with the comic specifically as a
medium in itself.

Sabin writes with two aims in view: the first is to contextualize
the medium which, according to the media at least, underwent a
'revolution' in 1986–7 when comics 'grew up'. The first two sections
of the book deal specifically, and sceptically, with this claim. Sabin
argues convincingly that 'the idea of comics suddenly "maturing" is
a myth' (p. 249), because the depiction of comics as juvenile, or just
for children, ignores the history and complexity of the art-form:

> we have identified a rich and complex history of adult comics
> stretching back over a century ... we can say that it is not they
> that are the historical aberration, but the fact that the medium
> was ever restricted to children at all.

(p. 249)

This history forms the bulk of the book. He locates the origin of
the modern comic in the late Victorian period: Sabin claims *Ally
Sloper's Half Holiday* – started in 1884, centred on the eponymous
'Victorian anti-hero' (p. 18) and aimed at an adult market – was the
first modern comic. From these roots he traces the history of
the adult comic to the present day. In the Anglo-American world
there are two developing strands to this history; the first is 'mainstream' comic history, the primarily economic story of comics as a
commercially successful industry. Sabin argues that the comic became
an art form perceived as appropriate only for children because of
specific historical and economic reasons. These include an expansion

into a successful children's market in the 1920s and 1930s and, in the 1950s, the Macarthyite panic and consequent backlash against a broadening spectrum of comics following the publication of *Seduction of the Innocent* (1955) in which psychiatrist Fredric Wertham claimed comics led to moral degeneracy. The second strand of this history, and more useful for Sabin's argument, follows the growth of the underground 'comix' (to distinguish themselves graphically from 'comics').

Sabin covers the development of American underground comix by such creators as Crumb, Shelton, Emerson and many others in the 1960s and 1970s. Uniquely he explores the history of the British underground from which most of the significant writers of the 1980s came. However, and this is a weakness in the book, he seems to write off the continuing 'underground' both here and in the US. The underground comics – political, angry, adult – are still with us, sometimes in a re-articulated form, perhaps more 'independent' than 'underground'. Some are better known, *Knockabout Comix* and *Big Bang*, both briefly mentioned in *Adult Comics*, others less so. Sabin bewails the lack of political involvement in comics yet the underground has become intensely political, from the ludicrous reworking of Hergé in *Tintin Breaks Free* to the serious and upsetting *Downside*, a comic about life in Tower Hamlets which is profoundly opposed not just to the establishment in general, but specifically and explicitly to the Conservative government. In the States too, the underground still provides a dissident voice, even if in a re-articulated form as 'independent': *Gay Comics*, for example, is growing in readership, as are a number of comics from oppositional political viewpoints.

These two developing strands, the commercially successful but limited comics and the radical, 'mature' comix of the underground, combined in the 1980s to make the comics 'revolution'. Sabin names three central texts from 1986–7, Miller's *Batman: The Dark Knight Returns*, Moore's *Watchmen* – both highly political 'superhero' revisionist texts – and Speigelman's harrowing Holocaust comic *Maus* – and shows how they, and other comics which benefited from the increased market they helped create, reintroduced the adult comic to public awareness. Comics didn't mature, the audience widened and was made aware that the scope of the medium was not limited to the superhero or the *Beano*. Perhaps more importantly, the constrictions of what could be done with the art form commercially were loosened by this success, as a number of comics since have shown: Alan Moore's *Big Numbers*, for example, concerns the effect of a new shopping complex on a Midlands town and its inhabitants. One of the fundamental problems in the medium has been the dominance of the superhero as subject-matter for commercially successful comics ever since *Seduction of the Innocent*. Sabin's historical perspective on both mainstream and underground comics shows how the essentially silly and politically dubious superhero is a historical accident, reducing the medium to immaturity when it is, has been, and most importantly will be, capable of so much more.

The third section of the book is a series of unconnected essays on world comics – especially European comics and Japanese Manga – women and comics, comics and other media (mainly film) and an exploration of the idea of the graphic novel. These case studies support the polemic of the previous sections.

Sabin's other intention is clear from the beginning of the book: *Adult Comics* was written to 'plug a gap ... a need for a primer-textbook that treats adult comics as an identifiable area for discussion' (p. 2) on courses primarily in the academies. There is no question that his book fills part of this gap. However, as Paul Dawson writes in 'Coming to terms with the graphic novel':

> We have hardly begun to sketch out an aesthetic appropriate to the form ... each (art form) must in the end be understood in its own particular terms.[7]

Sabin's book provides an extensive, detailed history, not a theoretical approach towards an aesthetic understanding of comics: for that book – and for a recognized area of study for which it will be a 'primer-textbook' – we are still waiting.

University of Wales, Lampeter

Notes

1 Reprinted in translation in Eco, *The Role of the Reader* (London: Hutchinson, 1981).
2 M. Barker, *A Haunt of Fears: The Strange History of the British Horror Comics Campaign* (London: Pluto Press, 1984). *Comics: Ideology, Power and the Critics* (Manchester: Manchester University Press, 1989) and, building on that, *Action: The Story of a Violent Comic* (London: Titan Books, 1990). Others in this Media Studies approach include Roberta E. Pearson and William Uricchio, *The Many Lives of the Batman: Critical Approaches to a Superhero and his Media* (London: BFI publishing/Routledge, 1991).
3 Richard Reynolds, *Superheros: A Modern Mythology* (London: B. T. Batsford, 1992).
4 In *Comics as Culture* (Jackson, Mississippi: University Press of Mississippi, 1990), p. xxi.

5 Peter Middleton, *The Inward Gaze: Masculinity and Male Subjectivity in Modern Culture* (London: Routledge, 1992).
6 Indeed, the status of comics in Europe and especially France – Bandes Desinées – is much higher than in the Anglo-American world: comics are the 'ninth art'; the Centre d'Etudes des Litératures d'Expression was founded in 1962 in Paris.
7 In *Stripsearch* (London: Camden Arts, 1990), pp. 5–7, a brochure for a graphic novel exhibition in Camden. Paul Dawson teaches a course on 'The Graphic Novel' at Manchester University.

Apology

The following review article originally appeared in *Textual Practice*, vol. 8, no. 1, 1994. Unfortunately the text as printed did not contain important revisions which were made after submission of the original article. The publishers and editors would like to apologize to Terri Ginsberg for this oversight and take the opportunity to reprint the revised text in full.

Mas'ud Zavarzadeh, *Seeing Films Politically* (New York: State University of New York Press, 1991), 267 pp., $16.95 (paperback)

Over the past several years, to pick up a scholarly book on film has meant being faced with writing informed by one of three modes of inquiry: neo-formalism, experiential culturalism, and new historicism. An inspection of the conditions of emergence of these modes of cultural theory finds them continuous with the enabling conditions of phenomena obtaining in other spheres of social (re)production, namely those of economic resources and state power, a disclosure coming as no surprise to theorists situated on the left, but one subject to vicious contestation by film theorists whose stakes are more aligned with programmes of the dominant sector, whether positioned in contemporary terms as 'liberal' or 'conservative'. This is because theorists of the left – also known as critical theorists or intellectuals – are concerned with how modes of knowing (including reading books and newspapers, or watching films, plays and TV), as part of the domain of cultural production, are linked in support of, negotiation with or resistance to the oppressive and exploitative functioning of global, transnational capitalism, a concern the effect of which *Seeing Films Politically*, by Mas'ud Zavarzadeh, forcefully and rigorously displays is none other than the realized possibility of dismantling and resituating – critiquing, or theorizing – the very foundations – the unspoken tenets, or ideology – of mainstream film theory.

Seeing Films Politically begins with an elaborate reading of these three modes, but because its theoretical approach is critique, the reader is spared the expected New Critical series of examples whereby the theorist cites the adequacies and inadequacies of each mode with respect to some *a priori* standard so taken for granted its principles need not be uttered, much less defended. Instead, *Seeing Films Politically* takes the citing of theoretical examples as the occasion for providing an explanation of not simply the 'details' of these discourses – their 'inner workings' or 'logics' – but of the complex ways in which they come to serve the perpetuation of capitalist social relations. In doing this, *Seeing Films Politically* refuses to take these examples – or those of the films it later reviews – as either fixed objects or intertextual matrices to be 'fetishized' and 'respected' as sacred entities against which harsh criticism ought not be levied due to their presumed existence as projections of the 'creative will'. *Seeing Films Politically* sees little time for such light-footed romanticism in the face of the grave urgencies presented by today's increasingly ominous global situation. Aware of the 'unpopularity' of its position amongst the die-hard figureheads of the dominant cinema studies regime of truth, *Seeing Films Politically* knows that the paradigm speaking these examples – along with its historico-political determinants – are nothing less than *its* enabling conditions, and it is firmly, unabashedly set on their overthrow.

Seeing Films Politically effects this veritable conceptual revolution through what it calls *renarration*, a critical practice enabling the production of alterior readings of filmic or written texts, readings that contest commonsensical 'interpretation' with a radical frame of comprehension that 'offcenters a film's tales and indicates their historical contingency' (p. 23). Crucial to this radical framework is *Seeing Films Politically*'s notion of the *tale* as not simply the aesthetic intersection of 'story' and 'plot' (as most theory has come to see it since Russian Formalism) but the effect of a *post-textual* endowment of meaning produced through struggles in the global social arena. *Seeing Films Politically* thus maintains the concept of the social totality in a way that film theory of the dominant order has disallowed since the (anti)foundations of poststructuralism provided the perfect alibi with which to relegate any attempt to read the matter of history past the confines of the 'local' or 'molecular' to the status of 'totalitarian' dogmatism. For such theory – the same decrying 'political correctness' – resistance and domination are but 'ludic' notions, delusions of paranoiacs and misguided conspiracy theorists who have not understood the 'fact' that a text, as 'autonomous object', contains in neo-Hegelian fashion its own, internal policing device and as such beckons nothing more than an 'appreciative' reception. *Seeing Films*

Politically discloses this 'fact' as none other than a discursive device transposing the mechanics of capitalist social relations into reified cultural fabric, and proffers in its stead the notion of *theory as resistance*, for which those social mechanics, in all their exploitativeness,are brought to the fore and subjected to the possibility of radical transformation.

Indeed, for *Seeing Films Politically*, one of the most occluded concepts of contemporary film theory is that of *possibility*. *Seeing Films Politically* finds that the dominant modes of contemporary film theory rest upon empiricist foundations, in that they assume an identity between the actual – the world 'out there' supposedly directly accessible to self-evident sensual 'experience' – and the real – the world as it is made knowable through frames of intelligibility enabled by prevailing social conditions and therefore subject to change in a way that the actual, immune to historical overdetermination, is not. When empiricist-based theory conflates these two fields, it privileges the terms of the former and naturalizes their referent as, *tel quel*, the real. As a result, any knowledge-practice attempting to re-situate the 'real' as an effect of intelligibility (our latter case) rather than sheer affect is presumed impossible. It is this kind of intellectual censorship *Seeing Films Politically* is working to counter.

For *Seeing Films Politically*, change is not a matter of flow and flux – of evolution – but of the stakes of capitalist social economy, of inclusion, exclusion and the politics of exploitation. In the postmodern academy, it is commonly thought that 'everything is political' in the pluralist sense for which all cultural phenomena are necessarily inflected with the 'biases' of specific, antagonistic 'points of view'. What such 'ethics' conveniently overlooks, however, are the invisible, i.e., non-obvious, systemic conditions of both the emergence and legitimation of any 'specificity', as well as the non-sovereign status of its 'specific' subjects – also known as 'individuals' – in light of their decentered positionality *vis-à-vis* the social arena. *Seeing Films Politically* replaces such ethics with politics, the struggle for control over the means of production in all social spheres, be they of state power, material resources, or cultural representation. These politics, we are reminded, are none other than those of class struggle, which on the plane of cultural criticism constitute what *Seeing Films Politically*, following Althusser, designates as *theory*. What allows pluralism to elide this designation is its refusal to consider social spheres as linked by anything but 'accident'. Such triviality then makes it very easy to decry systemic thinking – attempts to forge conceptual links in terms of social economy – as 'totalizing'. Change for pluralism obtains merely on the specific, or 'local' level of reform rather than at the global level of transformation.

Rejecting the limitations of the Foucauldian 'specific intellectual', then, *Seeing Films Politically* suggests that for a critical text to make a political rather than ethico-aesthetic intervention, it must call attention not merely to its conditions of 'existence' but to those of its possibility. In other words, for theory to make a *real* difference, it must construct a frame of reference in the face of which readers are enabled to come to *other*, larger explanations of presumed 'objects' of criticism, to 'show the "other" tale that is not told' (p. 24) and thereby to take such tale, 'as a cultural mode of exchange, back from the "professionals" and make it, once again, part of active ideological struggles for social transformation' (p. 25).

One of the strategies of *Seeing Films Politically*'s renarration in this regard is its undermining of bourgeois 'subtlety' through the articulation of *crudeness*. Recalling the marxian reading of the bourgeoisie as a social regime working to insure its survival by mystifying its enabling conditions, *Seeing Films Politically* refuses to stake its claims politely, realizing that 'a kinder, gentler administration' of knowledge is merely a dissimulation of the untold terror and exploitation wreaked by such neoliberal projects as the 'New World Order'. Instead of miming the significance of transnational capital, *Seeing Films Politically* stages a relentless attack against the dominant logic of oppression and exploitation by articulating the terms of its struggle as often as possible. This articulation is effected by a strategy of repetition, which to those theorists uncomfortable with such bold display of the political implications of their writing seems 'exasperating' or 'prosecutorial' but to *Seeing Films Politically* is simply part and parcel to the critique of the bourgeois discourses of scholarly etiquette: 'tone', 'style', and 'readability'. The effect of this strategy is a repositioning of the reader in a manner likened to Brecht's well-known *verfremdungs machen*, the praxis of estranging, or distancing the reader *not* from her affections, as would be the case for a Sartrean 'self-alientation', but from the mode of intelligibility through which she currently makes sense of, or appropriates, the real. As such, the reader is carried 'outside' the confines of the text 'itself' into the arena of post-textual, or non-discursive, social struggle and differentiation, where she is enabled to see not merely what the text 'is' but what it 'isn't', not merely where it sits, but how and why it leads. *Seeing Films Politically*'s mode of repetition hence takes the reader to the (material, not mystical) territory of unseen possibility in the face of which repetition is no longer a matter of the 'eternal return' of existential phenomenology but of the transformative movement of radical critical theory.

It is deducible from this explanation that the 'form' that a text takes is not so much the cognitive 'expression' of an ideal 'essence' but the barometer of its *situatedness*, of the significance of the stakes it claims within the social arena. As *Seeing Films Politically* is a decidedly interventionist text, its 'form' too is indicative of its place-ment-in-struggle and indeed dramatizes this battle in terms of the radical dismantling it endorses of dominant film theory. Rather than immediately provide the reader with analyses of selected films, thus formulating a relative degree of 'abstraction' from the 'concrete base' of the films' 'objecthood', *Seeing Films Politically* opens onto three chapters dealing strictly with theory and only afterwards stages an engagement with films on that basis. But, following Marx: 'The first part of the book is not a literal "exposition" and "preparation" for the second part but a matrix of signifiers that are enabling conditions of the "meanings" of the signifieds of the second part' (p. 149). *Seeing Films Politically*'s acknowledgement and foregrounding of its enabling conditions is not the humble apology for and genuflection to a fixed 'model' of critical normativity but the *politically reflexive dis-*articulation of that which prompts a radical critique of these films in the first place. In this way, *Seeing Films Politically* deconstructs the tenets of empiricism and idealism in one fell swoop.

The films selected for critique continue this radical agenda. Not only are they shown to be texts among others (e.g., critical texts) but, in this light, further occasions for the symptomatic reading of contemporary social struggle. Because, for example, the empiricism of much film theory is articulated through discourses of 'desire' and 'pleasure', whereby the notions of 'relationship' and 'love' are ideal-ized, or placed 'beyond' history, *Seeing Films Politically* focuses its reading on film texts the meanings of which it finds overdetermined by those ultimately nostalgic and politically complacent discourses whose critical sitings are ironically *un*pleasurable to those theorists whose professional (among other) stakes are in danger of being yanked by the implications of such attention. By focusing on social discourse rather than sheer form, moreover, *Seeing Films Politically* effectively avoids the pitfalls suturing the writing of perhaps the most outspoken and prolific neo-formalist/historian of the dominant cinema studies regime, David Bordwell, whose pithy term for critical theoretical frameworks – 'SLAB theory' – functions to bracket real possibility and thereby position his writing firmly within the domain of the reactionary and censorial. In contrast, while *Seeing Films Politi-cally* places brackets around the paradigms it contests, it never forgets that, far from being superfluous, they engage and appropriate highly powerful and productive discourses for the purposes of perpetuating an oppressive, hegemonic system. Rigour will not permit *Seeing Films Politically* to facilely relegate its opponents to the status of nonsense, as it knows such sophisticated will to ignorance, and not its own position, constitutes the field of the 'totalizing', 'politically correct', hermetically sealed intellectual vacuum.

It is always unfortunate that books like *Seeing Films Politically* are necessary, but likewise fortunate that theorists such as Mas'ud Zavarzadeh proceed to take up arms at the intellectual front, even and especially during times like the present in which the very possibility of publishing books such as his has been seriously jeopardized by a conservative wave of anti-intellectualism that denigrates anything 'smacking' of theory to the level of the 'unpractical', 'ineffective', 'naïve', 'illogical', and 'ridiculous'.[1] In the face of such utter discrimination and exclusionism as it masquerades in the regalia of liberal openness, we must know that it is only through books such as *Seeing Films Politically* that, as theorists of culture, we might be given the tools not merely to interpret the world, but to change it.

New York University

Note

1 See Zavarzadeh's ' "Argument" and the Politics of Laughter', *Rethinking Marxism*, Vol. 4, no. 1 (1991), pp. 120–31.

Arachnē

Arachnē is an interdisciplinary journal which publishes essays that deal with the connections among literature, philosophy, film, art history, psychology, classics, rhetoric, law, architecture, history, and language.

□ HIGHLIGHTS OF VOLUME ONE

Debate on Canadian perspectives of postcolonialism
Debate on law and literature between Peter Goodrich and
        Brook Thomas
Review essay of Daniel Boyarin's *Carnal Israel*

□ HIGHLIGHTS OF VOLUME TWO

Symposium on John Milbank's *Theology and Social Theory: Beyond
        Secular Reason.* Participants: Eve Tavor Bannet, Daniel
        Boyarin, Toby Foshay, Alan Jacobs, David Lyle Jeffrey,
        Sheila Kappler, John Milbank, Alan Shandro
Special issue on film. Participants include: Marta Braun, Jonathan
        Crary, Dan Streible, Virginia Wright Wexman

Subscription information and inquiries should be addressed to:
Editor, *Arachnē*, Laurentian University, Sudbury, Ontario P3E 2C6 CANADA
Tel. 705-675-1151, ext. 4344. Fax: 705-675-4887. arachne@nickel.laurentian.ca
One-year subscription (2 issues): $20CDN, outside Canada: $20US/EU.

♠♠♠♠♠♠♠♠♠♠♠♠♠♠♠♠♠♠♠♠♠♠♠♠♠♠♠♠♠♠♠♠♠♠♠♠♠♠

Social Semiotics

Social Semiotics is a transdisciplinary journal in functional linguistics, semiotics and critical theory, and is published twice each year.

Contributions are welcome.

We particularly seek articles which bring an interdisciplinary and socially critical approach to the analysis of texts—in the widest sense of these terms—and articles which develop new methods of semiotic analysis or new theoretical approaches to social semiotics.

We see social semiotics as connected to contemporary social theory, poststructuralist social science, feminist theories, psychoanalysis, deconstruction and a variety of approaches to cultural studies.

Papers in Vol 3/2 by:

Tara Brabazon   Tony Bex   Ulrike Meinhof   Jacob Mey   Toby Miller

Alec McHoul   Tony Schirato   Stef Slembrouck   Paul Thibault

Subscription Rates:
Individuals A$32 for one year (2 issues) A$70 for three years (6 issues)
Libraries A$50 for one year (2 issues) A$110 for three years (6 issues)
All prices quoted in Australian dollars
Overseas subscribers: add A$10 for mailing costs per year

All correspondence should be sent to:

Professor David Birch
Social Semiotics
Department of Communication & Media Studies
Central Queensland University
Rockhampton Qld 4702
Australia

Phone: (079) 309 403 Fax: (079) 309 501 Email - d.birch@cqu.edu.au

Social Semiotics

 Renaissance and
Modern Studies

Colin Heywood and Mark I Millington
Editors

Renaissance and Modern Studies selects a topical debate for each of
its annual issues. The theme is examined in a variety of settings and
from the perspective of a number of disciplines. Recent issues have
ranged from Latin America to Eastern Europe, and from the
Medieval period to the present day. Inspired by recent developments
in critical theory, the journal seeks a firm theoretical perspective on
its debates, drawing in the process from such disciplines as
sociology, theology, anthropology and above all history and literary
criticism. Each year specialists in these fields are invited to
contribute essays.

Foucault and Beyond
Vol 37 (1994)
Essays on: Gambling, Chance and the Discourse of Power in *Ancien
Régime* France ▪ Eugenic Theory and the Thematics of Sin ▪ Foucault
and Deleuze ▪ Discourses of Education ▪ Homosexuality and the
Middle Ages ▪ Foucault and a Guilt-Edged Europe ▪ Contingency,
Ambiguity and the Gender *Dispositif* ▪ Theories of law

Recent and forthcoming issues:
Vol 34 (1991) *Writing in Exile*
Vol 35 (1992) *Visions and Experiences of the Americas*
Vol 36 (1993) *Catholicism and Politics*
Vol 38 (1995) *Minorities*
Vol 39 (1996) *Space and Gender*

Published annually by The University of Nottingham. Subscriptions and
individual issues £10.50 (including postage); non-EU subscribers add £5 for
postage. Payment to be drawn on a British bank or by international money
order. Send order with cheque or money order payable to The University of
Nottingham to: The Business Manager, *Renaissance and Modern Studies*,
Department of Hispanic and Latin American Studies, The University of
Nottingham, Nottingham NG7 2RD, UK. Tel: +44 (0)115 951 5800, Fax:
+44 (0)115 951 5814.

Finitude's Score

Essays for the End of the Millennium
Avital Ronell

"This collection is stunning. Ronell has achieved a work of thinking at the highest level. She knows the score."—John P. Leavey Jr., author of *Glassary*

Avital Ronell writes about the demands that reading makes on readers: to pay attention, to follow along and make sense, to take the work seriously. She looks at the limits of the literary and the borders between words, art, and contemporary politics where significance points to matters beyond signs. Suspending the distinction between headline news and high theory, these essays examine diverse figures of finitude in our modern world: war, guerrilla video, trauma TV, AIDS, music, divorce, sadism, electronic tagging, rumor. £32.95 hb

University of Nebraska Press c/o Academic and University Publishers Group
1 Gower Street • London WC1E 6HA